The Acquisition of Egyptian Arabic as a Native Language

Georgetown University Classics in Arabic Language and Linguistics
Karin C. Ryding and Margaret Nydell, series editors

This series makes available seminal publications in Arabic language and linguistics that have gone out of print. Chosen for their quality of research and scholarship, these books will serve the growing national and international need for reference works on Arabic language and culture, as well as provide access to quality textbooks and audiovisual resources for teaching Arabic language in its written and spoken forms.

The Acquisition of Egyptian Arabic as a Native Language
Margaret K. Omar

Arabic Language Handbook
Mary Catherine Bateson

The Arabic Language Today
A. F. L. Beeston

The Arabic Linguistic Tradition
Georges Bohas, Jean-Patrick Guillaume, and Djamel Kouloughli

A Basic Course in Iraqi Arabic with MP3 Audio Files
Wallace M. Erwin

A Basic Course in Moroccan Arabic with MP3 Files
Richard S. Harrell with Mohammed Abu-Talib and William S. Carroll

A Dictionary of Iraqi Arabic: English—Arabic, Arabic—English
English—Arabic edited by B. E. Clarity, Karl Stowasser, Ronald G. Wolfe
Arabic—English edited by D. R. Woodhead and Wayne Beene

A Dictionary of Moroccan Arabic: Moroccan—English/English—Moroccan
Richard S. Harrell and Harvey Sobelman, Editors

A Dictionary of Syrian Arabic: English—Arabic
Karl Stowasser and Moukhtar Ani, Editors

Eastern Arabic with MP3 Files
Frank A. Rice and Majed F. Sa'id

Formal Spoken Arabic Basic Course with MP3 Files, Second Edition
Karin C. Ryding and David J. Mehall

Formal Spoken Arabic FAST Course with MP3 Files
Karin C. Ryding and Abdelnour Zaiback

Modern Arabic: Structures, Functions, and Varieties, Revised Edition
Clive Holes

The Modern Arabic Literary Language: Lexical and Stylistic Developments
Jaroslav Stetkevych

A Reference Grammar of Syrian Arabic with Audio CD
Mark W. Cowell

A Short Reference Grammar of Iraqi Arabic
Wallace M. Erwin

A Short Reference Grammar of Moroccan Arabic with Audio CD
Richard S. Harrell

The Acquisition of Egyptian Arabic as a Native Language

Margaret K. Omar

Georgetown University Press / Washington, D.C.

Georgetown University Press, Washington, D.C. www.press.georgetown.edu

Library of Congress Control Number: 2007927039

♾ This book is printed on acid-free paper meeting the requirements of the American National Standard for Permanence in Paper for Printed Library Materials.

14 13 12 11 10 09 08 07 9 8 7 6 5 4 3 2

First printing

Printed in the United States of America

To the memory of
Abdel-Hakim Omar
1898–1968

CONTENTS

FIGURES AND TABLES

FOREWORD TO THE GEORGETOWN CLASSICS EDITION

Margaret K. Omar Nydell's *The Acquisition of Egyptian Arabic as a Native Language*, published in 1973, is a comprehensive study of the speech of thirty-one children in an Upper Egyptian village who ranged in age from six months to fifteen years. Based on observation and elicitation exercises, the book details the order of acquisition of lexicon, phonology, syntax, and morphology. The study not only characterizes the patterned acquisition of features in this dialect comparing children's speech with that of adults in the same village, but it also sets up universal patterns of L1 acquisition based on study of an extensive body of published research on children's acquisition of other languages and on language universals theory, comparing these children's acquisition of Arabic with universal patterns. It is a sensitive treatment with many insights into the influence of environment, psychology, and other nonlinguistic factors on language learning.

The Acquisition of Egyptian Arabic as a Native Language was a pioneering work when first published; it is still today a valuable basic reference, and Georgetown University Press performs a service to the profession by republishing it in this new edition.

Ernest N. McCarus
University of Michigan

PREFACE

This study of Egyptian children's acquisition of Arabic was done in 1968 as part of a group effort on the part of dissertation writers from many universities across the United States. The goal was to obtain information about primary language acquisition in non-Western languages; at that point, data existed only for English, Spanish, and Russian.

Dr. Dan Slobin of the University of California at Berkeley edited a book for use in the field, *A Field Manual for the Acquisition of Communicative Competence* (Berkeley: 1967, second draft) with contributions from prominent linguists engaged in studying primary language acquisition. This superb guidebook included, for example, methodology and design of a field study, problems and categories to be studied, recording and elicitation techniques, samples of elicitation tests, samples of note taking, and posited universal strategies to be checked. He has since produced a five-volume series titled *The Crosslinguistic Study of Language Acquisition* (Mahwah, NJ: Lawrence Erlbaum Associates, 1985–1997).

This was the first study of child language acquisition in a Semitic language. It was followed by studies of Moroccan and Hebrew, and now we have material available for Lebanese, Palestinian, Jordanian, Saudi, Kuwaiti, Qatari Arabic, and undoubtedly several other varieties, in monographs, journal articles, and books. Of particular interest in Arabic are the acquisition of noun plurals, the simplified strategies used for verbs, and the use of numbers. The original dissertation, on file at the Georgetown University Lauinger Library, includes transcriptions of the raw data that were not included in the published version.

The field of primary language acquisition has grown enormously since 1968–69. This study is a straightforward analysis of child language as compared with the target adult language, and lacks many of the theoretical paradigms now in use. In the early years, I had a considerable amount of correspondence with others who intended to study Arabic and Hebrew. I hope that the republication of this book proves useful as an early example of research and analysis.

ACKNOWLEDGMENTS

I owe thanks to many persons for their advice and assistance to me while I was carrying out research for this project.

I am especially grateful to Professors Daniel P. Dato and Wallace M. Erwin of Georgetown University for their guidance, and to Mr. and Mrs. Mohamed Ali Yousef of Sheikh Mubarak village, U.A.R., for their hospitality and help during the research period. Assistance received from Miss Fatma Omar and the late Omar H. Omar in the preparation of the research design is also much appreciated. And finally, I thank my husband, Hanai, for his patience and encouragement during the entire time the project was being completed.

Margaret K. Omar
April, 1970

SYMBOLS

Symbols will be listed according to the chapter and section in which they are introduced.

Chapter 3

/ /	Slant lines enclosing phonemic transcription
[ ]	Brackets enclosing phonetic transcription
' '	Single quotes enclosing glosses (translations)
{ }	Braces enclosing a morpheme
^{a}/ /	Slant lines enclosing an allomorph
–	Hyphen indicating a point of affixation
m.	Masculine
f.	Feminine
pl.	Plural
sing.	Singular
C	Consonant
V	Vowel
$\bar{V}$	Long vowel
′	Primary stress
vs.	Versus, as opposed to
∼	Alternating with
>	Becomes, is realized as
+	Plus, indicating obligatory concatenation of elements in a construction
.	Syllable boundary

Chapter 5

5.1. Early Stages of Syntactic Development

S	Sentence
P	Pivot class word
O	Open class word
W	Word
N	Noun
N_{def}	Definite noun
N_{indef}	Indefinite noun
NP	Noun phrase
V_{neg}	Negated verb
Adj	Adjective

Adj_{desc}	Descriptive adjective
Adj_{dem}	Demonstrative adjective
Adj_{quant}	Quantifying adjective
Adj P	Adjective phrase
Pron	Pronoun
$Pron_{indef}$	Indefinite pronoun
Num	Numeral
Loc Part	Locative particle
H	Head
Mod	Modifier
Neg	Negative
Pred	Predicate
Pred P	Predicate phrase
→	Is rewritten as
( )	Parentheses indicating an optional element in a construction
{ }	Braces indicating alternative elements; only one of the enclosed symbols occurs in the position in the construction

5.2. The Acquisition of the Negative

V	Verb
V_{imper}	Imperative verb
V_{pres}	Present tense verb
Partic	Participle
Prep	Preposition
Prep P	Prepositional phrase
Subj	Subject
Obj	Object
$Pron_{pers}$	Personal pronoun
Aux	Auxiliary
⇒	Is transformed to
$T\ opt\ N_{1a,b,c}$	Optional negative transformations with /miš/
$T\ opt\ N_{2a,b,c,d,e,f,g}$	Optional negative transformations with /ma-. . .-š/
$T\ opt\ N_3$	Optional negative transformation with /læʔ/

5.3. The Acquisition of the Interrogative

VP	Verb phrase
QW	Question word
#	Falling terminal juncture
//	Rising terminal juncture
1	Low level of pitch
2	Mid level of pitch
3	High level of pitch
$T\ opt\ Q_1$	Optional interrogative transformation, 'yes-no' type
$T\ opt\ Q_{2a,b}$	Optional interrogative transformations, question word type

Chapter 6

6.2. The Acquisition of Inflectional Affixes for Noun Plurals

Ns	Noun stem
Af	Affix
N_{fs}	Feminine singular noun
N_{ms}	Masculine singular noun
N_{pl}	Plural noun
N_{sing}	Singular noun
Opt Rule Dual	Optional dualizing morphophonemic rule
Opt Rule Pl_1	Optional pluralizing morphophonemic rule, regular
Opt Rule Pl_2	Optional pluralizing morphophonemic rule, collective
Opt Rule Pl_3	Optional pluralizing morphophonemic rule, irregular
Opt Rule Num	Optional enumeration morphophonemic rule

6.3. The Acquisition of Inflectional Affixes and Agreement for Adjectives

Adj s	Adjective stem
Adj s_1	Adjective of color
Adj s_2	Comparative adjective
Adj_{ms}	Masculine singular adjective
Adj_{fs}	Feminine singular adjective
Adj_{pl}	Plural adjective
N_d	Dualized noun
N_{inan}	Inanimate noun
N_{coll}	Collective pluralized noun
Opt Rule $F_{1,2}$	Optional feminizing morphophonemic rules
Opt Rule Pl_1	Optional pluralizing morphophonemic rule, regular
Opt Rule Pl_2	Optional pluralizing morphophonemic rule, irregular
Opt Rule $Comp_{1,2}$	Optional comparison rules
Opt Rule Sup	Optional superlative rule
Opt Rule Adj Mod_1	Optional adjective modification rule, number
Opt Rule Adj Mod_2	Optional adjective modification rule, inanimate nouns
Opt Rule Adj Mod_3	Optional adjective modification rule, collective nouns
Opt Rule Adj Mod_4	Optional adjective modification rule, definiteness

1

INTRODUCTION

1.1. SCOPE OF THE STUDY

This study was undertaken to investigate some developmental stages by which children acquire Egyptian Arabic as a native language. Children were observed at various ages and stages of linguistic development. In addition to linguistic data, certain relevant ethnographic data were gathered, in order to provide additional information about socialization as related to primary language learning and the effects of social and environmental factors on linguistic development.

The case study technique was followed. The inhabitants of one small village were selected for study, which provided an insight into a real, complete social and linguistic unit. All inhabitants of the village shared approximately the same standard of living and had approximately the same occupations, daily routines, education and income. Because of this, there were fewer socio-economic variables which had to be considered in evaluating family setting, child-rearing attitudes, or children's performance than might be found in a more densely populated, urban area.

1.1.1. *Goals of the Study*

Both general and specific goals of the study were based on suggestions for this type of field research project outlined in the publication, *A Field Manual for the Cross-Cultural Study of the Acquisition of Communicative Competence*,[1] hereafter referred to as the *Field Manual*.

The general goals were to determine the rate and order of linguistic development of the children studied. The specific goals included investigation of:

1. the basic characteristics of the physical and social environment in which the native language was learned;
2. the characteristics and development of early communication and speech;

[1] Dan I. Slobin, ed., *A Field Manual for the Cross-Cultural Study of the Acquisition of Communicative Competence*, 2nd draft (Berkeley, Univ. of California Press, 1967).

3. the stages and rate of development of the phonological system;
4. the stages of development of two syntactic transformations, the negative and interrogative transformations;
5. the stages of development of two complex morphological inflections, the plural of nouns, and the gender and plural of adjectives;
6. comparison of findings with those reported in studies of other languages, and testing hypotheses and generalizations about the acquisition of language by children.

1.1.2. *Need for the Study*

The variety in the structure of natural languages is so great that information is needed about language acquisition in languages structurally different from 'western' languages. Most hypotheses and theories about primary language acquisition have been based on data gathered from children learning English and other Indo-European languages.[2] There also have been proposals that certain grammatical structures are universal and that certain universal cognitive abilities are likely to be involved in language learning. These findings and proposals should be compared to those obtained in observations of the language learning process in non-western languages.

Arabic is a Semitic language, with a structure very different from English. I know of no investigation that has been made to date regarding primary language acquisition in Arabic or any other Semitic language.

1.2. DURATION AND LOCATION OF THE STUDY

1.2.1. *Duration*

The field work was carried out from June through September, 1968. Most of this period was spent in the village, with daily contacts with its residents. While in the village, interviews, examinations, and taping sessions were conducted daily.

1.2.2. *Location*

The village selected for study was Sheikh Mubārak, an extremely small village by Egyptian standards, with only about thirty families. They are families of small landowners, tenants, agricultural workers, or craftsmen, who work for the local landlord or in the surrounding area.

[2] A list of studies of primary language acquisition in 21 languages is presented in Slobin, 1967, pp. 224–225.

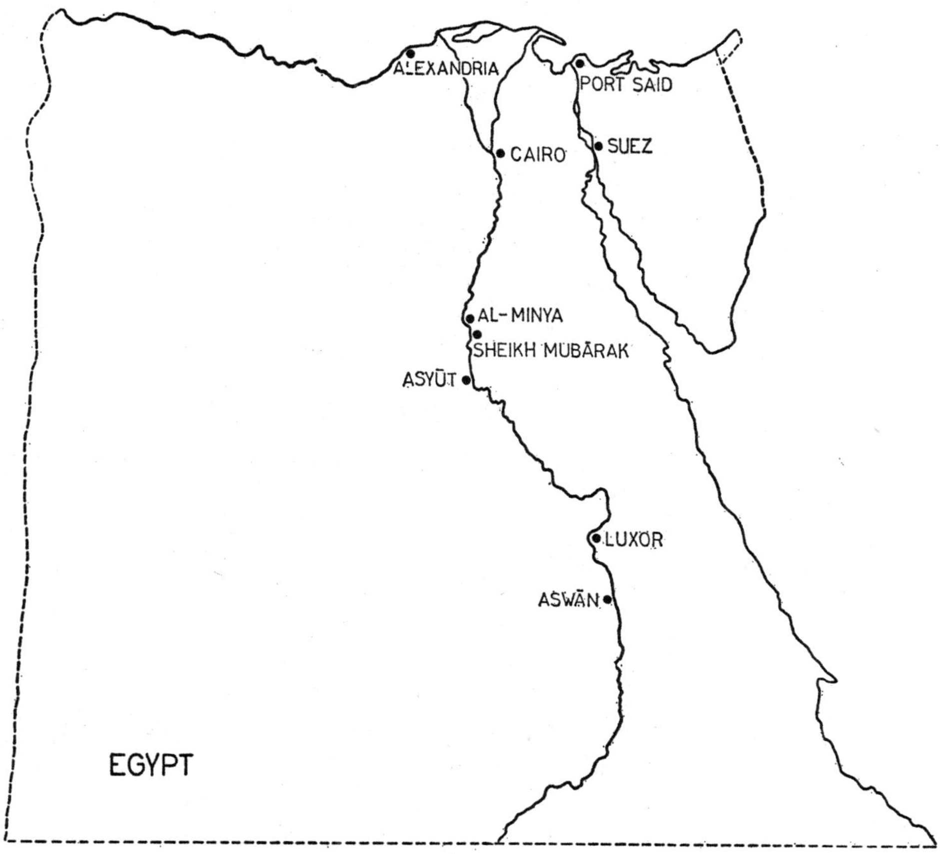

Figure: Map of Egypt, Showing Location of Sheikh Mubārak, Site of the Fieldwork

The village of Sheikh Mubārak is located in the district of Abu Qurqās, province of Al-Minya. This province is approximately in the middle of the country, about halfway between Alexandria and Aswan. It is considered part of Upper Egypt, which includes the whole area south of Cairo. The village is about five miles from the nearest town, Abu Qurqās, and about twenty miles south of the city of Al-Minya, the provincial capital and a major city in Upper Egypt (see Figure).

The village is composed of a compact group of 35 houses, arranged along three lanes, and surrounded by a high mud-brick wall. Outside this enclosure and across the road to the east are the water pump and well, mosque, and roads leading to the fields, Abu Qurqās, and the Government Cooperative Unit. North of the wall is the landlord's house. To the west lies West Village, /ʔil-ɣarb/, another large group of houses connected with a neighboring farm. In this village is located the local school. To the south of the village are fields.

1.3. METHODOLOGY FOLLOWED

1.3.1. *Recordings and Transcriptions*

The procedure followed was to select children ranging in age from approximately six months to 15 years and to record their utterances on tape and in phonetic transcription. Because of the short duration of field work, several children representing each age group or level of linguistic development were selected.

Utterances were later analyzed to discover patterns and stages in development approaching the adult model.

1.3.2. *Types of Speech Observed*

Smaller children were recorded in dialogue situations and free conversation. Comprehension and imitation tests were administered to children up to age 7, and grammar elicitation tests were administered to all children in the study. The four children under age 2½ were too young to be tested.

1.3.3. *Children in the Study*

Altogether 37 children were included in the study. All resided in Sheikh Mubārak village except the children of one family who lived in West Village (Children 16 and 25) and one child (Child 3) who lived in the landlord's house because his mother was a servant there (she is a native of Sheikh Mubārak). They were of at least normal health and intelligence, and all knew each other and had daily contact with each others' families.

Table 1 shows the children studied, their age and sex, and which tests were administered to each child. The spelling of names is regularized, not in phonemic transcription. (The symbol /ʕ/ denotes the voiced pharyngeal fricative consonant.)

1.3.4. *Families in the Village and in the Study*

Table 2 shows the families in the village studied and the children in each family.

1.3.5. *Approach Used with Village Residents*

The problems involved in being 'accepted' and receiving cooperation in a small community like this cannot be underestimated. 'Fitting in' is hard enough for any outsider, whether from a nearby town or from Cairo, and of course problems are greater for an American, especially in light of recent political events.

Table 1

Children studied and tests administered

Name	Age, Sex	Imitation 1	Imitation 2	Imitation 3	Comprehension	Negation	Interrogation	Nouns	Adjectives
A. Nadya Lamʕi	0.6-F	(Babbling stage)							
B. Abdalla	0.8-M	(Babbling stage)							
C. Sharbāt	1.0-F	(Stage I of phonemic development)							
D. Hasan	1.5-M	(Stage I of phonemic development)							
E. Zakiya	11.1-F	(Intermeditae stage in phonemic development; one-word stage)							
F. Suʕād	2.3-F	(Intermediate stage in phonemic development; one-word stage)							
1. Manāl	2.8-F	×	×	×	×	no	no	×	×
2. Wafā	3.0-F	×	×	×	×	×	no	×	×
3. Jamāl	3.6-M	×	×	×	×	no	×	×	×
4. Sanā	3.6-F	×	×	×	×	no	no	×	no
5. Abdel-Fattāh	4.0-M	×	×	×	×	×	no	×	×
6. Sabāh	4.0-F	×	×	×	×	no	×	×	×
7. Amāl	4.6-F	×	×	×	×	no	no	×	×
8. Yūsef	5.0-M	×	×	×	×	×	×	×	×
9. Ahmad	5.0-M	×	×	×	×	×	×	×	×
10. Niʕmat	5.6-F	×	×	×	×	no	no	×	no
11. Jirjis	6.0-M	×	×	×	×	×	×	×	×
12. Sarāya	6.0-F	×	×	×	×	×	×	×	×
13. Mohamed Mūsa	6.0-M	×	×	×	×	×	×	×	×
14. Tahiya	6.6-F	×	×	×	×	×	×	×	×
15. Zakariya	6.6-M	×	×	×	×	×	×	×	×
16. Kāmel Ridwān	7.0-M	×	×	×	×	×	×	×	×
17. Zeynab	7.0-F					×	×	×	×
18. Azīza	7.0-F					×	×	×	×
19. Mohamed Hilmi	8.0-M					×	×	×	×
20. Saʕdiya	8.0-F					×	×	×	×
21. Kamla	8.0-F					×	×	×	×
22. Hoda	8.6-F					×	×	×	×
23. Aliya	9.0-F					×	×	×	×
24. Mohamed Tagāwi	9.0-M					×	×	×	×
25. Nadya Ridwān	10.0-F					×	×	×	×
26. Wahība	11.0-F					×	×	×	×
27. Abdel-Raʕūf	12.6-M					×	×	×	×
28. Ali	13.0-M	×	×	×		×	×	×	×
29. Kāmel Saʕd	13.0-M					×	×	×	×
30. Sayyid	14.0-M					×	×	×	×
31. Abdel-ʕāl	15.0-M					×	×	×	×

Table 2

Families in the village and in the study

Family		
1.	Head:	Zohry – M, age 50
	Wife:	Fayza – F, age 40
	Child:	Amāl – F, age 4.6 (Child 7)
2.	Head:	Tawfīg – M, age 45
	Wife:	Fatma – F, age 35
	Child:	Tahiya – F, age 6.6 (Child 14)
3.	Head:	Mounīr – M, age 30
	Wife:	Farīda – F, age 28
	Children:	Wahība – F, age 11 (Child 26)
		Sādig – M, age 6 (retarded)
		Ibrahīm – M, age 0.4
4.	Head:	Abdu – M, age 70
	Wife:	Naʕīma – F, age 60
	Son:	Saʕd – M, age 42
	Son's Wife:	Mounira – F, age 32
	Son's children:	Kāmel – M, age 13 (Child 29)
		Kamla – F, age 8 (Child 21)
		Zakariya – M, age 6.6 (Child 15)
		Niʕmat – F, age 5.6 (Child 10)
		Zakiya – F, age 1.11 (Child E)
5.	Head:	Hasan – M, age 55
	Children (by first wife, deceased):	Ahmad – M, age 21
		Mustafa – M, age 17
		Safiya – F, age 14
		Ali – M, age 13 (Child 28)
		Aliya – F, age 9 (Child 23)
	Wife:	Hosniya – F, age 35
	Child:	Sharbāt – F, age 1.0 (Child C)
	Ahmad's wife:	Aida – F
6.	Head:	Khalaf – M, age 55
	Wife:	Nafīsa – F, age 42
	Children:	Anas – M, age 23
		Ibrahīm – M, age 16
		Azīza – F, age 7 (Child 18)
	Anas' wife:	Naʕīma – F, age 19
	Anas' children:	Wafā – F, age 3 (Child 2)
		Amāl – M, age 0.6

(Table 2–Continued)

Family		
7.	Head:	Hilmi – M, age 33
	Mother:	Baxīta – F
	Wife:	Amīna – F, age 32
	Children:	Abdel-ʕāl – M, age 15 (Child 31)
		Mohamed – M, age 8 (Child 19)
		Sabāh – F, age 4 (Child 6)
		Hasan – M, age 1.5 (Child D)
8.	Head:	Ahmad – M, age 38
	Mother:	Sulha – F
	Wife:	Wahība – F, age 28
	Child:	Abdel-Fattāh – M, age 4 (Child 5)
9.	Head:	Abdallah – M, age 43
	Wife:	Saʕdiya – F, age 28
	Children:	Etimād – F, age 11
		Manāl – F, age 2.8 (Child 1)
10.	Head:	Andarawz – M, age 62
	Wife:	Arāda – F, age 50
	Children:	Samīr – M, age 21
		Bishāy – M, age 16
		Mourīda – F, age 10
		Yūsef – M, age 5 (Child 8)
11.	Head:	Mūsa – M, age 40
	Mother:	Zeynab – F
	Wife:	Najafa – F, age 28
	Children:	Suʕād – F, age 8
		Mohamed – M, age 6 (Child 13)
		Ahmad – M, age 5 (Child 9)
		Mahmoud – M, age 3.6 (retarded)
12.	Head:	Ridwān – M, age 60
	Wife:	Fatma – F, age 50
	Children:	Mohamed – M, age 25
		Sakkīna – F, age 15
		Hōda – F, age 8.6 (Child 22)
	Mohamed's wife:	Baxīta – F, age 18
	Mohamed's children:	Sanā – F, age 3.6 (Child 4)
		Nāsir – M, age 1.0
13.	Head:	Ahmad – M, age 30
	Wife:	Ixwāt – F, age 25
	Children:	Sarāya – F, age 6 (Child 12)
		Mohamed – M, age 2.6 (retarded)
		Abdalla – M, age 0.8 (Child B)

(Table 2–continued)

Family		
14.	Head:	Lamʕi – M, age 48
	Wife:	Saddīga – F, age 35
	Children:	Jirjis – M, age 6 (Child 11)
		Nadya – F, age 0.6 (Child A)
15.	Head:	Mahmoud – M, age 18
	Mother:	Fawā – F
	Brothers:	Abdel-Raʕūf – M, age 12.6 (Child 27)
		Mohamed – M, age 9 (Child 24)
	Sister:	Baxīta – F, age 14
16.	Head:	Amīna – F, age 30
	Child:	Zeynab – F, age 7 (Child 17)
17.	Head:	Sālim – M, age 68
	Wife:	Nafīsa – F, age 40
	Children:	Sayyid – M, age 14 (Child 30)
		Saʕdiya – F, age 8 (Child 20)
		Suʕād – F, age 2.3 (Child F)
In West Village:		
Family		
1.	Head:	Ridwān – M, age 40
	Wife:	Saniya – F, age 36
	Children:	Najāh – F, age 16
		Rifāʕ – M, age 15
		Nadya – F, age 10 (Child 25)
		Kāmel – M, age 7 (Child 16)
		Fathi – M, age 5
		Sharbāt – F, age 2
In landlord's house:		
Family		
1.	Mother:	Insāf – F, age 28
	Children:	Nawāl – F, age 11
		Jamāl – M, age 3.6 (Child 3)

Being an American female, I was aware that a careful introduction of myself and my purpose had to be made. Two factors contributed greatly to my success in being accepted–ability to speak Arabic fluently, and my husband's acquaintance with the villagers through conducting previous economic research. Still, it seemed advisable to spend about a week greeting the adults and visiting their homes before attempting to begin the research. The women and children were friendly but a little puzzled about my attitude and interest in them.

The landlord, Mr. Ali Yousef, was most helpful in making my purpose known, especially to the men. He explained not that I was making 'scientific research' about language learning, which would have been hard to understand, but that I was a 'teacher of Arabic', and would have daily sessions with the children to tape their speech and help them improve their Arabic. At the same time, I would investigate how small children learned to speak, and discuss children's development with adults.

Children were very anxious to be recorded and hear their voices re-played, so there was no problem recruiting them. Adults, too, were cooperative during discussions and interviews.

1.3.6. *Assistance Received in Conducting the Study*

Interpreting and translating assistance was not required in preparing tests or speaking with adults and children.

As already mentioned, the landlord in the village was very helpful in introducing the purpose of the study and conducting interviews with men. His wife, Selwa, helped in conducting some interviews with women, and in recording free conversation of some small children. Both provided background information about residents of the village, such as approximate age, social status, and types of occupations. They also made valuable comments about some social customs and aspects of village culture.

1.4. STRUCTURAL SKETCH OF THE LANGUAGE

1.4.1. *The Root and Pattern System*[3]

Arabic, like all languages in the Semitic language family, is characterized by a 'root system' of forming words. Related words are regularly formed using a skeletal structure of three consonants called a 'root'. By combining a particular root with various vowel 'patterns' to form a 'stem', many related concepts can be expressed. Affixes may be added to the stem, but more often there is a change in position and quality of vowels which occur in combination with consonants of the root. For example, some words derived from the root *K–T–B* 'to write' are: /KæTæB/ 'he wrote', /Kǣ̄TiB/ 'a writer', /KiTǣB/ 'a book', /mæKTaBa/ 'a library'. Occasionally a root may have more than one general range of meaning. Whereas roots have general lexical meanings, patterns carry recurring gram-

[3] Based on the presentation in Ronald G. Wolfe, *An Introduction to the Arabic Language for Americans* (Washington, D. C., American Friends of the Middle East, Inc., 1965).

matical meanings.[4] The vowel pattern /CæCiC/, for example, expresses the active participle, the 'doer' of an action: /KæTiB/ 'a writer', /RæKiB/ 'a rider'.

Most tri-consonantal roots are 'sound', or regular. Irregular roots may contain a semivowel or glottal stop as one of the consonants in the root, or two of the consonants may be the same, resulting in minor modifications in the form of the stem when the root is combined with a vocalic pattern. Roots composed of four and even five consonants do exist but are not common. Sometimes a four-consonant root is 'reduplicated', i.e., consists of two identical syllables, as /TaBTaB/ 'to beat a rhythm'.

A few words are 'solid stems', and do not have a root-and-pattern structure. Words of this type are mostly prepositions, pronouns, and other particles. Examples are: /ʔiḥna/ 'we', /bæss/ 'only', and /kæm/ 'how much'.

1.4.2. *Phonology*

The phonology of the village dialect is described in Chapter 3.

1.4.3. *Morphology*

The morphology of the language is characterized by much inflection, usually the addition of prefixes and suffixes.

Nouns are either masculine or feminine. They are inflected for gender (usually /-a/ is added to the masculine form to make it feminine) and number (singular, dual, plural). The inflection of number for nouns is often irregular and very complex. The development of this was investigated and is described in Chapter 6 in some detail.

Adjectives are inflected like the nouns they modify, for gender and number. Some are inflected for comparison. This was also investigated and is described in Chapter 6. Most adjectives follow the nouns they modify. Notable exceptions are numerals and some adjectives of quantity and measure, such as /šwayya/ 'little bit', and /raṭl/ 'a pound'. An adjective may be used as a noun.

Verbs are inflected for person (first, second, third), number (singular, plural), tense (present, past), gender (masculine, feminine), and mood (indicative, imperative). Verbs which contain a semivowel, glottal stop, or two identical consonants in the root have irregular forms.

There is no infinitive form of the verb. The future tense is formed by prefixing /ḥa-/ to the present tense form. The prefix /ʕam-/ (or /ʕa-/) added to the present tense form expresses habitual or continuous action. The imperative is

[4] Wallace M. Erwin, *A Short Reference Grammar of Iraqi Arabic* (Washington, D.C., Georgetown Univ. Press, 1963) p. 48.

the stem form of the verb alone, inflected for gender and number. The passive voice is formed by adding the prefix /it-/ to the past tense form of the verb.

There are three productive verbal root patterns, which may be exemplified by the following verbs: /ʕæmal/ (CVCVC) 'he made', /dærris/ (CVCCVC) 'he taught', and /sǣfir/ (CV̄CVC) 'he traveled'. Each has approximately the same inflections.

Personal pronouns are inflected for person (first, second, third), number (singular, plural), and second and third person singular pronouns are inflected for gender (masculine, feminine). The personal pronouns are as follows:

	Number	Person	Gender	Subjective Case (free)	Possessive-Objective Case (bound)	
'I'	Sing.	1	M or F	/ʔæna/	/-ni/	(objective)
					/-i/	(possessive)
'you'		2	M	/ʔinta/	/-ak/	
		2	F	/ʔinti/	/-ik/	
'he'		3	M	/huwa/	/-u/	
'she'		3	F	/hiya/	/-ha/	
'we'	Pl.	1	M or F	/ʔiḥna/	/-na/	
'you'		2	M or F	/ʔintu/	/-ku/	
'they'		3	M or F	/humma/	/-hum/	

Personal pronouns may be the subject of an equational sentence (see below) or included for emphasis in a verbal sentence.

There is one relative pronoun, /ʔilli/ 'who, which, that', which introduces a relative clause. Demonstrative pronouns, expressing 'this' or 'that', are inflected for gender and number: /di/ feminine singular, /da/ masculine singular, and /dōl/ plural.

1.4.4. *Syntax*

There are three main types of sentences. The nominal sentence begins with a noun, for example: /ʔir-rājul šǣf ʔil-wād/[5] 'The man saw the boy'. The verbal sentence begins with a verb, for example: /šuft ʔir-rājul/ '(I) saw the man'. The 'equational' sentence is composed of a subject and a predicate with no verb. In an equational sentence, the subject is always definite and present tense is implied, for example: /ʔir-rājul kæbīr/ 'The man (is) big', /huwa hina/ 'He (is) here'.

[5] Hyphens and spaces between words in phonetic or phonemic notation do not represent pauses or changes in articulation; they mark boundaries between morphemes.

Negation is expressed by the free form /miš/ or by the affixation of its allomorphic bound form /ma- . . . -š/ to words. This is further discussed in Chapter 5.

Interrogation is expressed by question words, which may be placed either at the beginning or end of the sentence. 'Yes-no' questions are simply the declarative sentence spoken with a rising intonation. This is also described in Chapter 5.

Since the verb is inflected for only past and present tenses, more complex verb phrases and conditionals are formed by combining several verbs, sometimes including the verb /kǣn/ 'was'. For example, the English concept *He was going to go* would be rendered in Egyptian Arabic /huwa kǣn ḥa-yrūḥ/, lit. 'He was will-go', using /kǣn/ plus the future tense form of the verb.

A special type of noun phrase is frequently used, called a 'construct phrase'.[6] This construction consists of two or more nouns immediately following one another. The first noun never has the definite article; the phrase is definite if the second noun is definite. The meaning of the construction is either that the first noun is 'possessed' by the second, or expresses various relationships expressed by *of* in English. Examples are: /ʔuxt ʔil-wād/ 'the boy's sister', lit. 'sister the-boy'; /bǣb ʔil-bēt/ 'the door of the house', lit. 'door the-house'. If either noun is accompanied by an adjective, the construct phrase is taken as a unit and the adjective must follow the entire construction, for example: /ʔuxt ʔil-wād ʔiṣ-ṣuɣayyara/ 'the boy's younger sister', lit. 'sister the-boy the-small'.

Definiteness is expressed by the prefix /ʔil/ 'the' affixed to the noun. There is no indefinite article; without the definite article, a noun is usually indefinite, for example: /kitǣb/ 'a book', /ʔil-kitǣb/ 'the book'.

[6] Based on presentations in Richard S. Harrell, *et al.*, *Lessons in Colloquial Egyptian Arabic* (Washington, D.C.: Georgetown Univ. Press, 1963) pp. 3.4–3.6; and Walter Lehn and Peter Abboud, *Beginning Cairo Arabic* (Austin, The Univ. of Texas, 1965) pp. 37–39.

2

BASIC CHARACTERISTICS OF THE PHYSICAL AND FAMILY ENVIRONMENT

2.1. THE PHYSICAL ENVIRONMENT

2.1.1. *The Village Surroundings*

This area has two seasons, a mild winter from November to April, and a hot summer from May to October. Rain is almost unknown, and dust is everywhere.

Although bounded by desert, the area around the village is in the Nile valley, and irrigation from the river surrounds the village with green fields in which many crops are grown, including vegetables, fruits, grains, sugar cane and cotton. Palm and other trees are plentiful.

Animals are kept near the village, many inside the residential area. These include water buffaloes, cows, donkeys, goats, sheep, poultry, and as pets, a few cats and dogs. No camels are used in this village, although they are common in surrounding villages.

2.1.2. *Family Homes*

Houses are made of sun-baked bricks consisting of mud and straw. A mortar of plaster is used to hold bricks together. Trunks of palm trees are used for roof beams. The houses have one doorway and few windows. They have one or more rooms, one of which may be used for animals. The flat roofs are covered with cotton stalks and dry corn stalks which are used as oven fuel. Washing is hung out on the roof, and poultry may be kept there.

Inside the houses, there is a low earth oven in one corner, and a few cooking pots, water jugs, and a basin. Every family has a 'teapot', even if it consists of a tin can with a wired handle. Some have plates and spoons. Only a few bits of furniture are found. There is a low rounded wooden table for eating. Most families sleep on straw mats which are rolled out at night, and most have quilts and pillows. If not, they cover with burlap sacks. There is usually a wooden storage chest, and a few families have beds, closets and chairs. Since there is no electricity inside the houses, every family has at least one kerosene lamp.

2.1.3. *The Government Cooperative Unit*

The cooperative unit is composed of a set of modern buildings with running water and electricity, constructed by the government to provide this and nearby villages with primary education, medical care, and agricultural extension services. It is about 1½ miles away. It has a clinic and a twenty bed hospital, and the extension center has an agricultural supervisor and social worker. There is also a recreation room with a television. The village children do not attend this center's school; they attend a closer one in West Village.

2.1.4. *Physical Characteristics of Children in the Study*

The children were measured for height, and any physical abnormalities were recorded. Children of average performance were found to be about the same height at the same age, with little difference between boys and girls. Children who performed well and were more active were often larger physically than others in their age group.

This may be related to the quality of early nutrition. A study reported by Scrimshaw has shown that there were positive correlations between body height and weight and test performance among children of poor families in rural Guatemala, which did not hold for well-nourished urban children.[1] It seems reasonable to assume that similar environmental circumstances may have had corresponding detrimental effects on the growth and development of some of the children in this study.[2] Their diet, state of health, and environment are often similar to those described in the Scrimshaw studies.

Intelligence could only be estimated, based on each child's performance and observations of its interactions with other children and adults.

In Table 3 the children's physical characteristics are described.

Table 3

Physical characteristics of children in the study

Name	Age, Sex	Height (inches)	Health	Intelligence	Speech Quality
D. Hasan	1.5-M	29.5	Fair		
E. Zakiya	1.11-F	29	Fair		
F. Suʔād	2.3-F	27.5	Fair		

[1] Nevin S. Scrimshaw, "Infant Malnutrition and Adult Learning", *The Development Digest* VII. 1 (1969); 20–24.

[2] The ages at which children in this study were observed to have acquired certain verbal skills are later than the ages at which the same skills were acquired by urban middle-class Egyptian children who were tested and observed in another study by the author, which is forthcoming.

(Table 3–continued)

Name	Age, Sex	Height (inches)	Health	Intelligence	Speech Quality
1. Manāl	2.8-F	35.5	Good	Av.	Good
2. Wafā	3.0-F	35	Pale, sickly	Av.	Exc.
3. Jamāl	3.6-M	36.5	Excellent	High	Poor (unclear)
4. Sanā	3.6-F	35.5	Good	Av.	Good
5. Abdel-Fattaāh	4.0-M	35.5	Poor	Low	Poor (lisps)
6. Sabāh	4.0-F	37.5	Fair	Av.	Good
7. Amāl	4.6-F	38.5	Fair	Av.	Good
8. Yūsef	5.0-M	43.5	Good	Av.	Good
9. Ahmad	5.0-M	41	Good	High	Good
10. Niˤmat	5.6-F	39	Fair	Low	Fair
11. Jirjis	6.0-M	41	Fair	High	Good
12. Sarāya	6.0-F	45	Good	High	Good
13. Mohamed Mūsa	6.0-M	46.5	Good	Av.	Good
14. Tahiya	6.6-F	45.5	Fair	Av.	Good
15. Zakariya	6.6-M	43.5	Fair	Low	Good
16. Kāmel Ridwān	7.0-M	46	Good	Av.	Good
17. Zeynab	7.0-F	45.5	Good	High	Good
18. Azīza	7.0-F	48.5	Fair	Av.	Good
19. Mohamed Hilmi	8.0-M	52	Fair	High	Good
20. Saˤdiya	8.0-F	48.5	Fair	High	Good
21. Kamla	8.0-F	48	Fair	Low	Good
22. Hoda	8.6-F	52.5	Good	Av.	Good
23. Aliya	9.0-F	50	Excellent	Av.	Good
24. Mohamed Tagāwi	9.0-M	50	Fair	Av.	Good
25. Nadya Ridwān	10.0-F	50.5	Excellent	High	Good
26. Wahība	11.0-F	51	Good	High	Good
27. Abdel-Raˤūf	12.6-M	51.5	Excellent	High	Good
28. Ali	13.0-M	53	Good	High	Good
29. Kāmel Saˤd	13.0-M	54	Fair	Low	Good
30. Sayyid	14.0-M	54	Good	High	Good
31. Abdel-ˤāl	15.0-M	62	Good	Av.	Good

Child 5 had a history of illness. He had had softening of the bones due to a calcium deficiency, and had only recently started walking. His speech was slow and not very clear, but satisfactory.

2.2. THE SOCIAL STRUCTURE

2.2.1. *The Extended Family*

The family unit in the village constitutes the basic framework within which the lives of the people, from birth to death, are worked out. The family not only provides its members with support and social orientation in childhood, but remains for them the primary vehicle for economic cooperation, social control, and mutual protection. The first loyalty of every individual is to his family, on whose wealth, welfare, and reputation his own are dependent. New economic reforms are shaking the old self-sufficiency of the family, and governmental institutions are pre-empting some of the welfare and control functions which in the past belonged solely to the family, and they may in time transcend the exclusive loyalty to the kin and local group. But in the meantime, many of the traditional patterns have been less uprooted than superficially weakened, and in the village the family preserves its essential character.

There are two kinds of grouping among kinsmen in the village. These are the household, an extended family consisting of several generations, and the lineage or clan, composed of a number of related extended families.

Even if an extended family of two or more generations does not live in the same house, social and economic ties are strong. Men seldom leave their family group. Sometimes girls marry outside the village and leave, but marriage as close to home as possible is preferred. This may be difficult for Christians, who are not numerous. Christian brides usually come from other villages, and daughters leave upon marriage.

Polygamy is technically allowed for Muslim males, but it is very rare in modern times, partly because of the expense involved in supporting more than one family. All married men in the village are monogamous.

A typical household consists of husband and wife, unmarried children, and often married sons and their wives and children. The husband's brothers, sisters, or other relatives may reside with the family; the bond is blood relationship to the head of the household.

The language has many terms of kinship, the most important of which are:

Term	Gloss
/ʔabūya/	'my father'
/ʔummi/	'my mother'
/sīdi/	'my grandfather'
/sitti/	'my grandmother'
/ʔuxti/	'my sister'
/ʔaxūya/	'my brother'
/ʔibn/	'son'
/bit/	'daughter'
/ʔammi/	'my (paternal) uncle'
/ʔammiti/	'my (paternal) aunt'
/xǣli/	'my (maternal) uncle'
/xælti/	'my (maternal) aunt'

Relationships such as cousins, nieces and nephews are expressed in two-word phrases, such as /ʔibn ʕammi/ 'the son of my paternal uncle' or /bit ʔuxti/ 'the daughter of my sister'.

2.2.2. *Roles of Family Members*

The father or head of the household controls family decisions relating to financial expenditures, education, and events such as marriage. He is accorded special respect by other members of the family. The mother is the more direct disciplinarian of children, and is largely responsible for their upbringing and welfare.

Older children usually care for younger children, often carrying them all day wherever they go, returning them to the home only to be fed and to sleep. Younger children are expected to show respect for older ones if the age difference is about five years or more, and sisters respect brothers. Most teaching of the younger children, linguistic or social, is done by older chidren. From them they hear stories and learn games and songs.

2.2.3. *Training of Children*

As soon as children can walk, they spend most of the day outdoors playing with others. Mothers have little time to do much more than feed them. A lack of individual attention probably does not have much effect on slowing linguistic development, since this is made up for by a complete lack of privacy for the children–no one is ever alone. Children are constantly surrounded by speech, most of the time that of other children.

There is usually little concerted effort put forth in training children. It is felt that the society and time will take care of this. Adults are very tolerant of mistakes made by younger children until about age 3, or when they are expected to understand directions. Discipline is usually physical, but not often harsh. It is not very effective because it is so common.

Children are not often corrected in their language usage by other children, and adults claim that they "don't hear mistakes". Adults frequently expand children's utterances, thus inadvertently correcting or completing phonemic or grammatical deficiencies.

When questioned, adults could not agree as to when children began to 'babble',[3] giving the age as ranging from one year to age 2½. They agreed that children were "all alike" in their early speech, beginning with babbling before using words, and that they understood speech before they could talk. After some hesitation, all confessed to using special 'baby talk' words, although men use them much less.

[3] The term used in the language is /yinǣγi/.

2.2.4. *Children's Daily Routines, Work, and Games*

A child's daily routine is affected by several factors, mainly by the child's age, physical capability, intelligence, the degree of its mother's attentiveness, and number of other children in the family. The child's routines follow two or three seasons: the seasons of work, no work, and school if the child attends.

In the cotton harvest season in late summer, all children over age 5 work daily, for two periods lasting about a week each. The children are up with their parents and, after tea, hurry to the field. Even while picking cotton, children often eat, usually pieces of bread. Some are sent home periodically to fetch bread, water, or cigarettes, but in general they work a full day, stopping only for meals in the field. The children's day ends earlier, at about 3 : 00 p.m., after which they are free to play on cotton bales and gather for games and singing in the evening. If the children's family owns some of the cotton gathered, they may sit and clean the cotton in the evenings. During this time, the children go to sleep early, at about 8 : 00 p.m.

Other seasons of work include the season of gathering corn and sugar cane, and children are especially helpful when the new cotton plants must be inspected and parasitic worms removed by hand.

Children between the ages of 6 and 12 are required by law to attend school for about eight months out of the year, or the parents pay a high fine. However, the fine is payable per absence, regardless of how many days it lasts, so children are often kept out of school to work for periods long enough to earn more than the equivalent of the fine. School is held every day except Friday. It begins at 8 : 00 a.m., with a break at about 10 : 30 for the children to return home for breakfast. School ends at 2 : 00 and after eating, most children go to the field to help their father until sundown.

Children who are capable and clever, or have few older brothers and sisters, begin helping in the field work as young as age 5. They also become responsible for feeding the family's animals, such as the buffalo and donkey. Boys may drive goats and sheep to grazing places. Girls are frequently sent to get water from the pump, and often help in the home. Other children may not be required to work until about age 8. By age 14, a boy is doing a man's work daily, and is considered an adult.

Younger children awake early, about 6 : 30 a.m., and after drinking milk or tea, go out to play. They do not usually remain at home or help their mother with her tasks. Most do not sleep in the afternoon.

Children of all ages play together, because most older ones are caring for younger ones. Most playing is done in the dust. Boys may draw fields in the dust, and some draw elaborate irrigation canals and bring water to 'irrigate' their field. They frequently draw pictures in the dust, of farm tools and machinery. Girls make 'bread' or dolls out of mud, and enjoy sitting and talking, pretending to be older women. Play-acting is popular with all children; they may take roles such as the landlord, or the village mayor, or a police officer.

Group games include some which seem to be enjoyed by children everywhere, such as 'cops and robbers', 'hide and seek', and 'leap frog'. When a ball can be had, boys may play a version of 'kick ball'.

2.2.5. *Formal Education*

In spite of the government's efforts in promoting and, in fact, requiring free primary education for all village children, in this village at least, the value of education has not yet been recognized by most families. Some do see a value in education, however, because it is helpful to be able to read the newspaper, weigh cotton, and do simple arithmetic figuring, besides the fact that education improves the individual's social position. Usually whether children are sent to school regularly depends on whether the family can afford financially to do without their work.

The school which the children attend is located in West Village, and is a large one-story building with about eight classrooms. Teachers are graduates of two-year teaching institutes and are sent by the government to teach in rural areas. Most are from Cairo, and the majority are young men.

The curriculum includes the following subjects: Arabic, arithmetic, religion (Muslim and Christian), sports, drawing, general science, health, hand crafts, Arabic culture, geography, and history. In the first year, the first five subjects are taught; in the second year, general science is added, and after the fourth year, all subjects are taught.

A great part of learning is by rote memorization, of grammatical rules and paradigms, arithmetic tables, Koranic passages, and important dates and facts. Because of the high absence rate, classes proceed slowly.

In language instruction, a big problem facing children learning to read and write is that they must learn 'Modern Standard Arabic', since the spoken dialect is not written. They learn the alphabet first, which 'fits' the language very well, although vowels are not always written. The children then begin reading drills, in which not all the words or grammar are familiar. Emphasis is placed on reading and writing, and the children do not get much beyond reading simple stories and history. Language instruction may be divided into grammar rules, composition, dictation, reading (aloud), and poetry. Little silent reading is done. There is no training in oral skills such as public speaking or conversation techniques.

If a family desires to send a child to 'intermediate school' or any higher level, the child must attend in the town of Abu Qurqās. Only boys would go beyond elementary school, and this is relatively rare.

Many children reach age 12 before they have completed requirements for the 'elementary certificate' and never receive it. Some are granted the certificate after several years although they are barely literate, and they soon forget their new skills.

In spite of a government campaign against rural illiteracy, many have not been convinced of the value of formal education.

2.2.6. *Effects of the Social Structure on Children*

Children growing up under the circumstances described tend to learn early that complete conformity is required for successful social relations. Originality is not encouraged; it is not felt to be important, since "no one can accomplish new things". It is best for children to listen to adults and obey them. A child who is /muʔæddab/ 'polite' is one who respects his elders and listens to their advice.

Children have little contact with the 'outside' through travel, mass media, or reading. To them, concepts like 'the government', 'Cairo', and 'the world' are vague, and they will in all likelihood grow up to be as narrow in outlook and confined by ignorance as the preceding generation. It is almost unthinkable to leave home, since kin ties are strong and there is little economic independence.

Most individuals marry young if possible, and slip into the old patterns of work, raising children, and struggling to provide adequate subsistence for their families. Girls are expected to be subservient to their husbands and other male relatives. All persons respect the opinions and authority of older family members, who retain a strong influence on their children even after they have grown up.

2.2.7. *Special Uses of Language*

2.2.7.1. *Story-telling and Singing*

Children in the village are fond of telling stories and singing songs, but adults seldom participate in either activity. Imaginitive story-telling is not 'proper' for men, and their narration of events only occurs in the course of ordinary conversation. Stories are "of no practical value" and if fathers told them to children, it might encourage too much intimacy, thereby lessening respect.[4] Boys know and tell many stories; girls do not. Story-telling sessions cease when an adult approaches.

Girls sing songs, mainly wedding songs, and while boys enjoy listening, they do not join in. To sing, the girls gather in a circle on the ground. One begins

[4] Hamed Ammar, *Growing Up in an Egyptian Village: Silwa, Province of Aswan* (London, Routledge and Paul, 1954) p. 161.

beating a rhythm on a drum or any flat surface, and the others clap. The older girls are leaders in the singing, but all girls sing as many songs and verses as they know.

No 'speech play' or 'language games' were observed.

2.2.7.2. *Memorization and Recitation*

Great importance is placed on memorization and recitation of Koranic or Biblical passages. It is not uncommon for illiterate children and adults to recite verses for long periods, often while not understanding the obscure words and thoughts expressed. Memorizing the whole Koran is not uncommon. Prayers are also memorized.

2.2.7.3. *The Zikr*

The most unique use of language in this society is in connection with the practice of *zikr*. This is a gathering for pseudo-religious purposes, in which Muslim men stand in a circle or in lines and chant over and over the name of God, /ʔaḷḷāh/, or other phrases. They establish a chant rhythm and begin to bend and sway their heads and bodies in unison, closing their eyes in concentration. This may continue for hours without cessation, until the participants have worked themselves into a high state of religious excitement. It is not uncommon for one or two to be overcome and fall to the ground in ecstasy or as if 'possessed'.

This is an old practice, although it is not sanctioned by orthodox Islam. The original purpose of it was /zikr ʔaḷḷāh/ 'invocation of God' or /zikr ʔawliyǣʔ ʔiṣ-ṣāliḥīn/ 'invocation of the righteous saints', and names of locally venerated 'saints' are frequently mentioned.

A *zikr* gathering is usually sponsored by a man who has reason to express gratitude to God; in fact, he may have pledged that if a certain misfortune were averted or good fortune granted, he would sponsor a *zikr*. It may be on the occasion of a good harvest, circumcision of a son, or restoration of someone to health. The cost is whatever the man can afford–at least, tea for the participants and on-lookers; at most, an animal may be slaughtered for a feast.

A *zikr* begins after the evening prayer, about 8 : 00 or 9 : 00 p. m., and lasts until midnight. Large ceremonies may last until 2 : 00 or 3 : 00 a.m. Boys age 10 and over may participate of they wish; anyone is welcome. Often women, girls, and small children gather to watch, and women may prepare food. It is an affair for the whole village, and one of the few psychological outlets available.

Men in Sheikh Mubārak and West Village participate in *zikr* ceremonies held in either village, and they are quite frequent. They used to be held once or twice a month, but have become more frequent in the last two years or so, now averaging about once a week. In a nearby farm village, a *zikr* is held every night.

Boys in the study, when gathered together and requested to tell stories or discuss a subject, often decided that they would like most of all to chant a *zikr* together.

3

THE DEVELOPMENT OF PHONOLOGY

In order to trace the development of the phonological system in the speech of the children studied, their utterances will be compared to the phonological system of the adult dialect.

3.1. THE PHONOLOGICAL SYSTEM IN ADULT LANGUAGE

The local variety of speech cannot be assigned to either the Lower Egyptian (Cairene) or Upper Egyptian (Aswan) varieties of Colloquial Egyptian Arabic, which are the two commonly recognized dialects.[1] Just as the village is situated between the two areas geographically, its speech variety is approximately mid-way between these two dialects linguistically, sharing some phonological traits with the Lower Egyptian and some with the Upper Egyptian dialect. Khalafallah distinguishes between "northern Saʕīdi" and "southern Saʕīdi" dialects in Upper Egypt;[2] this is of the northern type.

3.1.1. *Consonants*

3.1.1.1. *Analysis and Classification*[3]

[1] Egyptian terminology for these dialects is /baḥari/ 'Lower Egyptian dialect' and /ṣacīdi/ 'Upper Egyptian dialect'.

[2] Abdelghany A. Khalafallah, "A Descriptive Grammar of Saciidi Colloquial Egyptian Arabic", Unpublished Ph. D. dissertation (Univ. of Texas, 1961) p. 2.

[3] Symbols used are those of the IPA system *(The Principles of the International Phonetic Association* [London, International Phonetic Association, 1964]) with the following exceptions:

IPA		Symbol Used	
ɾ	j	/r/	/y/
t̪ d̪ s̪ z̪ l̪		/ṭ ḍ ṣ ẓ ḷ/	
dʒ	ħ	/j/	/ḥ/
ʃ	ʕ	/š/	/c/

Table 4

Consonant Phonemes

Manner of Articulation	B	L–D	D–A	E–A	A–P	P	V	U	Ph	L	Point of Articulation
Stop			t	ṭ			k	q		ʔ	B: Bilabial
	b		d	ḍ			g				
Affricate					j						L–D: Labio-Dental
Fricative		f	s	ṣ	š		x		ḥ	h	D–A: Dental-Alveolar
			z	ẓ			ɣ		c		
Flap			r								E–A: 'Emphatic' Alveolar
Lateral			l	ḷ							A–P: Alveo-Palatal
Nasal	m		n								P: Palatal
Semivowel	w					y					V: Velar
											U: Uvular
											Ph: Pharyngeal
											L: Laryngeal

3.1.1.2. *Realization*[4]

The following consonants are articulated in the same or approximately the same position as in English, with the exception of /r/:

1. /b/ Voiced bilabial stop; may be voiced or voiceless before voiceless obstruents.
2. /t/ Voiceless dental or alveolar stop.
3. /d/ Voiced dental or alveolar stop.
4. /k/ Voiceless stop; palatal before front vowels, velar before back vowels.
5. /g/ Voiced stop; palatal before front vowels, velar before back vowels.
6. /j/ Voiced alveo-palatal affricate.
7. /š/ Voiceless alveo-palatal fricative; may be voiced before voiced obstruents.
8. /f/ Voiceless labio-dental fricative; may be voiced or voiceless before voiceless obstruents.
9. /s/ Voiceless alveolar fricative.
10. /z/ Voiced alveolar fricative.
11. /h/ Voiceless laryngeal fricative; may be voiced or voiceless before voiced obstruents and between vowels.
12. /l/ Voiced alveolar lateral; voiceless after voiceless obstruents; often has nasal resonance.
13. /m/ Voiced bilabial nasal; labio-dental before /f/; may be voiceless after voiceless obstruent.

[4] Consonants which are shared with the Cairene dialact are described approximately as described in Harrell. Richard S. Harrell, *The Phonology of Colloquial Egyptian Arabic* (New York, American Council of Learned Societes, 1957).

14. /n/ Voiced non-labial nasal; dental before vowels or when final; before consonants, variable in place of articulation according to articulation of the consonant; may be voiceless after voiceless obstruents.
15. /w/ High back rounded semivowel.
16. /y/ High front unrounded semivowel.
17. /r/ Voiced apico-alveolar flap; voiceless after a voiceless obstruent.

The following consonants are articulated with 'emphasis':

18. /ṭ/ Voiceless emphatic alveolar stop.
10. /ḍ/ Voiced emphatic alveolar stop.
20. /ṣ/ Voiceless emphatic alveolar fricative.
21. /ẓ/ Voiced emphatic alveolar fricative.
22. /ḷ/ Voiced emphatic lateral.[5]

The remaining consonants are 'back consonants':

23. /q/ Voiceless uvular stop.
24. /ʔ/ Glottal stop.
25. /x/ Voiceless velar fricative.
26. /ɣ/ Voiced velar fricative.
27. /ḥ/ Voiceless pharyngeal fricative.
28. /ʕ/ Voiced pharyngeal fricative.

3.1.1.3. *Allophones*

Allophonic variation of consonant phonemes occurs in the environment of an emphatic consonant.

Defining the phenomenon of 'emphasis' (/tæfxīm/, lit. 'thickening') in Arabic has long been a linguistic problem.[6] The point of articulation of the consonant is the same as for a non-emphatic consonant, while the tongue is flattened and the back of the tongue raised, so that the upper surface of the tongue is concave. The effect is velarization of the consonant, and rounding of the mouth and throat which results in more resonance than in non-emphatic consonants. The term EMPHASIS is a traditional one and should not be taken literally to mean that these consonants are articulated more forcefully than others. VELARIZATION is probably a more accurate term.

[5] For a justification of treating /ḷ/ as an independent phoneme, cf. Charles A. Ferguson, "The Emphatic L in Arabic", *Language* 32 (1956): 446–452. I have analyzed /ḷ/ as a separate phoneme in this dialect for approximately the same reasons.

[6] Selim summarizes several disagreements among linguists regarding emphasis in Egyptian Arabic in his Notes to his article, "Some Contrasts between Classical Arabic and Egyptian Arabic", *Linguistic Studies in Memory of Richard Slade Harrell*, ed., D. G. Stuart (Washington, D.C. Georgetown Univ. Press, 1967) pp. 145–146.

If emphasis is defined in terms of distinctive features, it may be stated as a flat-plain opposition, the emphasized consonant being "flattened" by contraction of the pharynx.[7] Harrell refers to Ferguson's notion that emphasis may be regarded as a distinctive feature of the vocalic or consonantal system, or as a suprasegmental feature.[8] Harrell states: "It [emphasis] never occurs as a feature of a single segment. The minimum range of emphasis is V(:)C or CV(:). These are merely the minimum ranges. Usually emphasis is a function of the entire syllable.[9] Emphasis is a feature of both vowels and consonants."[10] Lehn also treats emphasis as a suprasegmental feature of the syllable.[11] Firth suggests that emphasis in Arabic may be treated as part of the prosodic rather than the phonematic system, suggesting that emphasis is a type of vowel or consonant harmony.[12] Emphasis will be treated here, however, as a feature of certain segmental consonant phonemes.

Five consonants in the dialect are emphatic phonemes themselves, contrastive with nonemphatic counterparts, and they cannot lose their emphasis. Every other consonant phoneme has an allophonic, emphasized counterpart in certain environments, except /x/, /ɣ/, /ḥ/, /ʕ/, and /q/. Only the five emphatic consonants will be marked as such in phonemic transcription.

1. An emphatic consonant causes emphasis of the whole syllable in which it appears, and may extend to the morphological word (the stem plus the maximum number of bound forms). Emphasis affects both preceding and following phonemes. Vowels become rounded and velarized, and surrounding nonemphatic consonants are usually velarized. For example:

/ṭabīb/ > [ṭaḅīḅ]	'physician'
/ḍarabna/ > [ḍaṛaḅṇə]	'we hit'

The emphasis may be modified when a new unemphatic syllable is affixed, for example:

/ḍarab/ > [ḍaṛaḅ] 'he hit' vs. [ḍaṛabak] 'he hit you (m. sing.)'

[7] Roman Jakobson, C. Fant, and Morris Halle, *Preliminaries to Speech Analysis* (Cambridge, MIT Press, 1963) p. 31. This opposition was used in describing "pharyngealized consonants".

[8] Richard S. Harrell, "A Linguistic Analysis of Egyptian Radio Arabic", *Contributions to Arabic Linguistics*, ed., Charles A. Ferguson (Cambridge, Harvard Univ. Press, 1960) p. 26.

[9] Harrell, 1957. p. 78.

[10] Harrell, 1957. p. 79.

[11] Walter Lehn, "Emphasis in Cairo Arabic", *Language* 39 (1963): 29–39.

[12] J. R. Firth, "Sounds and Prosodies", *Readings in Linguistics II*, ed., Eric P. Hamp, Fred W. Householder, and Robert Austerlitz (Chicago, Univ. of Chicago Press, 1966) p. 184.

2. All voiced consonants may be, and usually are, emphasized before and after the vowel /a/.

[w̦al̦ad̦]	'child'	vs.	[wɪlǣd]	'children'
[yəl̦l̦ə]	'let's go'	vs.	[yūsɛf]	'Joseph'
[m̦ām̦a]	'Mama'	vs.	[mɪlk]	'property'

3. Consonants occurring in a cluster with /r/ or separated from /r/ by /a/ tend to be slightly emphasized.

3.1.1.4. *Morphophonemic Alternation*

Phonemically and morphemically conditioned alternation of consonant phonemes occurs when the phonemes are assimilated in certain environments. The most important instance is the assimilation of the definite article.

In the definite article, the prefix /ʔil-/, the /l/ is assimilated before dental-alveolar and emphatic consonants, and may or may not be assimilated before velar stops (in free variation). The assimilating consonant is geminated. Examples of allomorphs of the definite article morpheme are:

{ʔil-}	ᵃ/ʔiṭ-ṭarabēza/	'the table'
	ᵃ/ʔis-sæna/	'the year'
	ᵃ/ʔir-rājul/	'the man'
	ᵃ/ʔik-kitǣb/ ~ ᵃ/ʔil-kitǣb/	'the book'

When not part of the definite article, /l/ preceding these consonants is not assimilated, for example:

/kæl sæmak/	'he ate fish'
/kæl roz/	'he ate rice'

3.1.1.5. *Distribution*

All single consonants can occur in initial, medial and final position in a word.

All consonants except /q/ and /h/ may be doubled, and will be considered geminated consonants, since the consonant is divided into two parts by a syllabic boundary.[13] When the consonant /r/ is doubled, it results in an apical trill. Geminated consonants are subject to the same rules of distribution as other consonant clusters, but do not occur in initial position in a word.

Besides gemination, there are nine types of consonant clusters permitted, i.e., stops, fricatives, and resonants in any combination. Possible combinations are limited only by the rules of assimilation noted above.[14]

[13] Bertil Malmberg, *Phonetics* (New York, Dover Publications, Inc., 1963) p. 77.

[14] For a list of all possible and impossible clusters in an Upper Egyptian dialect, cf. Khalafallah, 1961, pp. 38–42.

Consonant clusters may occur across morphological boundaries. No clusters of more than two consonants occur. Consonant clusters can occur in initial, medial and final position in the word.

3.1.2. *Vowels*

3.1.2.1. *Analysis and Classification*

Table 5

Vowel phonemes

Short Vowels	Front	Central	Back	Long Vowels	Front	Central	Back
High	i		u	High	ī		ū
Mid	e		o	Mid	ē		ō
Low	æ	a		Low	ǣ	ā	

3.1.2.2. *Realization*[15]

1. /i/ /ī/ High front unrounded vowel.
2. /e/ /ē/ Mid front unrounded vowel.
3. /æ/ /ǣ/ Low front unrounded vowel.[16]
4. /a/ /ā/ Low central unrounded vowel.
5. /o/ /ō/ Mid back rounded vowel.
6. /u/ /ū/ High back rounded vowel.

3.1.2.3. *Allophones*

Vowels have a much wider variation than vowels in English. The allophone of a vowel is determined by its environment. Only the major allophones will be discussed here. There is no major allophonic variation in the realization of long vowels.

[15] /ē/ and /ō/ are derived from diphthongs /ai/ and /au/ in early Arabic. In many descriptions of Egyptian Arabic, these two vowels are described as occurring only in long form; in these descriptions, /e/ is treated as an allophone of /i/, and /o/ as an allophone of /u/.

[16] Contrary to most descriptions of Colloquial Egyptian Arabic, the sound /æ/ is treated here as a separate phoneme, rather than allophone of /a/, because of the occurrence of such nearly minimal pairs as: [bāba] 'Papa' vs. [bǣb] 'door', or [māma] 'Mama' vs. [mǣt] 'he died'. In neither pair is the vowel affected by an emphatic consonant, so it cannot be an allophonic variation. This vocalic inventory is consistent with Selim, based on Mitchell's analysis.

1. /i/.

[i] occurs only in post-stress, word-final position.

/sīdi/ > [sīdi] 'my grandfather'

[ɪ] occurs elsewhere.

/bit/ > [bɪt] 'girl'

2. /æ/.

[ɛ] occurs before and after /r/. [ɛ] may occur in free variation with [æ] elsewhere, although [æ] is more common before /w/ and /y/.

/bærd/ > [bɛrd] 'cold'

[æ] occurs elsewhere, but never occurs in the environment of emphatic consonants.

/mæla/ > [mælə] 'he filled'

3. /a/.

[ə] may occur in unstressed position, especially when final in a word.

/gutṭa/ > [gutṭə] 'cat'
/jæmal/ > [jæməl] 'camel'

[a] occurs before and after /q/, /ḥ/, /ʕ/, and emphatic consonants, and often before and after /r/.

/ʕala/ > [ʕalə] 'on'
/bælaḥ/ > [bælaḥ] 'dates (food)'
/maḍa/ > [ṃaḍa] 'he signed'
/barra/ > [baṛṛa] 'outside'

4. /u/.

[ɔ] occurs after /ḥ/; in /uCC/ environment before or after /ḥ/, /ʔ/ or labials; and when the following syllable contains /a/.

/ḥubb/ > [ḥɔbb] 'love'
/ḥukm/ > [ḥɔkm] 'judgment'
/mudda/ > [mɔddə] 'period of time'
/ʔuwaḍ/ > [ʔɔwaḍ] 'rooms'

[u] occurs only in post-stress, word-final position.

/šǣfu/ > [šǣfu] 'he saw him'

[ʊ] occurs elsewhere. In /uCC/ environment, allophones range from [ʊ] to [ɔ] in free variation.

/ʕuluww/ > [ʕʊlɔww] ~ [ʕʊlʊww] 'height'
/full/ > [fʊll] ~ [fɔll] 'jasmine'

3.1.2.4. *Morphophonemic Alternation*

1. In an environment where a sequence of more than two consonants would occur, this is prevented by the insertion of an 'epenthetic' vowel. If the word ends in two consonants and the next word begins with a consonant, the vowel [ə] is inserted at the juncture.

{bit} ᵃ/bit/ 'girl' vs. ᵃ/bitᵊ kwayyisa/ 'good girl'
{šuft} ᵃ/šuft/ 'you (m. sing.) saw' vs. ᵃ/šuftᵊ mīn/ 'you (m. sing.) saw who?'

2. Unless a sequence of three consonants would be brought about, unstressed /i/ and /u/ are dropped out under two conditions. They are dropped in the last syllable of a word before the final consonant when a suffix beginning with a vowel is added:

{širib} ᵃ/širib/ 'he drank' vs. ᵃ/širbu/ 'they drank'
{yākul} ᵃ/yākul/ 'he eats' vs. ᵃ/yaklu/ 'they eat'

Elision occurs in the first syllable of a word when it is pronounced in close association with a preceding word which ends in a vowel:

{fī} ᵃ/fī/ 'in' vs. ᵃ/f betna/ 'in our house'

3. Long vowels are shortened to their short counterpart except when occurring in isolation, at the end of a word, or in a closed syllable (CVC). If non-final and non-isolated, a long vowel must occur in an open, stressed syllable.

{šǣfit} ᵃ/šǣfit/ 'she saw' vs. ᵃ/šæfitak/ 'she saw you (m. sing.)'
{bēt} ᵃ/bēt/ 'house' vs. ᵃ/betna/ 'our house'

3.1.2.5. *Distribution*

A vowel cannot occur in initial position in a syllable. It is preceded by a consonant, at least by a glottal stop. All vowels occur in medial position. All vowels except/ō/ occur in final position.

There are six diphthongs in this variety of Egyptian Arabic,[17] all with /i/ or /u/ as the second component, which are realized as /y/ and /w/ when occurring before another vowel (to prevent a tripthong). The /y/ and /w/ are not distinct phonemes from the vowels, however, because no pair is distinguished by the fact that one case has a phoneme realized as a consonant and the other has a vowel.[18]

[17] Adapted from Harrell *et al.*, 1963, P–7, P–8. He lists five dipthongs, analyzing /æy/ as an allophone of /ay/.

[18] Adapted from Jean Cantineau, "Esquisse d'une phonologie de l'arabe classique", *Etudes de linguistique arabe* (Paris, Librairie C. Klincksieck, 1960): 193–194.

Four diphthongs occur in medial and final position in a word:

1. /æy/.

/ʔǣya/	'verse (in the Koran)'
/šǣy/	'tea'

2. /ay/

/mayya/	'water'
/ray/	'irrigation'

3. /aw/

/ʕawza/	'she wants'
/ʔaw/	'or'

4. /iw/

/niwṣal/	'we arrive'
/xiliw/	'emptiness'

Two diphthongs occur in medial position only:

5. /iy/

/miyya/	'hundred'

6. /uy/

/buyūt/	'houses'

3.1.3. *Functional Load of Phonemes*

3.1.3.1. *Consonants*

Tomiche has made a statistical count of the relative frequency of occurrence of phonemes in the Cairene dialect, based on a sample of running words containing 10,010 phonemes.[19] Frequency of occurrence of consonants was as follows:[20]

1. Dental-alveolar (/t/, /d/, /s/, /z/, /l/, /n/, /ṭ/, /ḍ/, /ṣ/, /ẓ/, /ḷ/)
   38.2%
2. Labial (/b/, /m/, /w/)
   18.7%
3. 'Pre-palatal' (/š/, /r/, /y/)
   14.5%

[19] Nada Tomiche, *Le Parler Arabe du Caire* (The Hague and Paris, Mouton, 1964) p. 72.

[20] In the village dialect, /j/ is substituted for /g/ here, and /g/ is substituted for /ʔ/ approximately one fourth of the time.

4. Laryngeal (/ʔ/, /h/)
   9.6%

5. Pharyngeal (/ḥ/, /ʕ/)
   7.6%

6. 'Post-palatal' (/k/, /g/)
   6.2%

7. Labio-dental (/f/)
   2.9%

8. Velar (/x/, /ɣ/)
   2.3%

The approximate frequency of occurrence of individual consonant phonemes was as follows:[21]

/l/	8%	/d/	2.5%	/ṭ/	1%
/m/	5	/ʕ/	2.5	/ṣ/	.9
/ʔ/	4	/k/	2	/x/	.9
/n/	4	/f/	2	/z/	.7
/b/	4	/ḥ/	1.5	/ḍ/	.5
/r/	4	/š/	1.5	/ɣ/	.5
/y/	3.5	/h/	1.5	/ḷ/	.4
/t/	3.4	/s/	1.5	/ẓ/	.2
/w/	3	/g/	1.5	/q/	.1

3.1.3.2. *Vowels*

The relative frequency of occurrence of vowels was as follows:[22]

/æ/	21%	/ī/	1%	[ə] 1.4% (an epenthetic vowel, or may occur after doubled or emphasized consonant)[23]
/a/	7	/ū/	.9	
/u/	3	/ē/	.8	
/ǣ/	1.5	/ā/	.5	
/i/	1	/ō/	.2	

Short vowels occurred approximately 75.17% of the time.[24]

Of the total, approximately 61.6% of the phonemes occurring were consonants, and 38.4% vowels.

[21] Tomiche, 1964, p. 64.

[22] Tomiche, 1964, p. 64. /e/ is analyzed as an allophone of /i/, and /o/ as an allophone of /u/.

[23] Tomiche, 1964, p. 50.

[24] Tomiche, 1964, p. 74.

3.1.4. *Syllable Types*

The following syllable types occur in this dialect of Egyptian Arabic:

CV	CCV
$C\bar{V}$	$CC\bar{V}$
CVC	CCVC
$C\bar{V}C$	$CC\bar{V}C$
CVCC	CCVCC

Tomiche has found that the frequency of occurrence of the syllable types in the Lower Egyptian dialect (which does not have initial clusters) is approximately as follows:[25]

CVC	42.5%
CV	40.2
$C\bar{V}$	8.6
$C\bar{V}C$	8.5
CVCC	.2

Syllables beginning with a consonant cluster occur only initially in a microsegment. Since a syllable cannot contain both a lengthened vowel and a doubled consonant or cluster medially, if these appear together in a word, the syllables are separated between the two consonants:

/ṭay · yā · ra/ 'airplane'

If they would appear together in final position in a word, the long vowel is shortened:

/fæk · kēt/ + /ma- . . . -š/ > 'I took apart' + morpheme of negation
/ma · fæk · ketš/ 'I did not take apart'

When a word begins with the syllable /ʔV/, the /ʔ/ may be dropped when it is pronounced in close association with a preceding word. If the word ends in a consonant, the /ʔ/ is dropped but the remaining vowel cannot begin a syllable, so it becomes part of the preceding syllable:

/ya wa · lad/ + /ʔis · kut/ > 'boy!' + 'be silent!'
/ya · wa · la · dis · kut/ 'boy, be silent!'

In the preceding word ends in a vowel, the following vowel will again become part of the preceding syllable, resulting in a diphthong. If both vowels are the same, a long vowel will probably not result; instead, the vowel will be shortened:

/ya/ + /ʔum · mi/ > vocative particle + 'my mother'
/yaum · mi/ 'oh, mother!'
/ma · ʕa/ + /ʔaḥ · mad/ 'with' + 'Ahmad' (proper name)
/ma · ʕaḥ · mad/ 'with Ahmad'

[25] Tomiche, 1964, p. 78.

3.2. THE BABBLING STAGE

3.2.1. *Theoretical Considerations*

As early as the end of the second month after birth, the normal infant begins the first phase of linguistic development, usually called the 'cooing phase'. The cooing sounds are fairly distinct from crying sounds, acoustically much like vowels. Leopold characterized sounds of this period as low front and center vowels (aæɛʌə) and high back vowels (uʊ).[26] Irwin and Chen found that vowels are more frequent than consonants in the first 30 months, five times as frequent in infancy, with the relative number of occurrences of consonants increasing gradually until the frequency is equal by age 2½.[27]

The babbling stage begins usually by the age of 6 months, and lasts until after the first year. New articulatory modifications appear, more phonetically diversified. Weir demonstrated that cooing and babbling are in part imitative, especially of the adult intonation system. As early as 5½ months, cooing or babbling sounds of babies whose "parent language" was tonal could be distinguished from those of babies in a non-tonal language environment.[28] Lenneberg points out that the child is reacting to whole patterns rather than to small segments, "so the intonation pattern of a sentence is the more immediate input rather than individual phonemes".[29] Intonation is closely linked with affective speech and emotions, and there is evidence that the child at age 3 months can distinguish between pleasant and unpleasant voice tones.[30] Intonation is used as a meaningful signal even by crying infants.[31] Lieberman reports the case of a 9-month-old child who responded to a phrase when uttered with exaggerated intonation but not when it was uttered with normal intonation; at 10 months, the child responded to the same phrase with normal intonation.[32] He also found that two children, ages 10 months and 13 months, spoke with lower fundamental

[26] Werner F. Leopold, "Patterning in Children's Language Learning", *Psycholinguistics, A Book of Readings*, ed., Sol Saparta (New York, Holt, Rinehart, and Winston, Inc., 1961) p. 353.

[27] Dorothea A. McCarthy, "Language Development in Children", *Manual of Child Psychology*, ed., L. Carmichael, 2nd ed. (New York, John Wiley and Sons, Inc., 1954) p. 509.

[28] Ruth H. Weir, "Some Questions on the Child's Learning of Phonology", *The Genesis of Language*, eds., Frank Smith and George A. Miller (Cambridge, MIT Press, 1966) p. 156.

[29] Eric H. Lenneberg, *Biological Foundations of Language* (New York, John Wiley and Sons, 1967) p. 279.

[30] Morris M. Lewis, *How Children Learn to Speak* (New York, Basic Books, 1959) p. 30. Philip Lieberman, *Intonation, Perception and Language* (Cambridge, MIT Press, 1967) p. 44.

[31] Lieberman, 1967, p. 44.

[32] Lieberman, 1967, p. 44.

frequencies when with their parents (apparently imitating them) than when alone babbling.[33] Chao reported that the Chinese-speaking child in his case study acquired tones very early.[34]

In the early period, Lewis distinguishes between "discomfort cries" and "comfort sounds",[35] each with three stages of development: vowel-like, earlier consonantal (mostly back consonants), and later consonantal (front consonants). Babbling itself occurs only in a state of comfort and is not an attempt to communicate verbally; rather, the child simply is enjoying producing sounds and is acquiring rudimentary vocal skills which will be used later in phonemic development. By 6 months, self-reinforcement encourages continued development (the essential "auditory feedback loop" is established),[36] and adult reinforcement also has an effect on the rate of development. Early babbling, however, is mainly unlearned and not dependent on reinforcement; it is observed even in deaf infants.[37]

In this period, sounds are not yet properly termed phonemes; they are not "speech sounds", acoustically, motorically, or functionally.[38] Even well-known babbling syllables such as /mama/, /baba/, and /papa/ are more properly "muscle exercises",[39] with no reference attached. Reduplicated monosyllables are very common in babbling,[40] babbling is more typically syllabic than phonemic.[41]

Irwin and Chen analyzed the pre-speech sounds of infants extensively, although apparently all subjects were in an English-speaking environment. Their findings agree closely with what I observed in an Arabic-speaking environment. They state that in the first two months, the child has a phonemic repertoire of approximately 7.5 "phonemes"–an average of 4.5 different "vowels"

[33] Lieberman, 1967, p. 45.

[34] Yuen Ren Chao, "The Cantian Idiolect. An Analysis of the Chinese Spoken by a Twenty-Eight-Months Old Child", *Semitic and Oriental Studies: A Volume Presented to William Popper*, ed., Walter J. Fischel (Berkeley, Univ. of California Press, 1951) p. 32.

[35] Morris M. Lewis, *Language, Thought and Personality in Infancy and Childhood* (New York, Basic Books, 1964) p. 15.

[36] D. B. Fry, "The Development of the Phonological System in the Normal and the Deaf Child", *The Genesis of Language*, eds. Frank Smith and George A. Miller (Cambridge, MIT Press, 1966) p. 189.

[37] Fry, 1966, pp. 189–190.

[38] Lenneberg, 1967, p. 277.

[39] Werner F. Leopold, "Study of Child Language and Infant Bilingualism", *Word* (1948) 4: 1.

[40] The CVCV pattern was also found by Weir to be very common in child soliloquies at age 1.3. Weir, 1966, p. 160.

[41] Charles E. Osgood and James J. Jenkins, "Diachronic Psycholinguistics–First Language Learning", *Psycholinguistics – A Survey of Theory and Research Problems*, ed., Charles E. Osgood and Thomas A. Sebeok (Bloomington, Indiana Univ. Press, 1965) p. 129.

and 2.7 different "consonants".[42] 50% of the consonants of newborns is /h/,[43] which may in part account for the finding of a predominance of "back consonants" by Lewis in his postulated "second stage", and for the generalization that earliest consonant development proceeds from back to front.[44]

While Lewis does not distinguish between cooing and babbling, I believe that only in Stage III ("later consonantal stage") can it be said that babbling has begun.

3.2.2. *Data Obtained in This Study*

In this study, speech samples of two infants were obtained, the earliest at 6 and 8 months, respectively. A 6-month-old girl, Nadya Lamʕi (Child A) was observed during and after feeding and while being spoken to by her mother. Her utterances, produced in a period of about 25 minutes, were transcribed as follows:

1. Child A–6 months

[ʔæ̃]	[ʔʊ̃]	[ʔə̃]	[ʔɛdɛ́̃]
[ʔapʰá]	[ʔabb]	[mmá]	
[ʔabb˺á]	[ʔʊɤə]	[ʔahé]	

The mother reinforced syllables similar to words such as /māma/ and /bāba/, but only after the child had produced the sounds. It is extremely doubtful that the child was imitating.

The 8-month-old boy, Abdalla (Child B), was observed with his mother and sister (age 6), and was addressed with typical 'baby words' such as /māma/ 'Mama' and /bāba/ 'Papa'. His utterances, produced in a period of about 35 minutes, were transcribed as follows:

2. Child B–8 months

[ʔaƀa][45]	[mū]	[mə]
[mbba]	[mámá]	[ʔaw]
[ʔʊh]	[ʔāya]	[b˺a]

[42] Cited in McCarthy, 1954, p. 509.

[43] Irwin and Curry, cited in McCarthy, 1954, pp. 511–512. McCarthy comments that perhaps /h/ cannot validly be listed as a consonant sound, since a sound like /h/ is automatically produced when the voice is held in the act of uttering any vowel, and in many utterances in the crying state. Early back consoants may also be related to the activities of sucking, swallowing, and chewing.

[44] Lewis, 1964, p. 17.

[45] Voiced bilabial fricative.

There were long periods of silence between utterances, and it was difficult to attract the child's attention. Both the mother and sister imitated the child's sounds, even some which are not in adult or baby talk vocabulary.

Compared to the stages found by Lewis for English-speaking infants, both children were in Stage III, producing mostly front consonants, mainly stops.

3.2.3. *Early Imitation*

In theory, a child may begin imitation in the period of 6 to 10 months of age, if it is sufficiently reinforced. Lewis divides imitation into three stages: "rudimentary" (3 to 4 months), then a lapse of imitation (4 to 5 months), and "accurate" (from 9 months on).[46] I feel that this is a bit early with reference to the two subjects in this study–it seems more likely that the babies' utterances have long been imitated by adults, and have consequently been standardized into 'baby talk' words by the society, rather than the infant actually having 'learned' words such as /māma/ 'Mama', /bāba/ 'Papa', or /mbū/ baby talk for 'water', by 8 or 9 months.

While Lewis, Leopold, Weir, and researchers mentioned in McCarthy's table have found imitation beginning at 6 to 10 months, I saw no convincing evidence of imitation until about the tenth month. A transcription of utterances of Child B at 10 months revealed 'nonsense' syllables, but also a beginning attempt to imitate some words:

1. Child B – 10 months

'Nonsense'			
[ʔazz]	[hɛb]	[ʔɛ̆]	
[zz]	[ʔavv]		
Imitation			
Sister:	[māma]		
Child:	[mm]	[mma]	[ʔámá]
Mother:	[bāba]	[bāba] (exaggerated lengthening of vowel)	
Child:	[ʔább^{h}a]	[ʔápa]	
Investigator:	[mbū]	[ʔambū]	
Child:	[mū]	[mu]	

This is consistent with what was reported by parents and adults in interviews, who stated that imitation and early speech begin at 8 months to one year.

Another important factor is that these babies receive much less individual attention and directed speech than do middle-class children, since parents have

[46] Lewis, 1959, p. 49.

little leisure time for such activity. Fry notes that speech in situations such as feeding, dressing, and bathing can have a marked effect on the acquisition of speech.[47] In this society, ritual bathing and changing of clothing does not occur. Even during breast feeding, which continues for at least a year, the mother is likely to be occupied with other tasks and does not commonly address the child.

In connection with this it may be noted that Fisichelli found that institutionalized infants of 6 to 18 months show retardation in speech development, presumably from lack of individual attention and reinforcement.[48] The fact that parents addressed babies in my presence does not imply that it is a regular practice.[49]

Fry points out that imitation is extremely important in the development of phonology, more so than in the later development of grammar.[50] After the phonological system begins to take shape, incorrect phoneme sequences (which would later have to be discarded) are not produced, as is frequently the case in early grammatical constructions. It is, however, extremely difficult to determine precisely when a very young child is imitating, especially when imitations are still far from accurate and are frequently interrupted by periods of inattention.

3.2.4. *Classification of Data*

An analysis of the early babbling samples obtained from Children A and B shows that the vowel- and consonant-like sounds uttered may be classified as follows:

Child A – 6 months	Child B – 8 months	Child B – 10 months
Vowels	Vowels	Vowels
	ū	u ū
ə ə̄ ʊ ʊ̄	ə ʊ	
ɛ e		ɛ ɛ̄
ǣ a	æ ǣ a	æ a

[47] Fry, 1966, p. 188.

[48] Cited by McCarthy, 1954, p. 511.

[49] Such "tuitional exposure" to language may accelerate language acquisition, but it is not necessary. What might be termed "normal" exposure is sufficient, in that it allows for primary and secondary reinforcement. Colin Fraser, "Discussion", *Psycholinguistic Papers*, eds., J. Lyons and R. J. Wales (Edinburgh, Edinburgh Univ. Press, 1966) p. 118.

[50] Fry, 1966, pp. 190, 196–197.

Consonants	Consonants	Consonants
p bb d ʔ	b bb ʔ	p b bb ʔ
	ƀ	
ɣ h		vv zz
	h	h
mm		m mm
	m	
	w y	

It is assumed that there was no imitation in Child A's utterances. There was no great variety in intonation–it was fairly monotone, possibly because long strings of syllables were not produced. The child would be placed in Lewis' Stage III, with mostly front consonants and many vowels. Vowels occurred more frequently than consonants. All sounds but two were stops, if /h/ be counted, and the /γ/ may well have been more an 'accidental' than controlled articulation. Vowels were front, central, and back, but high vowels were not recorded.

In the utterances of Child B, there was little evidence of imitation of intonation, which was sometimes quite exaggerated by the adult, as in the form: /bā/ba/, accompanying the exaggerated lengthening of the long vowel in this word. At 8 months, his utterances consisted of a variety of vowels and mainly front consonants. I think it may be assumed that this child was capable of producing some dental and possibly back consonants (other than /h/). He does not appear to be advanced over Child A, who was two months younger. An interesting consonant in his repertoire is /ƀ/, not part of the adult phonemic system, and probably a good example of a child producing a sound for the sheer pleasure of the experience. Two months later, notable additions to his repertoire of sounds were two fricatives, both held at some length, /zz/ and /vv/. The /z/ sounded as if it were produced behind the dental area, in the alveolar region, while the production of /v/ (somewhat unsteady) required the use of his new teeth. /z/ is an adult phoneme, while [v] exists only as an allophone of /f/. The lengthened or forcefully articulated sounds /mm/ and /bb/ in the second sample occurred in imitated words and intervocalically. In imitation of the words /māma/ and /bāba/, the initial consonant was usually omitted. One consonant cluster was not imitated, and it is assumed that consonant clusters had not yet appeared.

Child B's vowels were front, central, and back, but here also the /i/ is conspicuously missing. I do not think it can be justifiably concluded that it is not in this child's repertoire. It seems doubtful, however, that vowel oppositions have begun to be established.

It has been suggested that there may be a correlation between the frequency of certain phonemes in adult language and their relative frequency of occurrence in babbling.[51] I do not think sufficient data were gathered to test this hypothesis. The sounds uttered seem to verify theories of the universal tendency to produce front sounds, usually stops, first in babbling.

Before turning to a discussion of the acquisition of phonemes by slightly older children, I wish to point out that apparently the development of the phonological system is not as gradual and smooth as with middle-class children. Poor health and consequent apathy seem to suppress much early verbal activity and experimentation, and it appears that at a certain age and turning point in state of health, the emergence of a rudimentary but surprisingly large phonemic inventory is quite sudden. This is discussed in the next section.

3.3. STAGES OF ACQUISITION OF THE PHONOLOGICAL SYSTEM

3.3.1. *Theoretical Considerations*

As sounds become more differentiated and new articulatory modifications are observed in a child's utterances, many sounds produced are not in the adult phonemic system. It has been suggested that some of the causes of the changes in articulation may simply be that the child is now able to sit up, and has begun acquiring teeth, which may affect the oral cavity.[52]

Many theorists feel that rather than the child at this stage LEARNING new sounds by imitation, his phonemic repertoire in fact develops by the use of some of the sounds he has already uttered in babbling, while others are gradually eliminated. Sounds which are not reinforced will cease.[53]

Phonemes begin to emerge not as stable units at first, but as large classes of sounds which contrast with each other, with wide allophonic variations possible within each phoneme. The first words are not composed of acoustically invariant sounds, but of "equivalence classes of sounds",[54] each class functioning as a primitive phoneme. Response to a particular sound is with the child's own particular sound, often far from a close imitation, and this often continues into the first few years of speech. (This has been investigated in this study through a series of items in imitation tests administered to older, pre-school children.) Velten states that this process of proceeding to smaller and smaller phonemic distinctions is "identical for children in all linguistic communities".[55]

[51] Slobin, ed., 1967, p. 94.

[52] McCarthy, 1954, p. 513.

[53] Gregoire, cited by McCarthy, 1954, p. 516. Also noted by Weir, 1966, p. 154, referring to Mowrer's theory of secondary reinforcement as a factor in the increase in the quantity and accuracy of the child's speech sounds.

[54] Lenneberg, 1967, pp. 279–280.

[55] H. V. Velten, "The Growth of Phonemic and Lexical Patterns in Infant Language", *Language* 19 (1943): 282.

Irwin and Chen found that in the first 1½ years, the average production of phoneme frequencies increases at a constant rate.[56] Fry and others have suggested that the order of acquisition of phonemes may be determined by two factors: "intrinsic difficulty" and statistical frequency and information load.[57] Vowels are more easily heard and more frequent; consonants carry a greater information load. We must also distinguish the tasks involved in the acquisition of phonology: mastery of articulatory movements, recognition of acoustic cues, and social uses of words to obtain desired responses, all of which affect the rate and order of the acquisition of phonemes.[58]

Jakobson and Halle have postulated a universal order of acquisition of phonemes, applicable regardless of sounds uttered in babbling or phonemes in the native language, which is useful as a base for comparing phonemic development in Arabic.[59] Babbling begins with a "labial stage", and a "nuclear syllable" /pa/, which represents the two extremes in articulation and acoustic energy. Stops precede constrictives (and are later frequently substituted for them).[60] The nasal /m/ may be introduced next, for a nasal-oral consonant opposition. This, however, may be preceded by a labial-dental stop opposition, resulting in a "primary triangle" of oppositions:

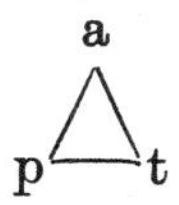

Early babbling sounds are agreed to be front labial sounds, usually stops, and vowels modified into syllables, usually resulting in the CV syllabic pattern.

It is assumed that 'baby talk' words in all languages take into account these early sounds, and early forms include consonants like /w/, /m/, /n/, /p/, /t/, /b/, and /d/.[61] This is true in the case of Egyptian Arabic. (A list of baby talk vocabulary is given in Chapter 4.)

Jakobson and Halle state that the next step is splitting of the "primary triangle" into two triangles, one of vocalic oppositions and one of voiceless consonantal oppositions (presumably with voiced allophones):

[56] Orvis C. Irwin and H. P. Chen, "Development of Speech During Infancy: Curve of Phonemic Frequencies", *Journal of Experimental Psychology* 37.2 (1947): 191.

[57] Fry, 1966, p. 194. D. L. Olmsted, "A Theory of the Child's Learning of Phonology", *Language* 42: 2. (1966) 531. Schultze, cited by Leopold, 1948: 4.

[58] Olmsted, 1966: 534.

[59] R. Jakobson and M. Halle, "Phonemic Patterning", *Psycholinguistics, A Book of Readings*, ed., Sol Saporta (New York, Holt, Rinehart and Winston, Inc., 1961) pp. 346–350.

[60] Leopold, 1961, p. 354.

[61] Lewis, 1959, p. 33.

The velar order has been added, and the front-back vowel opposition. Jakobson postulates that if there is a pharyngeal-non-pharyngeal consonant contrast, it will be acquired still later.[62] This was the case in Arabic, and the emphatic-nonemphatic contrast was also late.

Lewis also found that voiced-voiceless opposition of bilabial and dental stops preceded velar stops. He listed as "comfort sounds" in Stage III /p/, /b/, /t/, and /d/.[63] Leopold reported that in English, velar and dental stops may be frequently substituted for each other, velar stops being produced phonetically but not acquired as phonemes until nearly the end of the second year.[64] For English-speaking children, he gives the following approximate ages of acquisition of the following phonemes:

Phoneme	Year and Month
/b/	.9
/d/	.10
/m/	1.2
/n/	1.7
/g/	1.7
/k/	1.8

He states that the labial-velar-dental opposition is acquired at approximately age 2. Ervin and Miller suggest that the /p/–/tk/ contrast is also easier because it has a more obvious visual cue than the /t/–/k/ contrast.[65]

Leopold found that the development of vowels began with high back and central vowels, which later disappeared. There was a low-high opposition of front vowels by the ninth month, which in the beginning is termed "experimental pre-patterning" with such utterances as /baba/ and /dididi/.[66] The /i/ was acquired in the tenth month, then /i–e/, a mid-high front vowel opposition, and last the back vowel opposition, the /i–a–u/ triangle, in the thirteenth month. In another study, the frequency of front vowels dropped from 72% to 47%, and back vowels increased from 2.3% to 37% by age 2½.[67]

[62] Jakobson and Halle, 1961, p. 348.

[63] Lewis, 1964, p. 17.

[64] Leopold, 1961, p. 354.

[65] Susan M. Ervin and Wick Miller, *Language Development*, Offprint of Chapter III of the 62nd Yearbook, Part I, of the National Society for the Study of Education (Chicago, Univ. of Chicago Press, 1963) p. 113.

[66] Leopold, 1961, p. 353.

[67] Irwin and Chen, cited by McCarthy, 1954, p. 509.

In general, then, the order of discrimination of phonemes seems to be first the discrimination of voicing and nasality, then friction and duration, and finally the point of articulation, with more errors respectively.[68]

The postulating of 'stages' of phonological development has been done in several studies, notably by Ferguson, who notes that a "diachronic contrastive analysis comparing stages $x_1\ x_2 \ldots x_n$ where x_1 is zero and x_n a full natural language is basic to the study of child language development . . .,"[69] and goes on to attempt to set up stages of phonological acquisition for two children, learning French and English respectively. His studies report on the same child at successive stages, while in this study, time did not allow for such an extended period to follow an individual child. Instead, based necessarily on the assumption that the children in the study are normal and are developing without gross differences, 'stages' will be postulated based on data from the speech of several children as found in various stages of development at the time of the study.

The stages observed in the study are set up on structural criteria pertinent to the acquisition of the phonemic system of this language.

3.3.2. *Stage I*

Two children were placed in Stage I of phonemic development. Child C, Sharbāt, is female and Child D, Hasan, is male; they were ages 1.0 and 1.5 respectively. Only a small quantity of material was elicited from each child, and although Child D was advanced over Child C in accuracy of imitation, they showed very similar phonemic repertoires. With a five-month difference in age, Child D appeared to have added only to the vowel contrasts. As Ferguson has pointed out, when vocabulary is small, the child's repertoire of contrasts is difficult to elicit,[70] and forms may not recur. The data gathered are as follows.

Child C – Age 1.0:

Utterances		Adult Form		Gloss[71]
1. [ʔāh]	[ʔʊh]	[ʕábdu]	/ʕábdu/	'Abdu' (proper name)
2. [ʔáya]		[ʔɪzzǣy]	/ʔizzǣy/	'how'
3. [ʔāw]		[gʊ́ṭṭə]	/gúṭṭa/	'cat'
4. [ʔǽpə]		[mbū]	/mbū/	baby talk word for 'water'
5. [mām]		[mm]	/mm/	said when lulling to sleep
6. [bāba] [babb]	[bápa]	[bāba]	/bāba/	'Papa'

[68] Olmsted, 1966: 533.

[69] Charles A. Ferguson, "Contrastive Analysis and Language Development", *Georgetown University Monograph Series on Languages and Linguistics* 21, ed., James E. Alatis (Washington, D.C., Georgetown Univ. Press, 1968): 101.

[70] Ferguson, 1968: 103.

[71] The glosses were provided by the child's mother.

Phonemic Inventory for Child C:

Consonants			Vowels
b (p)			[æ] a [ʊ]
m			
		ʔ	
w	y		

Child D–Age 1.5:

Utterances	Adult Form		Gloss
1. [māma]	[māma]	/mə̄mə/	'Mama'
2. [bāba]	[bāba]	/bāba/	'Papa'
3. [mʊm]	[mʊmm]	/mumm/	baby talk word for 'food'
4. [mbū]	[mbū]	/mbū/	baby talk word for 'water'
5. [hʊb]	[hʊbb] [hʊ́ba]	/hubb/ /huba/	said when picking child up
6. [bʊ́bi]	[bōbi]	/bōbi/	baby talk word for 'dog'

Phonemic Inventory for Child D:

Consonants		Vowels		Consonant Cluster
b		i	u [ʊ]	mb-
	h			
m		a		

Both children showed very limited phonemic repertoires, mostly front, bilabial consonants and simple vowels. Child C had no consonant clusters; Child D had one, but neither had a single-double consonant contrast. The evidence in the data does not seem sufficient to credit Child C with more than one basic vowel phoneme. Child D had developed a rudimentary vowel inventory, using each vowel correctly in an actual word, but did not have the long-short vowel opposition.

Child C omitted the back consonant /ʕ/ and the cluster /bd/ in her imitation of the word /ʕabdu/, and omitted the fricative /zz/ in /ʔizzǣy/. The cluster /mb/ in /mbū/ was rendered as [p], or phonemically /b/ (/p/ does not occur in the adult system). /māma/ and /bāba/, which seem to be agreed upon by all informants as the earliest utterances to appear, were well articulated.

Child D articulated phonemically simple words. There was one initial consonant cluster, /mb-/, but probably at this point was the only one in the child's repertoire. There was no evidence as to whether medial and final clusters had been acquired.

The following phonemic inventory can be drawn up for Stage I:

Stage I

Children C and D

b		ʔ[72]	i	u
		h		
m			a	
w	y			

Stage I, therefore, shows the following characteristics of phonemic development:

1. All three bilabial consonants are present.
2. Both laryngeal consonants are present.
3. The only other consonant is /y/, a semivowel.
4. There is no voiced-voiceless contrast.
5. The vowels attained are the basic vocalic contrasts, Jakobson's first "vocalic triangle".

3.3.3. *Stage II*

The child determined to be in Stage II of phonemic development also happened to be Child 1 in the general study, a girl, Manāl, age approximately 2.8. After an outline of her phonemic inventory and reasons for calling this a 'stage', examples will be given of the repertoires of two other children, Child E and Child F, who were 'intermediate' between Stages I and II.

Child 1 was recorded on tape in conversation with her mother, and in imitation and elicitation tests. Examples of words in her utterances which illustrate phonemic development are as follows:

Child 1–Age 2.8:

Utterances	Adult Form		Gloss[73]
In conversation with mother			
1. [ʔīdi]	[sīdi]	/sīdi/	'my grandfather'
2. [ʔæmīn]	[ʕábdɛl ʕaẓīm]		
	/ʕábdel ʕaẓīm/		'Abdel Azim' (proper name)

[72] /ʔ/ is acquired late in medial and final position. Since /ʔ/ and /h/ are both sounds which may be produced simply in conjunction with vowel onsets or off-glides, their status as phonemes at this stage is open to question.

[73] Glosses were provided by the child's mother, often inadvertently, when 'reinforcing' and expanding the child's utterances.

Utterances	Adult Form		Gloss
3. [xǽli]	[xǣli]	/xǣli/	'my uncle'
4. [wāṭə]	[wárdə]	/wárda/	'Warda' (proper name)
5. [ʔǽyza ʔǣwa]	[ʕǽyzə ḥalǣwə]	/ʕayza ḥalǣwa/	'I want some sweets'
6. [yíbli sǽnna]	[yjíbli sándəl]	/yjíbli sándal/	'He gets me some sandals'
7. [jɪbləbíyə]	[jæləbíyə]	/jælabíya/	'dress, robe'
8. [ʔʊ́xti bǽnə bíbti]	[ʔʊ́xti ʔɪʕtɪmǣd ḥabíbti]	/ʔúxti ʔiʕtimǣd ḥabíbti/	'my dear sister Etimad'
9. [mǣt hǣdə] [mǽt-ɪs ḥǽdə]	[ma-ʕamǽlt-ɪš ḥǣjə]	/ma-ʕamǽlt-iš ḥǣja/	'I didn't do anything'
10. [kæt nah]	[kælt naḥ]	/kælt naḥ/	'I ate "meat"' (baby talk word)
In imitation tests			
11. [sʊ́ftu]	[ʔǽnə šʊ́ftu]	/ʔæna šuftu/	'I saw him'
12. [stūs]	[ma-šʊftʊ́h-š]	/ma-šuftúh-š/	'I did not see him'
13. [mágalə]	[bágarə]	/bágara/	'cow'
14. [hɪb]	[ʕa-yḥíbb]	/ʕa-yḥíbb/	'he likes'
15. [kɛt] [dækɛ́t]	[jakɛ́ttə]	/jakítta/	'jacket'
16. [máyə sʊ́xnə] [sʊ́kənə]	[ʔɪl-máyyə sʊ́xnə]	/ʔil-máyya súxna/	'The water is hot.'
17. [huwa ṣi]	[hʊ́wa ʕa-yṣīḍ]	/húwa ʕa-yṣīd/	'He is fishing.'
18. [mǽdlæs] [mǽsælə] [mǽlæsə]	[mǽdrəsə]	/mǽdrasa/	'school'
19. [hu ʔadál]	[hʊ́wa ʕa-yɪtḍáṛab]	/húwa ʕa-yitḍárab/	'He is being hit.'
20. [sǣli]	[sæhl]	/sæhl/	'easy'
21. [hasfūla] [ʔasūla]	[ʕaṣfūrə]	/ʕaṣfūra/	'bird'
22. [hǣlə]	[ḥílwə]	/ḥílwa/	'sweet'
23. [gʊ́ttə]	[gʊ́ṭṭə]	/gúṭṭa/	'cat'
24. [ʔásələ]	[ʕášarə]	/ʕášara/	'ten'
25. [tīf]	[laṭīf]	/laṭīf/	'nice'
26. [sʊɣl]	[šuɣl]	/šuɣl/	'work'
27. [zɪbn]	[jíbnə]	/jíbna/	'cheese'

The following phonemic inventory can be drawn up for Child 1, representing Stage II:

Stage II
Child 1

b	t	d			k	g	[ø]		ʔ
				[j, d, z]					
f	s	z		[s]	x	ɣ		[ḥ, h, ʔ] [ø, ʔ]	h
m	n								
w	[l]	y							
	l								
[ɪ]	i		u	[ʊ]					
[ɛ]	e	[ə]	o	[ɔ]					
		a							

Five diphthongs occurred: /æy/, /ay/, /iy/, /uy/ and /aw/. Several consonant clusters occurred in the data. Initially, two clusters occurred, /st-/ and /ht-/. Medially, the following clusters occurred:

/-yz-/	/-ft-/
/-bl-/	/-xn-/
/-xt-/	/-dl/[74]
/-bt-/	/-sf-/

Final clusters were: /-bn/ and /-ɣl/.

However, many consonant clusters were omitted or simplified. They are as follows:

Cluster	Child's Utterance	Model
/-rd-/	[wāṭə]	[wárdə] /wárda/
/-nd-/	[sǽnna]	[sándəl] /sándal/
/yj-/	[yíbli]	[yjɪbli] /yjíbli/
/-lt-/	[mǽt-ɪs]	[ma-ʕamǽlt-ɪš] /ma-ʕamált-iš/
/-hš/	[stūs]	[ma-šʊftʊ́h-š] /ma-šuftúh-š/
/-yḥ-/	[hɪb]	[ʕa-yḥíbb] /ʕa-yḥíbb/
/-yṣ-/	[ṣī]	[ʕa-yṣīḍ] /ʕa-yṣīd/
/-tḍ-/	[ʔadál]	[ʕa-yɪṭḍaraḅ] /ʕa-yitḍárab/
/-hl/	[sǣli]	[sæhl] /sæhl/
/-lw-/	[hǣlə]	[ḥɪlwə] /ḥílwa/

[74] This occurred in utterance 18, a substitution for /-dr-/ in the model word.

In many cases, these consonant clusters contain a phoneme not yet in the child's inventory. Some, however, are probably articulated. It appears that the mastery of consonant clusters is still very incomplete and in a state of fluctuation. Probably many more clusters can be produced than are actually present in the data, as may be seen in some items which are repeated, once with a cluster and once without, e.g., utterance 21, [hasfūla] and [ʔasūla] for the model [ʕaṣfūrə].

In determining this child's phonemic inventory, the problem arises as to when to include a sound which is still in a state of flux as a phoneme in the system. This child sometimes articulated /j/ and /ḥ/, but usually substituted another sound for them. I feel that caution is best in 'recognizing' phonemes. Minimal pairs were not observed to prove doubtful phonemic contrasts, and analysts of child language have usually agreed that even if a sound is phonetically acceptable in an isolated item, it should be consistently realized correctly before being treated as a phoneme.[75] Leopold aptly states that "the phonetic capacity of the child can be well ahead of the phonemic development".[76] At the same time, "archaisms" may appear in the child's speech, words in which an already-established phonemic contrast is not observed.[77]

This caution is also appropriate in the analysis of this child's distinctions between single and doubled consonants, and short and long vowels. A few geminated consonants occur, but more often they were simplified to a single consonant, indicating that the contrast was not yet established. Similarly, none of the long vowels were well established, so it is unlikely that the short-long vowel contrast had been attained.

In general, Stage II was marked off as a 'stage' because of the following characteristics of phonemic development:

1. Pharyngeal consonants have not been acquired. /ḥ/ is variously realized as [ḥ], [h], or [ʔ]. /ʕ/ is realized as [ʕ] or [Ø].
2. Alveo-palatal consonants /š/ and /j/ have not been acquired. /š/ is realized as [s]; /j/ as [j], [d], or [z].
3. The emphatic-nonemphatic consonant opposition has not been established. Emphatic consonants are almost always realized as their nonemphatic counterparts.
4. Lateral /l/ and flap /r/ are treated as one phoneme, with /l/ consistently substituted for /r/.
5. The uvular stop /q/ is not realized at all.

[75] Leopold, 1961, p. 355. Olmsted, 1966, 534.
[76] Leopold, 1961, p. 355.
[77] Ervin and Miller, 1963, p. 115.

6. Geminated consonants and long vowels have not been established as phonemically distinct from their simple counterparts. Sometimes they are articulated correctly; usually they are simplified.
7. Consonant clusters and diphthongs are in a state of fluctuation, and not all have been mastered.

Phonemes which had been acquired since the last stage were:

1. The series of voiced-voiceless stops, /t/–/d/ and /k/–/g/.
2. Two sets of voiced-voiceless fricatives, /s/–/z/ and /x/–/ɣ/.
3. The labio-dental fricative /f/.
4. The alveolar nasal /n/.
5. The lateral /l/.
6. Three vowels, /æ/, /ē/, and /ō/.

The phonemic inventory, however, was not stable. Even sounds which are usually accurate and have phonemic status were not always articulated accurately. The data show several examples of this. For example, while /s/ was usually articulated correctly, the word [sīdi], utterance 1, was realized as [ʔīdi], with [ʔ] substituted for /s/. /b/ is one of the earliest phonemes; nevertheless, in utterance 13, [bágarə] was realized as [mágalə], [m] being substituted for /b/. The word [sóxnə], in utterance 16, was repeated once correctly, once as [sókənə], [k] being substituted for /x/.

Only one stop is missing, the very rare /q/. Of the other phonemes not yet acquired, four are fricatives. The other is the flap /r/, which is one of the last sounds acquired by every child observed.

This child was said to represent a 'stage' of development because she had rather neatly acquired the simpler phonemes, and was just on the verge of acquiring the distinctions of emphasis, vowel length, and consonant gemination but had not yet done so.

3.3.4. *Two Intermediate Case Studies*

Two children observed, Child E and Child F, showed phonemic development intermediate between Stages I and II.

Child E, Zakiya, was a girl age 1.11, whose utterances were recorded in phonetic transcription in a conversation with her sister, age 8. Many words were imitations.

Child E–Age 1.11:

Utterances		Adult Form		Gloss
1. [kūkə]		[læklūkə]	/læk lūka/	'piece of bread; food'
2. [mbū]	[ʔambú]	[mbū]	/mbū/	baby talk word for 'water'
3. [daḥ]		[daḥḥ]	/daḥḥ/	baby talk word for defecation

Utterances		Adult Form		Gloss
4. [bíhə]		[bíḥḥə]	/bíḥḥa/	'duck (female)'
5. [wízzə]		[wízzə]	/wízza/	'goose'
6. [ḥūs ə bɪt]		[ḥūš ʔɪl-bɪt] /ḥūš ʔil-bit/		'Make the girl stop.'
7. [dízə]		[bízzə]	/bízza/	'female breast'
8. [ʔǽnə]		[ʔǽnə]	/ʔǽna/	'I'
9. [táti]		[bɪtǽʕti]	/bitǽʕti/	'mine'
10. [bǽyə]		[báṛṛə]	/bárra/	'outside'
11. [mam]		[mʊmm]	/mumm/	baby talk word for 'food'
12. [dídi]		[sīdi]	/sīdi/	'my grandfather'
13. [həwə́wə]	[həyǽyə]	[ḥəlǣwə]	/ḥalǣwa/	'sweets'
14. [bah]		[bæləḥ]	/bǽlaḥ/	'dates (food)'
15. [dǽmə]		[jǽməl]	/jǽmal/	'camel'
16. [dʊ́t]		[gʊ́ṭṭə]	/gúṭṭa/	'cat'
17. [hǣy] [xǣy]		[xǣli]	/xǣli/	'my uncle'
18. [ɤa]	[ʔáya]	[ṣʊɤáyyar]	/ṣuɤáyyar/	'small'
19. [ʔapú[	[ʔafūlə]	[ʕaṣfūrə]	/ʕaṣfūra/	'bird'

The following phonemic inventory can be drawn up for Child E:

Phonemic Inventory for Child E:

b	t	d		k		[d]	[Ø]		ʔ
			[d]						
[f, p]	s	z	[s]	[x, h]		[ɤ,ʔ]	[ḥ, h]	[Ø]	h
m		n							
w		[y, r]		y					
		[w, y, Ø]							
[I]	i			u	[ʊ]				
		[ə]							
	æ		a						

Child E has several 'gaps' in her phonemic inventory, as compared with Stage II.

/l/ and /f/ were missing. While /k/ was a phoneme, the voiced counterpart /g/ was still realized as [d]. The velar fricatives, /ɤ/ and /x/, were not firmly established; in fact, only three fricatives were consistently present. The sound /q/ was not elicited.

Child E had added the vowel /æ/, not present in Stage I, but had not developed the vowel repertoire further. /ē/ and /ō/ did not occur in the data.

/mb/ was the only consonant cluster in the data, in two positions. It seems very likely that the child could articulate at least several other combinations;

in the model words in the data, few consonant clusters happened to occur. No diphthongs occurred in the data, so the child's progress could not be observed.

Child F, Suʕād, was a girl age 2.3, who was recorded in conversation with her brother, age 14, and sister, age 8. Many of her utterances were imitations, and many were expanded by the brother and sister after being uttered. A few utterances, marked with asterisk, were not heard, but were reported by the older sister.

Child F–Age 2.3:

Utterances	Adult Form	Gloss
1. [mbú]	[mbū] /mbū/	baby talk word for 'water'
2. [kʊx]	[kʊxx] /kuxx/	baby talk, when child dirties itself
3. [daḥ]	[daḥḥ] /daḥḥ/	baby talk, when showing where one is hurt
4. [bízzə māma]*	[bɪzzə māma] /bízza māma/	'the breast, Mama'
5. [dæməlǽt]*	[jæməlǣt] /jæmalǣt/	'Jamalat' (proper name)
6. [sʊád]	[suʕād] /suʕād/	'Suʕad' (proper name)
7. [bēḍə]	[ḅēḍə] /bēḍa/	'an egg'
8. [mɪdǽmɪs]	[mɪdǽmmɪs] /midǽmmis/	'boiled beans'
9. [xǽlt æmīna]	[xǽlti ʔamīnə] /xǽlti ʔamīna/	'my aunt Amina'
10. [xǣli]	[xǣli] /xǣli/	'my uncle'
11. [nah]	[naḥḥ] /naḥḥ/	baby talk word for 'meat'
12. [bʊf]	[bʊff] /buff/	baby talk word for 'bread'
13. [bísbɪs] [bísə]	[bísbɪs] [bíssə] /bísbis/ /bíssa/	baby talk words for 'cat'
14. [bába dɪh]	[bāba jɪh] /bāba jih/	'Papa came'
15. [māma dæt]	[māma jæt] /māma jæt/	'Mama came'
16. [dǽwə] [ʔǽwa] [hæyǽyə]	[ḥəlǣwə] /ḥalǣwa/	'sweets'
17. [díyə]	[saʕdíyə] /saʕdíya/	'Saʕdiya' (proper name)
18. [lɔz ya bābə]*	[rɔz ya bāba] /roz ya bāba/	'rice, Papa'
19. [nātɛm]	[ṭamaṭɛm] /tamaṭem/	'tomatoes'
20. [tātə]	[baṭāṭɪṣ] /baṭāṭis/	'potatoes'
21. [báṣa]	[ḅáṣaḷə] /báṣala/	'an onion'
22. [ʕāk]*	[məʕāk] /maʕāk/	'with you (m.sing.)'
23. [hūt]	[maḥmūd] /maḥmūd/	'Mahmoud' (proper name)
24. [ʔǽnə būyə bíyə]	[ʔænə yə abūyə jæləbíyə] /ʔæna ya abūya jælabíya/	'I, father, want a dress.'
25. [sáya]	[ṣʊɣáyyar] /ṣuɣáyyar/	'small'
26. [ʔənnɛ́h]	[ʔaḷḷāh] /ʔaḷḷāh/	'God'
27. [sǽmə]	[ʔɪš-šæms] /ʔiš-šæms/	'the sun'

The following phonemic inventory can be drawn up for Child F:
Phonemic Inventory for Child F:

b	t	d		k	g			ʔ
			[d]					
f	s	z	[s]	x	[ø]	[ḥ, h]	[ʕ, ø]	h
m	n							
w	[l]	y						
	l							
[ɪ]	i			u	[ʊ]			
[ɛ]	e	[ə]	o		[ɔ]			
	æ	a						

Child F had almost reached Stage II in phonemic development. She lacked only one consonant found in Stage II, the /ɣ/. This was simply omitted.

Vowels had reached complete development. In fact, Child F seems to be closer to a distinction of vowel length than the older child in Stage II.

Diphthongs did not appear in the data; the child articulated one, [ʊa], as a result of omitting the /ʕ/ in the model word [suʕād] in utterance 6. Few consonant clusters occurred in the data, so no indication is given of how many can be articulated. Those which appeared in model words were articulated, except for two other medial clusters, /-ʕd-/ (utterance 17) and /-ḥm-/ (utterance 23). No final clusters occurred in the data.

3.3.5. *Stage III*

Stage III, or adult mastery, can be said to be attained by approximately age 5. This age was arrived at by analyzing results of imitation tests. A dividing line can be drawn between Child 8 and Child 9. Child 9, age 5, had mastered all the adult phonemes, with the possible exception of /q/.

Although at this age /q/ may not be mastered, this phoneme is so rare that I feel its mastery is not necessary to qualify a child as having a complete adult phonemic system. Most children learn to pronounce this phoneme after conscious attention in school, when they learn the alphabet. It seems safe to assume that most of them are not aware of its existence before then, and some children in this study could not imitate it at ages 6 and 7. To my knowledge, the only familiar words in which /q/ occurs are the name of the letter /qāf/ and the word [ʔɪl-qʊrʔān] 'the Koran', which is a retention of the Classical Arabic pronunciation of this word. In the present-day dialect, /g/ is regularly substituted for the Classical Arabic /q/ phoneme.

Child 9 will be considered the first in the study to have acquired definite mastery of the adult phonemic system. His phonemic inventory would be that of the complete adult system, with /q/ in a state of fluctuation, sometimes realized as [k]. All diphthongs and consonant clusters are articulated correctly, and there is a clear distinction of vowel length and consonant gemination.

Speech samples of Children 2 through 8 will be used to determine relative intermediate development leading to a complete phonemic system.

3.4. ORDER OF ACQUISITION OF PHONEMES

3.4.1. *Individual Phonemes*

In this section the general order of acquisition of the segmental phonemes is outlined. The data were obtained from conversations, elicitation tests, and a series of imitation tests, discussed in the following section.[78]

It must be pointed out that for each phoneme, the age of acquisition can be determined only approximately and relative to other phonemes, because of the many children in the study. 'Slips' in pronunciation are common at later ages, and phonetic realization of phoneme sounds sometimes occurs at an earlier age than that at which mastery appears certain.

Based on the data, phonemes appear to be acquired at the following ages and in the following relative order.

1. /b/ /m/ /w/ /y/ /ʔ/ /h/ /a/ /i/ /u/ Age 1.5

These phonemes, the inventory in Stage I, are the earliest to develop, and most appeared in the data as early as age 1.0. Although it is not evident here, /b/, /m/, and /a/ may appear first, if it is assumed that the children develop in a pattern similar to children learning other languages.[79]

It is common for the children to omit final consonants, but there is no evidence that all the vowels and consonants thus far acquired cannot be articulated in all positions. One exception is /ʔ/, which occurs only initially at this age. Evidence from older children indicates that this phoneme is late in being articulated in medial and final positions. /ʔ/ in medial position began to occur at about age 3.6, in imitation test Item 11, and was usually articulated by children older than this. However, it was occasionally missed by some children at ages 5, 6, and 7, so it is probably stabilized at about age 4.0.

[78] Templin found, in a series of comparative tests, that there was no significant difference in children's articulation of phonemes while imitating, as compared with spontaneous articulation. Mildred C. Templin, "Spontaneous versus Imitated Verbalization in Testing Articulation in Preschool Children", *Journal of Speech and Hearing Disorders* 12 (1947): 293–300.

[79] Cf. Ferguson, 1968: 104; Jakobson and Halle, 1961, pp. 346–347; Lewis, 1964, p. 17.

2. /t/ /d/ /s/ /z/ /n/ /k/ /æ/ Age 2.0

This group of phonemes appeared next in the data, in the speech of Child E, age 1.11. Since there is a gap of some six months between the age of this child and Child D of Stage I, it cannot be determined with certainty the order in which the individual phonemes were added to the child's inventory. Again based on data from other languages, it seems likely that /t/, /d/, and /n/ were added, then /k/, before the two sibilants. /k/ was probably late because in several items, /t/ was substituted for /k/, as in the word [tælb] for [kælb] 'dog', uttered by Children 3 and 4, age 3.6.

The sibilants occur less frequently than the four stops in adult language, which would also support the assumption that they are acquired later. In any case, all of these phonemes were acquired between ages 1.5 and 1.11. Probably all of these phonemes can occur in all positions.

3. /f/ /l/ /x/ /g/ /e/ /o/ Age 2.3

Since these phonemes are in the inventory of Child F, age 2.3 and only four months older than the previous child, again they must be considered as a group, and the relative order of acquisition cannot be definitely determined.

The fact that /e/ and /o/ are the last vowels to occur correlates with their relative infrequency of occurrence in adult language. Errors in imitation indicate that /o/ is the least stable, so it is probably the latest to develop.

/g/, however, was not consistently articulated. Interesting substitutions for it were made by Child 3, age 3.6, who said [bákʰə] for [bágərə] 'cow', and Child 4, age 3.6, who said [dádᵊ] for [gáʕdə] 'sitting'. /f/ was once realized as [s], in Child 3's articulation of [næfīsə], a proper name, as [nsīs], but otherwise was a very stable phoneme for all children, once it was attained.

/x/ may develop later than the other three consonants here, because it appears to be less stable in the data obtained from children under age 4. In the speech of Child 3, [færxə] 'chicken' was realized as [fǽkʰə], and [xænzīr] 'pig' was realized as [ʔænzi].

4. /ɣ/ Age 2.6

This consonant was added in Stage II, where the child was age 2.8, five months older than the previous child. Thus, the acquisition of this phoneme can be placed at approximately age 2.6. After acquisition, the phoneme is stable. Its occurrence in adult language is quite rare, and less frequent than the voiceless counterpart, which is acquired first.

From this point, the theory of the development of phonemes will be based on the data from the speech of children 'intermediate' between Stages II and III. This includes Children 2 through 8, ranging in age from 3.0 to 5.0. Examples from imitation tests will be given. Utterances of older children will be referred to where errors were made, especially for the 'difficult' consonants.

5. /ḥ/ Age 3.0

This phoneme was definitely established in the speech of Child 2, age 3.0, and thereafter. Only occasionally was it articulated as [h], although this occurred in the speech of Child 7, age 4.6, in imitation test Item 2 and in the speech of Children 8 and 9, age 5.0, in imitation test Item 3. In general, however, this phoneme was articulated accurately in all three positions in words beginning at age 3.0.

6. /ṣ/ /ẓ/ Age 3.6

Beginning with Child 3, age approximately 3.6, the phoneme /ṣ/ was correctly distinguished from its non-emphatic counterpart. In free conversation several items with /ṣ/ were uttered by children, and after age 3.6, errors (realizing it as non-emphatic) were rare.

/ẓ/ is extremely rare in the language, so it seldom occurred in the data. From age 3.6, it was correctly imitated in the word [ẓakɛttə] or [jækɛttə] (both pronunciations are correct) in imitation test Item 8.

7. /ṭ/ /ḍ/ /ḷ/ Age 3.6

Imitation test Items 5 and 10 show /ṭ/ as a phoneme in the speech of Child 4, age 3.6, but not in the speech of Child 3, age 3.6. Since age of acquisition cannot be exactly determined, it may be that Child 4 is slightly older; in any case, /ṭ/ seems to appear slightly later than /ṣ/ and /ẓ/. Imitation test Item 14 indicates that /ḍ/ is a phoneme after age 3.6.

The phoneme /ḷ/ is relatively rare, and was elicited only in an item in the noun plural examination. In item 16 the word [ḷaṭīf] 'nice' was given as an adjective accompanying the noun. It was not repeated by the younger children, so no exact determination can be made as to its status. It was correctly repeated by age 5, but without evidence to the contrary, it seems most likely that it is acquired along with other emphatic consonants, at approximately age 3.6 or 4.0.

8. /j/ Age 4.0

This phoneme was acquired early by some, later by others. Child 3, age 3.6, and all others had acquired /j/ in the word [jɪbnə] in imitation test Item 7. In Item 17 in the word [sajarə], the /j/ was realized as [d] by Child 4, age 3.6, and Child 7, age 4.6. There is no doubt that /j/ was a phoneme, although it was not entirely stable, often realized as [d]. Evidence here indicates that /j/ may be more stable initially than medially.

In the Upper Egyptian dialect, /d/ is a regular substitution for the /j/ of this dialect, and the children may be exposed to the Upper Egyptian dialect periodically. Likewise, /j/ is realized regularly as /g/ in the Lower Egyptian dialect of Cairo. In some words /g/ was articulated in place of /j/, depending on the amount of the child's exposure to this dialect, often through radio broadcasts.

9. /ʕ/ Age 4.6

/ʕ/ is a difficult consonant to analyze. It is very frequent and continued to be mispronounced (as [ʔ] or [Ø]) in isolated cases long after its acquisition as a phoneme. Evidence in the imitation tests shows that in the majority of items imitated, /ʕ/ was present by about age 4, but not before. Various imitation test items produced different results. In Items 12 and 15, /ʕ/ occurred medially and was pronounced correctly after age 4; in Items 4, 11 and 17, /ʕ/ occurred initially and was pronounced correctly at age 4.6 or 5 and after. Words from free conversation showed /ʕ/ being realized as [ʔ] or omitted occasionally in the speech of much older children. This happened, for example, in the speech of Child 10, age 5.6, who articulated [saʕd], a proper name, as [sad], and Child 7, age 4.6, who articulated [ʕayze ʕarabɪyə] 'I want a [toy] car' as [ʔayze ʔaləbɪyə]. It even occurred once in the speech of Child 28, age 13, when pronouncing his name, [ʕali], twice as [ʔali].

10. /š/ Age 4.6

This phoneme, like /ʕ/, showed a good deal of variation in the age of acquisition and, after acquisition, was not always articulated correctly. Even older children at times substituted [s] for /š/ and it, along with /r/, was cited by adults to be one of the latest consonants acquired.

Virtually all children under age 4 substituted [s] for /š/ in every word; the imitation test Items 1, 12, 16 and 18 show that it was quite well articulated by age 4 and after. Items 1 and 13 showed consistent articulation by age 5. Child 7, age 4.6, had not acquired /š/ in her speech, and never articulated it either in conversation or in tests. After acquisition, /š/ occurred in all three positions.

11. /r/ Age 5.0

The substitution of [l] for /r/ was observed for every child under age 5, and sometimes after this age. This is reported by adults to be 'universal' in children learning Egyptian Arabic, regardless of dialect. Imitation test Items 2, 6 and 18 show /r/ being articulated correctly after age 5, with the exception of Child 6, age 4, who did have /r/ as a phoneme at this age. Child 3, age 3.6, occasionally achieved phonetic articulation of /r/, although it alternated with [l] No other children under age 5 articulated it at all.

12. /q/ Age 6.6

/q/ was elicited only in imitatio n test Item 6 in the word [qʊrʔān] 'the Koran'.

Two children articulated it correctly at age 6, and several who were age 6.6 and 7. The lateness in acquisition is no doubt due to the extreme rarity of this phoneme. It was consistently articulated correctly after age 7.

13. Long Vowels Age 3.0

The phonemic distinction of vowel length is acquired quite early. Even before age 3 it is articulated, although not consistently. Many imitation test items confirm that at age 3, represented by Child 2, and after, long vowels were correctly distinguished and imitated.

14. Geminated Consonants Age 3.6

Geminated consonants are sometimes articulated before age 3.6, but imitation tests showed no consistency in correct imitation and distinction until age 3.6. Some consonants are geminated correctly a higher percentage of the time than others, and this seems to correlate with the general order of acquisition of the single consonant counterparts. For example, /tt/, /kk/, /mm/, and /yy/ are quite well pronounced by age 3, while /ṭṭ/ and /ɣɣ/ are pronounced well by age 3.6.

3.4.2 *Phoneme Combinations*

1. Diphthongs: Age 3.0

Four of the six diphthongs, /æy/, /ay/, /iy/, and /əw/, were acquired by the child in Stage II at age 2.8. The other two, /iw/ and /uy/, are more complex, composed of high front and back vowels with low back and low front semivowels respectively. These may be acquired later than the others; they are also infrequent in occurrence. Since they occur in the speech of Children 2 and 3, ages 3.0 and 3.6, it may be assumed that, on the whole, diphthongs are acquired quite early, by about age 3.0.

2. Consonant Clusters: Age 1.5–5.0

Since almost any two consonants can occur together in a cluster, a very large number are theoretically possible. Some clusters occur very early, such as /mb/, and a few occurred in Stage II. The first to occur are composed of the early-articulated consonants, such as those in Stage II, like /bl/, /bt/, /st/, and /bn/. However, some rather 'difficult' clusters also occurred, such as /ɣl/, /xt/, and /lw/, so that there does not seem to emerge a general order of ability to articulate consonant clusters. Young children sometimes articulated clusters and sometimes omitted or simplified the same ones in a different utterance, as can be seen in the data for Child 1, Stage II. Some clusters which contain difficult consonants were late in developing, for example /šr/ in Item 18, which was not articulated correctly until age 4 and after.

Isolated examples of a cluster being simplified or broken with epenthetic vowels can be found in the speech of older children in certain words.

It seems safe to assume that, in general, consonant clusters are acquired early, at about the same age that the constituent single consonants are acquired.

3.4.3 *Summary*

In summary, the approximate age of acquisition and order of acquisition of the phonemes was found to be as follows. It may be noted that most consonants in the first three groups of consonants acquired are also among the most frequent in occurrence in adult language.

Consonants	
1. /b/ /m/ /w/ /y/ /ʔ/ /h/	Age 1.5
2. /t/ /d/ /s/ /z/ /n/ /k/	Age 2.0
3. /f/ /l/ /x/ /g/	Age 2.3
4. /ɣ/	Age 2.6
5. /ḥ/	Age 3.0
6. Vowel length	Age 3.0
7. Consonant gemination	Age 3.6
8. /ṣ/ /ẓ/	Age 3.6
9. /ṭ/ /ḍ/ /ḷ/	Age 3.6
10. /j/	Age 4.0
11. /ʕ/	Age 4.6
12. /š/	Age 4.6
13. /r/	Age 5.0
14. /q/	Age 6.6

Vowels	
1. /a/ /i/ /u/	Age 1.5
2. /æ/	Age 2.0
3. /e/ /o/	Age 2.3

Combinations	
1. Diphthongs	Age 3.0
2. Consonant clusters	Age 1.5–5.0

3.4.4. *Comparison with Phonemic Development in Other Languages*

These findings may be compared briefly with findings regarding phonemic development in other languages and with some theoretical generalizations that have been made.

Albright and Albright found that a 1-year-old child learning English had a phonemic inventory consisting of the consonants /b, d, g, m, n, ʔ, h/; vowels

/ɪ, ɛ, ə, ʊ, a/; and two diphthongs.[80] Leopold reported that the front vowels /i, e, æ/ were acquired before the front-back vowel contrast.[81] He found that the /a/–/i/–/u/ contrast began at age 1.1, with /u/ definitely established at about age 1.6.

Fry states that in English the general order of acquisition of consonants is first /m/ and /b/, then /p/, /t/, /d/, /n/, then /k/, /g/, /w/, and last /r/, /θ/, /ð/, /s/, /h/, and /f/.[82] Templin's study confirmed that at age 3, 90% of the English-speaking children studied could articulate /n, t, g, m, b, d, w, h, p, k/, 70–80% could articulate /f, ŋ, l, s, y/, 50–60% could articulate /v, r, š, j, č/, and only 10–49% articulated /z, θ, ð, h, w/ correctly. As late as age 6, 10% still did not articulate /s, š, ð, z, ž, h, w, č/ correctly.[83]

Lyamina and Gagua reported that the following were easy consonants for children of age 1½–3 learning Russian: /p, b, t, d, m, n, g, k, v, l/, and the following were difficult: /z, s, ž, š, č, kh[x], f, r/.[84]

In an old but fairly clear study, Kroeber reported that a 24-month-old boy learning Zuñi had acquired "all five vowels", and the consonants /p, t, m, n, l, w, h, ʔ/. He had not acquired the palatalized stops /k, ky, kw/, affricates /ts, tš/, fricatives /s, š/, the voiceless lateral, or the glottalized series /kwʔ, kʔ, kyʔ, tsʔ/.[85]

Menyuk has carried out preliminary investigations to determine the order of acquisition of consonants in terms of Jakobson and Halle's matrix of distinctive features.[86] She found that both American and Japanese children mastered the features of nasality, gravity and voice before the features of diffuseness, continuance and stridency, indicating that this may be a universal hierarchy of feature distinction. Especially common is non-observation of distinctions between sounds when they differ from each other by only one feature, e.g., place of articulation. For each consonant substitution, all feature attributes were maintained except one in each instance.

In Arabic, the order of acquisition of phonemes is about the same as in English. Front stops and nasals are first, back stops a little later, and /š/, /j/ and

[80] Robert W. Albright and Joy B. Albright, "The Application of Descriptive Linguistics to Child Language", *Journal of Speech and Hearing Research* 1.3 (1958): 260.

[81] Leopold, 1961, p. 353.

[82] Fry, 1966, p. 195.

[83] Study cited by Carroll. John B. Carroll, "Language Development in Children", *Psycholinguistics, A Book of Readings*, ed., Sol Saporta (New York, Holt, Rinehart and Winston, Inc., 1961) p. 335.

[84] Study abstracted by Slobin. Dan I. Slobin, "Abstracts of Soviet Studies of Child Language", *The Genesis of Language*, eds., Frank Smith and George A. Miller (Cambridge, MIT Press, 1966) pp. 374–375.

[85] A. L. Kroeber, "The Speech of a Zuñi Child", *American Anthropologist* 18.4 (1916): 532.

[86] Paula Menyuk, "The Role of Distinctive Features in Children's Acquisition of Phonology", *Journal of Speech and Hearing Research* 11.1 (1968): 138–146.

/r/ are late. In Arabic, however, /s/, /z/ and /h/ are early. Since /h/ in Arabic is not restricted in occurrence as in English, this may explain its being acquired earlier. /f/ also poses little difficulty for Arabic-speaking children.

In English, the liquids, /r/ and /l/, are acquired late; in Arabic, the /l/ is relatively early. Leopold found that /l/ in medial position occurred at age 2.5, very close to the age of its appearance in Arabic, and that /r/ was acquired at age 4.[87] It is interesting to note that the Arabic /r/, although a flap and not a liquid, is likewise among the latest consonants to be acquired.

Fry states that the frequency of occurrence of individual phonemes in the language will help determine the order of acquisition, and particularly, the occurrence of minimal pairs facilitates acquisition.[88] Obviously, the frequency of occurrence and the information load of the phonemes of Arabic which are shared with English are not the same, and this may be an important factor in accounting for differences in the acquisition patterns of Arabic- and English-speaking children studied. There are far fewer minimal pairs in Arabic than in English, and consonants do not have as important a functional load as English consonants do; vowels are fewer than in English and have a higher functional value. This is probably why they are all acquired early, earlier than in English. It has been noted that there is a positive correlation between frequency of occurrence of phonemes in Arabic and the order of acquisition found in these data.

I think that the similarities in order of acquisition of Arabic phonemes far outweigh any differences with acquisition order in English, considering the dissimilarities of the two phonemic systems involved. Ages of acquisition are quite different, however; vowel distinctions are acquired earlier in Arabic, while the consonantal system as a whole is completely attained as much as a year later, compared with studies made of English-speaking children.

3.5. IMITATION

3.5.1. *Theoretical Considerations*

Imitation is the characteritic behavior of every normal child, although this does not lead to the assumption that it is an inborn ability; imitation has to be learned.[89] Perhaps its importance as a device in language acquisition has been overestimated, because the child must acquire more than the surface aspects of the language which are available to be imitated. Imitation is more important as an indication of the child's linguistic competence.

87 Leopold, 1961, p. 355.
88 Fry, 1966, p. 195.
89 Lewis, 1964, p. 22.

A great deal of time in learning to speak is spent in imitation. Studies reported by Ervin have shown imitation helpful in acquiring vocabulary and accurate phonology, but there is no evidence that imitation is significant as a source of grammatical progress.[90] Miller and Dollard hold that imitation helps only in providing new combinations of responses which have already been learned by other means.[91]

It has been widely noted that in imitating words, it is common for children to omit some phonemes, especially final phonemes. Leopold found that fricatives were commonly omitted in final position; in fact, his child had two sets of fricatives for a time, one initial set and one terminal set.[92] Fry states that in imitation, no incorrect phonemic sequences are produced.[93] This was upheld in the data.

Ervin and others have noted that if a child cannot or does not imitate the whole utterance, it is most likely to repeat the last words or stressed words in an utterance, and that words usually are imitated in the same order as given.[94] This was only partially upheld in the data gathered. Many examples of repeating final and stressed parts of words can be seen in the utterances of Child 1, and Children E and F, presented above.

Slobin and Welsh have carried out a study of imitation with a 2-year-old child learning English.[95] Controlled, elicited imitations were analyzed to discover the child's underlying linguistic competence. Function words and inflections were often omitted in her imitations, and phenomena such as inversions of word order and substitutions were observed.

3.5.2. *Data Obtained in This Study*

In this section, examples will be given of imitation by children of various ages in the study, some of utterances of older children or adults in conversation, and some of standardized utterances in imitation tests. It will be seen that substitutions and omissions of phonemes follow rather consistent patterns, and there is a clear development of more accurate imitation with age. Data

[90] Susan M. Ervin, "Imitation and Structural Change in Children's Language", *New Directions in the Study of Language*, ed., Eric Lenneberg (Cambridge, MIT Press, 1964) p. 172.

[91] Cited by Carroll. Carroll, 1961, p. 333.

[92] Leopold, 1961, p. 355.

[93] Fry, 1966, p. 197.

[94] Ervin, 1964, p. 169. Roger Brown and Ursula Bellugi, "Three Processes in the Child's Acquisition of Syntax", *New Directions in the Study of Language*, ed., Eric Lenneberg, (Cambridge, MIT Press, 1964) p. 136.

[95] Dan I. Slobin and Charles A. Welsh, *Elicited Imitation as a Research Tool in Developmental Psycholinguistics* (→ Working Paper No. 10, Language-Behavior Research Laboratory (Berkeley, Univ. of California, 1968).

here are important in helping to determine the approximate age at which certain phonemes are acquired, and the order in which they are acquired, discussed in the previous section. Phonological development will be emphasized here; aspects of grammatical development in imitation will be discussed in Chapter 5.

A few examples may be taken first from the utterances of Children C, D, E, and F, already cited. All of these are single-word utterances.

Child C:

Utterances	Model Imitated	Gloss
1. [ʔáya]	[ʔɪzzǣy]	'how'
2. [ʔǽpə]	[mbū]	baby talk word for 'water'
3. [ʔāw]	[gʊ́ṭṭə]	'cat'
4. [bāba]	[bāba]	'Papa'

In Item 1, the child omitted the fricative consonant, as it was not yet in her phonemic repertoire; the last consonant of the word, however, was reproduced, probably because it occurred in the last, stressed syllable. Item 2 is interesting in that the bilabial stop was imitated, but the stress was moved before the consonant, and there was no attempt to reproduce the consonant cluster. There is also evidence that the child has only one phonemic vowel; the long /u/ at the end was ignored. Item 3 shows very rudimentary imitation; no stops were even articulated. Item 4 was correct imitation, and represents the polarity of sounds given by Jakobson and Halle as the earliest sound distinction. It is not surprising that this reduplicated syllable was easy to imitate.

Child D:

Utterances	Model Imitated	Gloss
1. [māma]	[māma]	'Mama'
2. [bāba]	[bāba]	'Papa'
3. [mʊm]	[mʊmm]	baby talk word for 'food'
4. [mbū]	[mbū]	baby talk word for 'water'
5. [hʊb]	[hʊbb]	baby talk word, said when picking child up
6. [bʊ́bi]	[bōbi]	baby talk word for 'dog'

Imitations of Child D were quite accurate, but unfortunately, all words given as models are words commonly used with children. They contain phonemes acquired early, no more than two syllables, and are of simple canonical form. The only noticeable error in imitation is Item 6, in which the long vowel was not reproduced, and presumably was not yet part of the child's phonemic repertoire. The consonant cluster, /mb/, probably the easiest one possible, was reproduced, and so were the final consonants of the words. Probably this child had had considerable practice in saying these words, and it would have been helpful to observe imitation of more difficult items. In the two-syllable words, the stress was correctly placed.

Child E:

Utterances	Model Imitated	Gloss
1. [kūkə]	[læklūkə]	'piece of bread, food'
2. [daḥ]	[daḥḥ]	baby talk word for defecation
3. [dízə]	[bízzə]	'female breast'
4. [táti]	[bɪtǽʕti]	'mine'
5. [bǽyə]	[ḅáṛṛə]	'outside'
6. [həwǽwə] [həyǽyə]	[ḥəlǣwə]	'sweets'
7. [dǽmə]	[jǽməl]	'camel'
8. [ɤa] [ʔáyə]	[ṣʊɤáyyar]	'small'
9. [ʔapú] [ʔafulə]	[ʕaṣfūrə]	'bird'

This child imitated difficult adult words, and was far from accurate, except for stress. It may be noted that for three-syllable words, often only the last, stressed part was reproduced. In Item 1, the consonant cluster was reduced and the stop, not surprisingly, was reproduced instead of the liquid, resulting in near reduplication of syllables. Item 2 was one of a few one-syllable words imitated; all retained the final consonant. Item 3 was quite accurate except for an unaccountable substitution of [d] for /b/ In Item 4, the /ʕ/ of the consonant cluster was omitted and the last two syllables only were repeated. Item 5 shows [y] substituted for medial /r/; in Item 6, /l/ was reproduced as both [y] and [w]. This is consistent with Leopold's generalization that /r/ and /l/ are often realized as semivowels.[96] In Item 6, a strong tendency toward reduplication of syllables is evident. Item 7 conforms with some general patterns of imitation; the affricate was replaced by a stop, and the final consonant was omitted.[97] In Item 8, at first the first syllable was repeated, which is not to be expected. This may be due to the fact that it contains /γ/, which is a sound not yet established for the child, and may have been a source of interest; the second repetition was typically of the last two syllables, omitting the final consonant. In Item 9, the first attempt was a repetition of the first two of the three syllables, with the substitution of a stop [p] for a consonant cluster of two fricatives. The second

[96] Leopold, 1961, p. 355.
[97] Leopold, 1961, p. 355.

attempt at imitation was more complete, substituting [ʔ] for /ʕ/ and simplifying the consonant cluster, although both constituents, /s/ and /f/, were in the child's phonemic repertoire.

Child F:

Utterances	Model Imitated	Gloss
1. [hūt]	[maḥmūd]	'Mahmoud' (proper name)
2. [lǽbən]	[lǽbən]	'milk'
3. [ʔənnɛ́h]	[ʔaḷḷāh]	'God'
4. [sʊád]	[suʕād]	'Suʕad' (proper name)
5. [mɪdǽmɪs]	[mɪdǽmmɪs]	'boiled beans'
6. [bába dɪh]	[bāba jɪh]	'Papa came'
7. [dǽwə] [ʔǽwa] [həyǽyə]	[ḥəlǣwə]	'sweets'
8. [dííyə]	[saʕdííyə]	'Saʕdiya' (proper name)
9. [ʔʊ́zz] [lōz]	[rɔz]	'rice'
10. [nātɛm]	[ṭaṃāṭɛm]	'tomatoes'
11. [tātə]	[baṭāṭiṣ]	'potatoes'
12. [sáya]	[sʊɣáyyar]	'small'

These imitations were on the whole quite accurate. Most errors can be accounted for as regular substitutions of phonemes not in the child's repertoire, and as omissions of the first syllable of two- or three-syllable words, as in Items 7, 8, and 11. Some three-syllable words were repeated fully, however, as in Items 3, 5, and 7; in Item 7, this was on the second try. Item 7 shows at least two substitutions for /l/–[d] and [y], although there is evidence that /l/ is a phoneme by this time. In Item 10, /m/ was replaced by [n] for the only time in all of this child's utterances, possibly because in this word, /m/ becomes emphasized in the environment of emphatic consonants. Similarly, emphatic /ḷ/ in Item 3 is rare, which may explain why it was replaced by [n].

Final consonants were not usually omitted; an exception was Item 11. Item 12, a complicated three-syllable word, was imitated as two syllables. The difficult consonant /ɣ/ was omitted, and apparently its occurrence in the second syllable caused that syllable to be entirely omitted, resulting in the first and third syllables repeated.

3.5.3. *The Imitation Tests*

Imitation tests were considered an essential tool in investigating children's phonemic development. They provided an opportunity for obtaining a large, diversified, controlled body of data, which is much more efficient than waiting for spontaneous utterances of various types.

Results from imitation tests administered to Children 1 through 16 (ages 2.8–7) show the gradual development of accuracy in imitation of individual sounds and words, as well as ability to imitate longer utterances more accurately. These tests were also administered to Child 28, age 13, to check that the model was consistent with standard adult speech.

Imitation Test 1 consisted of 11 short, simple sentences, and was designed mainly to elicit as many individual phonemes as possible. Results are summarized, discussing children's imitation of each of the model sentences.

1. Model. [ʔǽnə ma-šʊftʊ́h-š] /ʔǽna ma-šuftúh-š/ 'I did not see him.'

In this sentence, the first notable error was the substitution of [s] for /š/ by Children 1–5 and Child 7. Children 1 and 2 omitted the final cluster /-hš/; Child 1 repeated only the second word and omitted the medial consonant cluster as well; her utterances were [stūs], [tus]. The sentence was accurately imitated by Children 10–16.

2. Model. [ʔíntə rāyɪḥ fēn] /ʔínta rāyiḥ fēn/ 'Where are you (m. sing.) going?'

The three youngest children did not repeat the sentence; instead, they repeated the last words, /rāyiḥ fēn/, and Child 2 repeated only one word at a time. All children repeated /ʔinta/ and /fēn/ accurately; /rāyiḥ/ was realized as [láhə] by Child 1, and [lāyɪḥ] by Children 2, 4, 6 and 7. Phonetic [r] appeared in the imiations of Children 3, 5, 8, and 9, although it was not yet established as a phoneme for the youngest children. Other children imitated the model accurately.

3. Model [ḥa-nḥʊ́ṭṭu fēn] /ḥa-nḥúṭṭu fēn/ 'Where will we put it?'

Imitation of the first word in the sentence showed some variation. Children 1–9 produced utterances of the type [ḥtu], [ḥʊttu], or [nḥʊṭṭu]. Children 1 and 2 did not articulate the geminated consonant in /nḥuṭṭu/, omitting the future prefix /ḥa-/ and sometimes the person marker /n-/. Children 10–16 imitated the model accurately.

4. Model. [di ʕarabíyə] /di ʕarabíya/ 'This (is) a car.'

This sentence contained the difficult phoneme /ʕ/. There is evidence that its articulation is still not consistent even after the child has learned the phoneme. The /ʕ/ was omitted or articulated very weakly in the imitations of Children 11, 12, 15, and 16. The two youngest children again imitated only the last word of the sentence. Child 1 at first imitated only the last two syllables, substituting [m] for /b/, saying [ʔɛmíy], [miyə], and [ʔabíy]. Children 2–5 and Child 7 produced [ʔaləbɪyə], substituting [l] for /r/. The other children imitated the model accurately.

5. Model. [híyə ṭawīlə (gáwi) (jíddən)]
/híya ṭawīla (gáwi) (jíddan)]
'She (is) very tall.'

Two words, /gáwi/ and /jíddan/, can be used to express 'very' in this dialect. At first, /jíddan/ was given, but when it was realized that this is rather formal in this dialect, /gáwi/ was used, which explains why there were two models for this item.

The /j/ was difficult for Child 1, who used three phonemes to substitute for it, and again repeated only the last word in the sentence. Her utterances were [mídyə], [ẓíddə], and [ʔíddə]. It is interesting that Child 2 mixed the order of words in her repetition of the sentence, and substituted [d] for the emphatic /ṭ/ which she could not yet articulate. Her utterance was [híyə jídə dawīlə]. Child 3 substituted [d] for /g/, repeating /gáwi/ as [dáwi], although he articulated /g/ elsewhere. All Children through Child 9 omitted the final consonant of the word /jíddan/. The first two words were easy to imitate for all children except the three youngest ones, and Children 10–16 imitated the sentence accurately.

6. Model. [ʔɪl-qʊrʔān ʔɪl-kærīm]
/ʔil-qurʔān ʔil-kærīm/
'The Holy Koran'

This was the hardest item phonemically in the test. The rare /q/ phoneme was introduced, in a standard phrase, in which the other word contained /k/, much like /q/. This confused almost all the children; the only accurate imitations were by Children 9 and 12, and Child 12 missed the second definite article. Child 9 was the first to articulate the /q/, at age 5. Younger children substituted [k], [g], or omitted it. For example, Child 1 produced [ʔān], Child 2 [kánə], Child 3 [kʊlʔá], and Child 5 [gʊrʔā].

Children 11, 14, and 16 made such a conscious effort to articulate /q/ that they also articulated the second word with /q/, as [qarīm], although it is a common word in their vocabulary and in other environments was pronounced correctly. Another source of difficulty was the medial /ʔ/ in the first word, which was omitted in imitations of Children 2 and 10.

Children 1 and 3 did not repeat the phrase; they attempted only one word at a time. Child 2 repeated the phrase a second time with the words in inverse order, as [ʔɪl-kælīm l-ʔān].

7. Model. [kǽlnə jɪbnə w zaytūn]
/kǽlna jíbna w zaytūn/
'We ate cheese and olives.'

Except for /j/, this sentence contained easy phonemes, and elicited three consonant clusters. Imitation, however, was extremely irregular. Child 1 repeated the sentence in parts, and substituted [ẓ] and [z] for /j/, which was not yet in her phonemic repertoire. She also substituted [d] for the sibilant /z/, although she had previously articulated /z/. Her utterances were [ẓɪbnə kǽlnə] [daytūn]. Neither she nor any of the children had problems imitating the consonant clusters.

Child 2 produced two imitations of the sentence, very different, and highly irregular. The first time, she rendered /zaytūn/ as [ftūn]; the second time she repeated only the last syllable, [tūn]. She articulated the first two consonant clusters, then simplified them in the second imitation, and substituted [dd] for the cluster /ln/, producing [kǽddə jínə w tūn].

Child 3 probably misunderstood at first, and blended two words into one nonsensical word, [jɪbtūn]; he then attempted to repeat the last word, as [zɪtúnə].

Child 4's first imitation of /jibna/ as [zíttə] was so poor that it seems likely she misunderstood the word, since she articulated it accurately the second time. Child 5 substituted [ʔ] for the phonemes /k/ and /t/, in [ʔálnə] and [zayʔ-ūn], although they are among the earliest phonemes acquired. Child 7 also had unusual phoneme substitutions, articulating /t/ in the last word as [x] and [k], in [zayxūn] and [zaykūn].

The vocabulary in this sentence is familiar; perhaps the meaning is not realistic. I can think of no other reason to account for this confusion in imitation.

8. Model. [hʊ́wə lǽbɪs žakɛ́ttə]
/húwa lǽbis jakítta/
'He (is) wearing a jacket.'

The allophone [ž] here is in free variation with /j/ ([j]) in the word /jakitta/. [ž] occurs rarely, in words of foreign origin. Since it is quite unfamiliar, as is the word, most children substituted [ẓ], and a few substituted [d]. Since older children also articulated the [ž] as [ẓ], as in [ẓakɛ́ttə], this will be taken as an alternative, acceptable pronunciation in this dialect.

Children 1 and 2 pronounced the word /jakítta/ as [dakɛ́tə] and [dakɛ́tt] respectively; Children 3, 5, and 8 produced [zakɛ́ttə], and Children 4, 6, and 9 [ẓakɛ́ttə]. Child 7's substitutions for [ž] are interesting; the first time she was probably concentrating on the initial substitution [d], and rendered the second consonant, /k/, as [d] also, in the utterance [dædɛ́ttə]; later she produced [dagɛ́ttə] and [zagɛ́ttə].

The first two words were easy for all children to imitate.

9. Model. [ʔɪl-ṃáyyə sʊ́xnə]
/ʔil-máyya suxna/
'The water (is) hot.'

This was an easy item, with only one difficulty, the consonant cluster /xn/. This was missed once by Child 1, and articulated once, in her utterances [sʊ́xnə] and [sʊ́kənə]. Otherwise, imitation was quite accurate. Child 3 pronounced the second word as [sʊx]. Child 5 articulated /s/ as [ṣ] in the word [ṣʊ́xnə]. All children imitated the first word accurately.

10. Model. [ʔabūyə fɪl-ɣēṭ]
/ʔabūya fil-ɣēṭ/
'My father (is) in the field.'

This sentence is uttered often by the children. Nevertheless, in a formal testing situation, some were hesitant. Child 2, for example, usually articulated /ʔabūya/ correctly, but here produced [ʔamūyə], and Child 5 could articulate /ɣēṭ/ correctly in conversation, but here said [ga]. This is a good illustration of how a formal situation can give a partially inaccurate indication of the child's phonemic development.

Children 1 and 4 imitated the sentence correctly, but omitted the prepositional phrase /fil/. Child 3 produced by [ɣɛy]. Other children imitated the model accurately.

11. Model. [híyə sǽʔælɪt ʕalēk]
/híya sǽʔælit ʕalēk/
'She asked about you (m. sing.).'

The second word, /sǽʔælit/, was difficult, due to the medial position of /ʔ/. It was not articulated by the three youngest children, and missed by some older ones. Children 1 and 2 produced [sǽlə] and [sælt] respectively; Children 8, 10, 11, and 12 produced [sǣlɪt]. Because /sǽʔælit/ was difficult for the children, some made unusual substitutions of phonemes or transposed their order, for example, Children 3 and 5, who said [sǽlətɪt] and [sǽlæʔɪt] respectively.

In the last word, the /ʕ/ was omitted and replaced by [ʔ] by Children 1–6 and 8–12, who said [ʔalēk].

Imitation Test 2 consisted of four items, mainly longer, complex sentences. Some new phonemes were elicited, and the abilty to imitate complex sentences was tested.

12. Model. [hʊ́wə ʕam-yíʕraf yíktɪb ʕašǣn ʕam-yrūḥ ʔɪl-mǽdrəsə]
/húwa ʕam-yíʕraf yiktib ʕašǣn ʕam-yrūḥ ʔil-mǽdrasa/
'He knows how to write because (he) goes to school.'

This long sentence could clearly be divided into two parts, and Child 6, age 4, was the first to repeat it completely. Older children, Children 5, 7, and 8, succeeded only after repeating both halves separately.

The word /mǽdrasa/ was difficult for Children 1 and 2, who repeated it with several variations, such as [ʔɪl-mǣsə], [mǽdlæs], [mǽsælə], [mǽlədæsə].

Child 2 omitted some words in her repetition, all of them less important grammatically; she actually said 'writes, goes to school', [ʔan-ʔíktɪb rūh

ʔɪl-mǽlədæsə]. Children 2 and 5 omitted the pronoun, /huwa/, which is optional grammatically. Child 1 repeated only the last word of the sentence, and Child 3 the last word of both halves, producing [yíktɪb] and [ʔǽdlæsə].

It may be noted that all children repeated the words in correct order.

13. Model. [ʔʊ́mmi mɪš ʔabūyə lli fɪl-bēt]
/ʔummi miš ʔabūya ʔílli fil-bēt/
'My mother, not my father, who (is) in the house.'

There were no difficult phonemes or words in this sentence; it was included because of its structural complexity.

Children 6, 8, 9, and 10 imitated it correctly; Child 11 twice mixed up *my mother* and *my father*. Child 5 simply said 'Not my father (who) is in the house'. Some of the confusion was very likely due to the fact that these children were in a testing situation and may have been somewhat tense and conscious of being recorded.

Younger children tended to imitate only the last part of the sentence. Child 2 said [mɪš ʔabūyə fɪl-bēt], and Child 3 [búyə bēt]. The other children imitated the sentence accurately.

14. Model. [hʊ́wə ʕam-yɪṭḍárab̩]
/huwa ʕam-yitḍárab/
'He (is) being hit.'

The passive voice used in this sentence is not commonly heard. Nevertheless, it was immediately comprehended and quite accurately produced, except by Child 3, who repeated [hʊ́wə díli]. The only phonemic difficulty was with the emphatic consonants. Children 1 and 2 said [ʔadál] and [mɪtdaləb], and Child 4 [ʔɪtdírɪb]. Other children repeated the sentence accurately.

15. Model. [ʔabūyə rāḥ ʔɪl-ɣēṭ fɪṣ-ṣʊbḥ bǽdri w ḥa-yírjaʕ fɪl-mǽɣrɪb]
/ʔabūya rāḥ ʔil-ɣēṭ fiṣ-ṣubḥ bǽdri w ḥa-yírjaʕ fil-mǽɣrib/
'My father went to the field in the morning early and will return at dusk.'

Although this sentence was as long as Item 12, it was easier to imitate because its contents made more 'sense', i.e., were a more real part of the child's life. Children 5 and 12, in fact, repeated what their father had really done that day, saying he went to the market, /ʔis-sūg/, instead of to the field. Children 2, 5, and 7 replaced the verb /yírjaʕ/ 'return' with the more common /yīji/ 'come'. Child 7 said her father went /ʔil-wakt/ 'now'. Many became confused in repeatin the long sentence; for example, Child 6 said 'My father went to the field at dusk', [ʔabūyə rāḥ ʔɪl-ɣēṭ fɪl-mǽɣrɪb], omitting the whole central part of the sentence. Child 8's confusion resulted in a nonsense statement, 'My father went to the field at dusk in the morning early'. Another example of confusion was Child 14's transposition of two phrases, which resulted in the utterance, 'My father went in the morning early to the field and returned'.

Younger children could not pronounce /rāḥ/, and substituted [l] for the /r/ phoneme, as in the utterances of Child 1, [la], Child 3, [laḥ], and Child 7 [lāḥ].

The consonant cluster in /bǽdri/ was repeated by Child 1 as [bǽdli]; Child 2 once articulated the cluster and once split it, saying [bǽdɛli]. Other children pronounced it correctly

The final /ʕ/ in /yírjaʕ/ was omitted by Children 4 and 9. Other younger children did not repeat it; older ones repeated it correctly.

The word /mǽɣrib/ was difficult for some to pronounce; many substituted [g] or [k] for /ɣ/. Child 1 did not try to imitate it; Child 2 produced [ʔɪm-mágrɛd], Child 3, [mæk], Child 4, [mǽg], Child 5, [mǽgrɪb]; the rest of the children pronounced it correctly.

Imitation Test 3 consisted first of two irregular sentences, both containing a word repeated twice, to see whether the children would repeat the sentence as given. The third item was composed of four sentences, in each of which was added a new adjective or phrase, to test ability to repeat a sentence of increasing length. The last item was a sentence repeated three times, each time with the sentence stress on a different word.

16. Model. [ʔɪš-šʊɣl šuɣl mɪš sæhl]
/ʔiš-šuɣl šuɣl miš sæhl/
'The work work (is) not easy.'

It was most common for children to reduce the sentence when imitating it, and most repeated the noun only once. Child 8, age 5, was the first to repeat the sentence accurately, and most of the children after this age did so.

The difficulties in pronunciation were two consonant clusters, /ɣl/ and /hl/. The first cluster was successfully imitated by all children but Child 2, who said [sʊ́ɣʊl]. The second cluster was often simplified, with one of the two consonants omitted. Child 1 produced the utterance [sǣli]; Child 3, [sǣh], Child 6, [sæl]. It was correctly produced by Children 2 and 4, and older children.

Child 7 was distracted during the testing, and she repeated a completely different word from the one given, so her utterance resulted in nonsense, 'The work is not under'.

17. Model. a. [šʊft ʕaṣfūrə]
/šuft ʕaṣfūra/
'I saw a bird.'

b. [šʊft ʕaṣfūrə ṣʊɣayyárə]
/šuft ʕaṣfūra ṣuɣayyára/
'I saw a small bird.'

c. [šʊft ʕaṣfūrə ṣʊɤayyárə fɪs-sájarə]
/šuft ʕaṣfūra ṣuɤayyára fis-sájara/
'I saw a small bird in the tree.'

d. [šʊft ʕaṣfūrə ṣʊɤayyárə ḥílwə fɪs-sájarə]
/šuft ʕaṣfūra ṣuɤayyára ḥílwa fis-sájara/
'I saw a small pretty bird in the tree.'

With regard to remembering words and their order, the first difficulty in repeating the sentence came in part (c). At this point, there were so many words that some children repeated them in mixed order, e.g., Children 2 and 4, who said [sʊft w sádələ ʔafsūlə] and [sʊft ʔaṣfūlə fɪs-sádəl ẓyállə]. Some omitted words or phrases, e.g., Child 5, who said 'I saw a tree', and Child 7, 'I saw a small one'.

Part (d) consisted of an additional adjective, added not at the end as other words had been, but inserted before the last phrase. The result was considerable confusion. Children 1, 4, 11, and 14 added the new word at the end according to the previous pattern of addition, saying 'I saw a small bird in the pretty tree'; Child 2 repeated the new word twice, omitting the earlier adjective; her utterance was [sʊft ḥílwə w zádələ l-ḥílwə]. Children 6 and 10 repeated no adjectives at all, whereas both had repeated the adjective in part (c). They simply said [šʊft ʕaṣfūrə fɪs-sájalə].

The word /ʕaṣfūra/ was mispronounced by many children. Children 1–7 omitted the initial /ʕ/, replacing it with [ʔ]. Children 1, 2, and 7 rendered /ṣ/ as [s]. Child 5 split the consonant cluster in parts (b), (c), and (d), saying [sufūlə], although he had articulated it in part (a).

The word /ḥílwa/ proved easy to pronounce. Only Child 1 mispronounced it, as [hǽlə].

/sájara/ contained two phonemes which are acquired late, /j/ and /r/. Child 1 imitated this word as [sájələ]. Child 2 imitated it as [sádələ] and [ságələ], Child 3 as [sád], and Children 5 and 7 as [sájələ]. In these cases, /j/ was replaced by [d] and [g], and /r/ by [l].

18. Model. [ʔɪn-nǣs ʕam-yíšrabu šǣy kull^{I} yōm]
/ʔin-nǣs ʕam-yíšrabu šǣy kull yōm/
'People drink tea every day.' (Repeated three times, with sentence stress on the first three words.)

Change of stress had no noticeable effect on imitation of this sentence, possibly because the sentence was too short or because its contents were too 'familiar' and easily remembered for repetition. In only one case did a child repeat the sentence differently from the first time; Child 2 repeated the word /šǣy/ 'tea' twice when it was stressed in the model sentence, saying 'Tea, everyone drinks tea'.

Children 4 and 7 changed the word order in their repetition, saying 'People every day drink tea'.

The consonant cluster /šr/ was difficult for younger children, since they had not acquired either one or both of the consonants. Children 1 and 3 pronounced the word /yíšrabu/ without a cluster, as [ʔísab]. Children 2, 4, 5, and 7 produced [yíšlabu].

Child 6 and older children pronounced the sentence correctly.

3.5.4. *Final Observations*

One phenomenon occurred in the data of imitation tests which I believe had not been noted or analyzed by previous researchers. Borrowing Labov's concept,[98] this may be termed "hypercorrection". Sometimes when a child was striving to articulate a difficult phoneme, his concentration on that articulation caused a nearby phoneme (which he could easily pronounce) to be articulated like the first, difficult one. The best examples of this were seen in Item 6. Several children, striving to articulate /q/ in the first word, /qurʔān/, also pronounced the second word in the phrase, /kærīm/, as [qarīm]. Another example is in the speech of Child 7 in Item 11. In trying to pronounce /jakitta/, she substituted [d] for /j/, and the following /k/ was also articulated as [d], resulting in [dædɛttə]. In subsequent tries, she corrected this.

The children performed in imitation about as expected, and their pronunciation of phonemes was consistent with their pronunciation in non-testing situations. There was a marked improvement with age, in articulation and in memory span. Only one child, Child 7, a girl age 4.6, seemed somewhat behind her age group. In conversation and playing with other children, she was very verbal, but when being tested, she had poor concentration. Unlike some children younger than she, she never articulated /š/ or /r/ in any utterances.

Consistent with theories about early imitation, phonemes which were omitted were usually in final position in a word. If a multi-syllabic word was not repeated as a whole, the stressed syllable was usually repeated. If a multi-syllabic word was repeated, stress was correctly imitated.

In imitation of sentences, if the children could not repeat the whole sentence, it was most common for them to repeat the final or stressed words. In complex sentences, words were often repeated in mixed order, and words or particles which were grammatically less important were omitted. Other processes which are commonly observed in children's imitation of sentences are present in

[98] William Labov, "Hypercorrection by the Lower Middle Class as a Factor in Linguistic Evolution", *Sociolinguistics*, ed., William Bright (→ *Janua Linguarum*, series major 20) (The Hague, Mouton, 1966) pp. 84–113. He describes hypercorrection as occurring when "lower middle class speakers go beyond the highest status group in their tendency to use the forms considered correct and appropriate formal styles" (p. 88).

these data, such as reduction of redundant material (Item 16), and addition of words or phrases not included in the model sentence (Item 15).

The relatively larger number of errors made by younger children and the fact that there is a positive correlation between success in imitation and age are evidence that errors are the result of limitations in the child's development and ability to encode and decode material at various levels of complexity. It must be kept in mind, however, that some mistakes in imitation of sentences may be due to more than limiting factors related to verbal development. Extraneous factors may interfere, such as lack of attention, noise, or inconsistent quality in the presentation of the model sentence by the tester, and may cause a poorer performance than that of which the child is capable. On the other hand, the child may sometimes repeat short segments of sentences well without actually having understood or 'processed' the information, and there is no way to determine when this is being done.

4

EARLY COMMUNICATION AND INITIAL VOCABULARY

4.1. COMPREHENSION

4.1.1. *Theoretical Considerations*

A newborn child is immediately surrounded by linguistic activity, much of it directed to him. The first responses to this are in the form of imitations, and very early there is evidence of rudimentary comprehension of some signals in the form of gestures, intonation patterns, and finally, verbal forms.[1] In the beginning, responses are gross and global, and gradually become differentiated and structured. The child learns to try new responses and to generalize, and to make the critical distinctions necessary in his language by an unconscious trial-and-error process.[2] The child understands items in the language before he uses the language himself. Fry has stated that "it is agreed by all observers of infant speech that recognition of words . . . precedes any deliberate attempt on the part of the child to say the word with reference to that situation".[3] Studies have shown that children respond to different gestures and commands from 9 to 12 months.[4]

Lewis states that intonation patterns are probably the first items distinguished.[5] Later the child links the intonation form with the corresponding phonetic form and situation, and finally, the phonetic pattern becomes dominant over intonation and gestures in evoking a response in the child. At this point, the child knows that a phonetic form refers to a particular object or event, and has understood a 'word'. Throughout language development, the child learns which verbal and gestural responses will obtain for him what he wants and fend off what he dislikes.[6]

The first evidence of recognition and understanding of certain symbolic gestures, intonations and words comes in the latter part of the babbling stage,

[1] Lewis, cited in Weir, 1966: 157.

[2] Carroll, 1961; 333.

[3] Fry, 1966, 192.

[4] McCarthy, 1954, 503.

[5] Morris M. Lewis, *Infant Speech: A Study of the Beginnings of Language* (New York, Humanities Press, 1951) pp. 115–116, 122.

[6] Carroll, 1961, 333.

at about 8 to 10 months. At this point the brain has matured to the level of development which has been called "speech readiness".[7] By 10 to 12 months, the normal child can differentiate some words and understand simple commands, and by 18 months, demands and prohibitions.[8] Usually a child can un derstand more than he can say. It is possible to learn to understand a language without learning to speak it, and this situation can be present for a time in normal primary language acquisition.

Carroll states that the over-all frequency with which items occur in speech heard by the child has an important relation to the developmental sequences in which items are learned, although it is possible that the frequencies heard by the child do not correspond to those in adult speech.[9]

When the early speaking stage begins, it still overlaps with babbling for some months. A word may be used by the child to cover a wide variety of meanings. For example, Leopold observed that *mama* was articulated by his child in the first year, but did not take on the referential meaning of 'mother' until 16 months. Similarly, *papa*, articulated at 7.5 months, took on referential meaning at 13 months.[10] Lewis states that *mama* is an early discomfort sound, and is later used in asking for something, and linked with food and sleep, as well as with the mother.[11]

Comprehension is very difficult to test, although with younger children of age approximately 18 to 36 months, there is a tendency for the child to run through his repertoire of capacities and thus give a fair indication of the extent of his vocabulary and comprehension.[12] From age 30 months and older, production is unreliable as an indicator of language capacities, since at all levels, children understand more features of language than they can actively use.[13] Chomsky's distinction of "competence" and "performance" must be kept in

[7] Leonard Carmichael, "The Early Growth of Language Capacity in the Individual," *New Directions in the Study of Language*, ed., Eric Lenneberg (Cambridge, MIT Press, 1964) p. 15.

[8] Carroll, 1961, 337. Also see chart of linguistic development in McCarthy, 1954, 501.

[9] Carroll, 1961, 334.

[10] Leopold, 1948, 1–2.

[11] Lewis, 1964, 30–32.

[12] Lenneberg, 1967, 285.

[13] Wick Miller and Susan Ervin, "The Development of Grammar in Child Language", *The Acquisition of Language*, eds., Ursula Bellugi and Roger Brown (Lafayette, Ind., Child Development Publication of the Society for Research in Child Development, 1964) p. 11. David McNeill, "Developmental Psycholinguistics", *The Genesis of Language*, eds., Frank Smith and George A. Miller (Cambridge, MIT Press, 1966) p. 76. Noam Chomsky, "Formal Discussion", *The Acquisition of Language*, eds., Ursula Bellugi and Roger Brown (Lafayette, Ind., Child Development Publication of the Society for Research in Child Development, 1964) p. 39. Henry Kahane, Renee Kahane, and Sol Saporta, "The Development of the Verbal Categories in Child Language," *IJAL* 24.4 (1954), Part II : 1.

mind; competence in a language is greater than what is indicated by performance.

Comprehension may be tested by giving the child commands, asking him to manipulate objects, or to name objects or pictures. Standardized pictures which depict minimal grammatical contrasts are also suggested,[14] although some contrasts cannot be clearly illustrated. The asking of questions is helpful, but not as systematic.

Care must be taken to eliminate as many distractions and contradictions in the situation as possible. Luria's experiments showed that for young children, words are not directive if the child is in a situation where the visual cue contradicts the verbal signal; the visual cue dominates the response.[15]

4.1.2. *The Comprehension Test*

In this study, a comprehension test was administered to young children, beginning with Child 1, age 2.8, through Child 16, age 7. The test contained 25 items, of several types, testing comprehension of vocabulary items, grammatical contrasts, and ability to follow directions. It was found that there were no errors after Child 11, age 6. The results of p erformance on the test items were as follows.

4.1.2.1.*Results: Part I, General Recognition of Objects*

Each item was accompanied by pictures. The child was told to point to the appropriate object. The first items were deliberately simple to get the child oriented to the testing situation.

1. Boy–girl: this item was done correctly by all children except Children 1, 7, and 10.
2. Big girl – little girl: this item was done correctly by all children except Child 3.
3. Cow – donkey: several children missed this item: Children 1, 5, 6, 7, and 10.
4. Dog – cat: this item was missed by Children 1, 2, 5, 6, and 10.
5. Fat man – thin man: only Children 4 and 10 missed this item.
6. Black cat – yellow cat: since this item involved recognition of colors, it was missed by several children, Children 2, 3, 5, 8, and 10.
7. Flowers – green, yellow, red, blue: every child from Child 1 through Child 10 inclusive missed at least one of the colors. The older children all performed perfectly except Child 15, age 6.6, who confused two colors.

[14] Slobin, ed., 1967, p. 27.

[15] Aleksandr R. Luria, "The Directive Function of Speech in Development and Dissolution, Part I: Development of the Directive Function of Speech in Early Childhood", *Word* 15 (1959): 342.

8. Girl carrying – stick, doll, water jug: this item was missed by Children 1, 2, 3, 4, 5, and 7.

4.1.2.2. *Results: Part II, Object Manipulation*

Because the children were not accustomed to dealing with pictures, some concepts were tested with the use of real objects.

9. (Prepositions) "Place the stone (beside, in, under) the cup". Only Children 7 and 10 missed this item.
10. (Colors; Subject-Object) "Make the red car push the green car." "Make the green car push the red car." This item was done correctly by all except Children 1, 3, 7, and 10.
11. (Numbers) "Give me (1, 2, 3, 4, 5) stones." All children performed correctly for the numbers 1 and 2.[16] For numbers 3 to 5, all children from Child 1 through Child 11 inclusive missed at least some items.
12. (Prepositions) "Give me the stone which is (on, under, beside) the cup." All children performed correctly except Chijdren 2 and 7.

4.1.2.3. *Results : Part III, Minimal Grammatical Contrasts*

Each item was accompanied by pictures on cards. The child was told to point to the correct one. This part was not administered to Child 3.

13. (Singular-Plural) "The (boy, boys) are playing ball." (This is a 'broken plural' form.) All children performed correctly except Children 1, 2, 6, 8, and 10.
14. (Present Progressive – Past Tense) "The boy (is falling, fell)." This item was missed by almost all the children, by Children 1, 2, 4, 5, 7, 8, 9, 10, 13, and 14.
15. (Affirmative – Negative) "The boy (is, is not) sitting." Only Child 2 missed this item.
16. (Word Order) "The girl is smaller than the boy." "The boy is smaller than the girl." This item was missed by Children 1, 2, 4, 6, 7, and 8.
17. (Present – Future Tense) "The girl (is drinking, will drink) water." This item was missed by Children 1, 2, 6, 7, and 14.
18. (Subject – Object) "The girl is hitting the boy." "The boy is hitting the girl." Only Children 1, 6, 10, and 13 missed this item.
19. (Animate – Inanimate) "(Who, What) is in the picture?" (A man and a tree) This item was missed by Children 1, 4, and 8.

[16] "2" was given in numeral form, as in /ˀiddi̅ni ˀitnēn/ 'give me two'.

20. (Singular – Plural) "Give me the picture of the (boy, boys)." This item was missed only by Children 1 and 5.
21. (Active – Passive) "The boy (hits, is being hit)." This item was done correctly by all except Children 1, 12, and 15.
22. (Subject – Object) "The dog is running after the cat." "The cat is running after the dog." This item was missed by several children, Children 1, 4, 5, 10, 11, and 15.
23. (Adjective Modification) "The big boy with a dog." "The boy with a big dog." This item was missed by Children 1, 2, 4, 5, 6, and 15.
24. (Affirmative – Negative) "The girl (is, is not) drawing water." This item was missed only by Children 4 and 10.
25. (Gender and Verb Agreement) "Someone is hitting (m., f. verb) him." This item was missed by Children 2, 4, 5, 8, 9, and 14.

4.1.3. *Conclusions*

There were no items in which none of the children erred in the answer. Some, however, were missed by so few that it may be assumed the objects or contrast were actually known by all children, and errors were due to inattention, effects of formality in the testing situation, or ambiguity of the illustrations accompanying the item. Some children, notably Children 5, 6, 7, and 10, missed so many items that it seems probable they did not properly understand the nature of the test or were inattentive throughout it, since children younger than they performed well. Child 1 missed many items also, but I feel not all errors were due to lack of knowledge; she was restless and in fact may not have comprehended the principle that illustrations represent real objects, since pictures and photographs are not commonly seen by these children.[17]

Child 3 was administered Parts I and II only because he was unwilling to continue the test.

All items were administered at the same time and the test lasted from 10 to 30 minutes. Children did not hear others answering the items; if older children were required to be present with younger ones, the older children were tested first, alone.

In Part I, because the errors were made by the same children in Items 1 through 5, they will not be considered as indicative of a lack of ability to distinguish between the objects if actually presented. I think errors were due to inadequacy of the illustrations and the fact that illustrations were used at all instead of real objects, which may have been difficult for some children. Therefore, these items will be treated as having all been answered correctly.

[17] Meerson observed that three-year-old Russian children often could not name pictures of objects but could name the objects when they were presented directly. Slobin, 1966, 377.

Items 6 and 7 tested colors, in which there was confusion. Item 6 gave a choice of two colors, so guessing could account for the fact that about half of the children were right and half wrong, through Child 10. Item 7 was a more valid test, depicting four colors from which the correct one had to be chosen; virtually all children through Child 10 missed at least one color. Of the four colors, if any one was correct, red was always included as one of them. In both items testing color, the errors were made by children through Child 10 and not thereafter, so it appears that basic colors are not mastered until about age 6.[18]

Item 8 required the child to distinguish three common objects. Most children through Child 7 missed at least one of the objects; perhaps in the pictures they were depicted too small, or the fact that a girl was present in each picture may have been distracting. It seems unlikely that the children did not know the actual objects tested.

Part II dealt with object manipulation, and three of the items were answered very well. Items 9 and 12 tested prepositions. Child 2 was the only one who apparently did not know the basic prepositions; Child 7 knew *beside* and *on*, but missed *in* and *under;* Child 10 put all stones 'inside' in Item 9, but performed correctly the second time. Child 7 was very inattentive during the test. I think the evidence here is that prepositions are acquired very early, probably before age 3.

Item 10 tested two colors again, and with real objects, performance was better, although guessing could have accounted for some right answers. Only 4 children missed this item.

Item 11, testing numbers through 5, proved to be the most difficult in the test. All children through Child 11 erred in at least some numbers. All knew 1 and 2. In subsequent errors, none knew 3 except Children 7 and 11; and only Child 11 knew 4. Children 9 and 11 gave three stones when asked for five; most of the other children gave two for all numbers above 2, or a random handful of stones. Results of this item would indicate that the numbers are not learned until age 6, which corresponds with the children's first attendance at school.

Part III tested minimal grammatical contrasts. Since it was necessary to elicit responses by pictures, the validity of the test cannot be determined, and for some items, there were so many errors that their validity is in question. In these questionable items, the desired grammatical contrast could not be illustrated clearly.

Items 13 and 20 tested singular and plural forms of a noun which has as plural a 'broken', irregular form, the word /wād/ 'boy', plural /wilǣd/ 'boys'.

[18] Lenneberg notes that "basic" colors are learned between age 2½ and 3½ by middle-class American children. Eric H. Lenneberg, "The Capacity of Language Acquisition", *The Structure of Language: Readings in the Philosophy of Language*, eds., J. A. Fodor and J. J. Katz (Englewood Cliffs, N. J., Prentice-Hall, 1964) p. 594.

This is a simple concept and a common word; errors were few, and made by children whose errors are not considered a valid indication of level of linguistic development. Only Child 1 may have actually not known the distinction; Child 2 missed the first but not the second time.

Item 19 tested the distinction between animate and inanimate nouns, through the use of pronouns. Errors were few. Only those made by Children 1 and 4 may indicate a lack of distinction of the items, but Child 2 was correct. Results are not clear, although it is evident that the distinction is not late in being acquired.

In Item 17 the present and future tenses of the verb were tested. While four children, Children 1, 2, 6, and 7 missed this item, it is most probable that only the two younger children may have lacked this contrast; the errors of Children 6 and 7 are more likely due to other factors. Item 14 tested the present progressive and past tenses of the verb. Since it was missed by so many children, it was considered invalid. This was possibly due to the difficulty in illustrating the contrast.

Items 15 and 24, testing affirmative and negative forms of the verb, were missed by few children. No child erred in both items, so this indicates that this contrast was probably known by all children.

Item 21 tested the active and passive voice of the verb. This was easier to illustrate, and the only error which may indicate that the contrast was not yet attained was made by Child 1. It is obviously attained early.

Item 25 tested the recognition of the gender of the verb form. A 'neutral' subject (/ḥadd/ 'someone') was used with the masculine and feminine inflections of the verb form, and the child had to determine the subject of the action by the verb cue only. This proved tricky. No answers were given by Children 1, 6, and 7. Others through Child 5 missed this item. It appears that this subtlety may not be acquired until about age 5.

Item 16 tested word order, and this contrast was apparently not attained by children through Child 8, or about age 5. A difficulty here may have been due to the fact that *smaller* was used as comparison; using *larger* as the adjective of comparison may have been easier.

Items 18 and 22 also tested word order, the distinction between subject and object. Errors were probably due to the poor illustrations or to distractions, because they were scattered through all age groups. Only Children 1 and 10 erred both times.

Item 23 tested adjective modification of the noun. In the two sentences given, both nouns are masculine with the masculine form of the adjective. Child 7 was not tested; all children through Child 6 missed the item, so that the age at which this contrast is attained appears to be about 4 or 4½.

4.1.4. *Effects of Other Factors on Performance*

It has been postulated that diet and health can affect linguistic development, and there was evidence of this from the comprehension test. Three of the children who routinely missed items have backgrounds which may explain their poor performance. Child 5 is a boy who is physically short for his age and is reported to have walked at age 3½, Child 7 is from one of the poorest homes in the village, and Child 10 is one of a large family, the largest in the village, where the children receive even less attention than usual and have a very poor diet.

To investigate the effects of environment and outside factors on performance, this test was also given to two other children. The first was a boy, Sādig (not included in the general study), age 6, whose height was 34 inches, one inch shorter than the 2- and 3-year-old children in the study. It was reported that he began walking and talking at about age 4, due to poor health and much illness. He was nursed until recently. The result has been at least temporary mental and verbal, as well as physical, retardation. On the comprehension test, this child performed so poorly that results could not be analyzed. He was not nearly as verbal as Child 1.

The second child to which the test was given was a girl, Heba, age 3.6, in a middle-class home in Cairo, who was in excellent health and exposed to much verbal attention. Her performance was perfect on all 25 items in the test, with answers given without any indication of misunderstanding the questions or the illustrations, and without hesitation.

4.2. EARLY SPEECH AND VOCABULARY

4.2.1. *Theoretical Considerations*

Early speech and the acquisition of vocabulary are, of course, closely linked with the development of comprehension and are dependent on it. Meaningful speech often begins before the end of the first year.

Between the ages of 10 and 18 months, the child begins to utter meaningful single words, and this is the period of the one-word sentence. Even phrases may be learned as units.[19] It must be remembered, however, that the first utterance of a word may not be its meaningful use; there is a gap between the utterance of a phonetic form and the symbolic use of the word in an appropriate situation.[20]

[19] Carroll, 1961, 338.
[20] McCarthy, cited in Carmichael, 1964, 9.

Early speech expresses mainly emotional and volitional meaning.[21] Sounds are repeated in particular situations to get desired responses; early speech is for social use. The first words refer to classes, not unique objects or events.[22] Lenneberg states that there is no evidence that onset and development of meaningful speech is affected by cultural and linguistic variations.[23]

Many studies have been made in which attempts were made to estimate the size of vocabulary for children of various ages. In most cases, the estimate was too low, for it is difficult to check completeness of elicitation of vocabulary. Lenneberg suggests that a normal child may have acquired some 20 vocabulary words by 18 months, and 200 words by 21 months.[24] After the appearance of the first few words, the growth in vocabulary is very rapid, and there is much individual variation. Lenneberg states that by 24 to 27 months, the child may have a vocabulary of 300 to 400 words.

Vocabulary may be analyzed according to the parts of speech of the items, or according to their content, determining the semantic domain of early words. It is difficult to determine the meanings of vocabulary words used, because the meaning of a word depends on the child's own experiences with it and may be more varied than the adult imagines. First acquisition of a word is just the first step, and meanings later are extended or limited.[25] As stated previously, earliest words are mainly emotional. In a study by Shirley of 336 children ages 2 to 5, the four most common concepts or semantic domains in early vocabulary were related to mother, father, siblings and home; the 11 most frequently used word concepts carried an emotional charge for the children, and 20% were expositional.[26] This emphasizes the importance of language for the child in expressing feelings and desires.

Piaget showed that much of the speech of preschool children is egocentric, and all utterances are either egocentric or socialized.[27]

The great majority of early vocabulary words are nouns. This is due to the fact that the child first goes through a 'naming stage', and has an active curiosity to know the names of objects. Vygotsky states that this is brought about when the development of speech and thought join to initiate this new

[21] Lewis, 1964, p. 37.

[22] Eric H. Lenneberg, "A Biological Perspective of Language", *New Directions in the Study of Language*, ed., Eric Lenneberg (Cambridge, MIT Press, 1964) p. 66.

[23] Lenneberg, 1964, 66.

[24] Eric H. Lenneberg, "The Natural History of Language", *The Genesis of Language*, Frank Smith and George A. Miller, eds., (Cambridge, MIT Press, 1966) p. 22.

[25] Lewis, 1964, 49.

[26] Cited in Mc Carthy, 1954, 528.

[27] J. Piaget and K. Paul, *The Language and Thought of the Child*, trans. Marjorie Gabain (New York, Meridian Books, 1955) pp. 58–68. Also discussed by Vygotsky (Lev S. Vygotsky, *Thought and Language*, ed., trans., Eugenia Hanfmann and Gertrude Vakar [Cambridge, MIT Press, 1965]) pp. 132–138.

form of behavior, and "speech begins to serve intellect".[28] Naming objects helps the child organize reality.[29] By the end of the second year, the child begins learning names rapidly, and due to a limitation in vocabulary, may use one word for a variety of situations. Homonyms may be common because the vocabulary outstrips the ability to make phonemic contrasts.[30]

Although there is a high proportion of nouns, the noun may be used as other parts of speech, and even as a sentence when the child is in the one-word stage. Interjections are also frequent. After the child has passed the naming stage and ceased the early use of interjections, he begins to combine words into sentences, and the proportion of parts of speech is more determined by conventional forms of sentence structure.[31]

Weir found that for a child age 2½, the breakdown of vocabulary words by parts of speech was as follows.[32]

1. Content Words:	Nouns	37.9%
	Verbs	26.7
	Adverbs	15.3
	Adjectives	7.9
	Pronouns	9.2
	Numerals	3.0
2. Function Words:	Articles	48.5%
	Prepositions	25.3
	Conjunctions	11.4
	Interjections	14.8

The percentage of nouns is less if the analysis is made of running conversation rather than total vocabulary.[33]

4.2.2. *Data Obtained in This Study*

A large-scale study of early vocabulary was beyond the scope of this project. Instead, initial vocabulary for some children was elicited, and adult-child conversations were observed to see how the adult named objects and 'taught'

[28] Vygotsky, 1965, 43.

[29] Aleksandr R. Luria and F. I. Yudovich, *Speech and the Development of Mental Processes in the Child*, trans. O. Kovasc and J. Simon (London, Staples Press, 1959).

[30] Velten, 1943, 287.

[31] McCarthy, 1954, 531.

[32] Ruth H. Weir, *Language in the Crib* (→ *Janua Linguarum*, series major 14) (The Hague, Mouton, 1962) pp. 76–78.

[33] McCarthy, 1954, 531.

the child. As suggested in the *Field Manual*,[34] an attempt was made to determine the extent of vocabulary and the semantic domain of early words.

The vocabulary of the youngest children was elicited, and siblings were questioned for additional items. Some of the data have been presented above already for phonemic analysis.

Child C's utterances were imitations, so cannot be considered as an indication of vocabulary.

Child D, age 1.5, produced six words, but the range of meaning is not clear. The meanings of the words were as follows:

Child D

1. 'Mama'
2. 'Papa'
3. baby talk word for 'food'
4. baby talk word for 'water'
5. baby talk word, said when picking child up
6. baby talk word for 'dog'.

The last four words are 'baby talk' words. All but one are nouns. Item 5, [hub], must mean 'pick me up' when used by the child. With such a limited vocabulary, it is probable that a word like /māma/ could be used when trying to get attention, and possibly to refer to other caretakers besides the mother. The informants were unable to verify these assumptions.

The utterances of Child E were mainly spontaneous, and only these will be presented.[35]

Child E

1. 'piece of bread, food'
2. baby talk word for 'water'
3. 'Mama'
4. 'Papa'
5. 'goose'
6. 'Make the girl go away.'
7. 'female breast'
8. 'I'
9. 'mine'
10. baby talk word for 'food'
11. 'my grandfather'
12. 'sweets'

If this can be considered a representative, though by no means complete, sample of this child's vocabulary, it may be noted that most items are nouns, names of things. They relate to basic needs of the child, chiefly food, as well as to her parents. The word [wízzə] 'goose' is probably one of several names she knows of familiar animals and objects around the household. The first person

[34] Slobin, 1967, 15.

[35] Some items, however, were also heard as imitations.

singular pronoun occurs, and the adjective [táti] 'mine' (inflected for person, lit. 'belonging me'), both referring to the self. It is likely that the pronoun is used in several situations. Only one verb phrase occurs here. Because there is no evidence of the use of other verbs, this verb phrase was probably learned and used as a unit. The noun [dízə] 'female breast' must mean "I want to eat', or be used in a situation when trying to get attention from the mother. Other imitated words were also chiefly nouns, names of objects familiar to the child.

Child F, age 2.3, produced 48 words, although some were imitations. This is probably a large part of her vocabulary, since the older siblings tried to 'fill in' with any additional words she had said. The child was in only fair health, and did not appear very verbal. The non-imitated words, and some items reported by her older sister as spontaneous utterances, were as follows.[36]

Child F:

1. baby talk word for 'water'
2. 'Mama'
3. 'Papa'
4. 'mother'
5. 'the breast, Mama'
6. 'give me'
7. 'an egg'
8. 'my grandmother'
9. 'my grandfather'
10. baby talk word for 'Mama'
11. baby talk word for 'bread'
12. baby talk word for 'cat'
13. 'It's hot, Mama'
14. 'Papa came'
15. 'Mama came'
16. 'sweets'
17. 'Saʕdiya' (proper name)
18. 'Sayyid' (proper name)
19. 'rice, Papa'
20. 'potatoes'
21. 'water buffalo'
22. 'with you (m.sing.)'
23. 'dress, robe'
24. 'I, father, want a dress'

The semantic range of vocabulary words for Child F is very similar to that of Child E. Items are mainly nouns referring to basic concepts such as members of the family, and foods. This child's vocabulary is mainly nouns, with several proper nouns, but she may be beginning to use verbs and to make small sentences (Items 14 and 15). The question is whether these are genuine noun-verb sentences, or whether they have been learned as units through imitation, since when she uttered them, the adults immediately repeated them several times, and said they frequently said this to the child when one of the parents entered the home.

The other sentences were elliptical and vocative, addressed to the parents. Item 5 linked two nouns, [bízzə māma] 'the breast, Mama' and Item 24 used the first person pronoun and two nouns, [ʔǽnə búyə bíyə] 'I, father, [want] a

[36] Some items were also heard as imitations.

dress', omitting the vocative particle [ya] and the verb, since the full adult form would be [ʔǽnə ya ʔabūyə ʕáyzə jæləbíyə] 'I, father, want a dress'. The other two sentences were of the structure Noun + Vocative Particle + Name (Addressee), calling the addressee's attention to the first noun:

[yaḥ ya māma]	'It's hot, Mama'
[lɔz ya bābə]	'rice, Papa'

[yaḥ] means 'it's hot' or 'hot thing', and cannot really be placed as a certain part of speech; it is baby talk and simply denotes the concept of hotness, and is therefore analyzed as a noun here. This child also used a prepositional phrase in Item 22, which in this language is expressed on the word level, [maʕāk] 'with you (m.sing.)' ([máʕə] 'with' + [-k] 'you (m.sing.)'). In the absence of other such prepositional words and inflections of this type, it seems most likely that this is still treated as a single unit in the child's system.

The vocabulary of Child 1 was elicited in conversation with her mother, and in spontaneous conversation when at play with other children. At first, the mother tended to give a word for the child to imitate, but on request, began eliciting items. Part of the conversation was as follows.

Mother	Child
"Manāl, say:" [bāba] ('Papa').	(Imitating) [bāba]
"Say:" [sīdi] ('my grandfather').	(Imitating) [ʔīdi]
"Who is your grandfather?"	[ʔīdi ʔæmīn] ('my grandfather Abdel Azīm')
(Expanding) [ʕábdɛl ʕaẓīm]?	[mm] ('yes')
"And your uncle?"	(Partially imitating) [xǣli] ('my uncle')
"His name?"	[hælī] ('Halīm')
(Expanding) [ʕábdɛl ḥælīm]	
"Raise your voice! What's wrong? What do you want?"	
(Offers a piece of candy)	[ʔyǽzə ʔǣwa] ('[I] want candy')
(Expanding) "Yes."	
[ʕáyzə ḥəlǣwə] ('[You] want candy'). "And what is the name of your grandmother?	
My mother." ([ʔúmmi ʔǽnə])	(Imitating) [ʔumǽnə] ('my mother')
"What is her name?"	[wāṭə] ('Warda')
(Expanding) "Her name is [wárdə]."	

Mother	Child
"What do you want? Candy?"	(Partially imitating) [ʔǽyza ʔǣwə] ('[I] want candy')
"Say:" [ʕayzə ḥəlǣwə] (Long vowel held to exaggerated length)	(Imitating) [ʔǣwə]
"All right. When you go to see your grandfather, what does he get you?"	[yíbli sǽnnə] ('He gets me sandals')
(Expanding) [yjíblɪk sándəl] ("He gets you sandals")?	
"And what else?"	[jɪbləbíyə] ('a dress')
(Expanding) "And a dress." [jælebíyə]	
"Raise your voice! What is your sister's name?"	[ʔúxti bǽnə bíbti] ('my dear sister Etimad')
(Expanding) [ʔúxtɪk ʔɪʕtɪmǣd ḥabíbtɪk] ("your dear sister Etimad")?	
"What is that?"	[líyə] ('car')
(Expanding) [ʕarabíyə] ("car")	
"This is a recorder. Say:" [mǽkənɪt tæsjīl].	(Imitating) [mǽkə zī]
"What did you do today?"	[mǣt hǣdə] ('I didn't do anything')

The child's mother was quite successful in eliciting vocabulary words and sentences, although obviously this is just a small part of the child's vocabulary. She expanded and corrected most utterances, and often asked the child to repeat items, articulating carefully.

Items elicited from conversation with other children were the following.

1. [ʔáywə]	'yes'
2. [xúdi]	'take (it)'
3. [hǣti]	'give (it to me)'
4. [xúdi ya bɪt]	'Take (it), girl'
5. [ʔǽyzə di]	'(I) want this (one)'.
6. [wáḥdə]	'one'
7. [ʔǽnə]	'I'

This child's utterances show considerably more variation as to structure and parts of speech. She was past the one-word stage, and her statements, especially in play, were quite explicit. The child's mother elicited names of family members, and some sentences of the pattern V + N:

[ʔǽyzə ʔǽwə]	'(I) want candy.'
[yíbli sǽnnə]	'(He) gets me sandals.'
[mǣt hǣdə]	'(I) didn't do anything.'

Although the articulation was quite poor, these sentences were grammatically complete. In play, the same type of sentence was produced.

[xǿdi ya bɪt]	'Take (it), girl'
[ʔǽyzə di]	'(I) want this (one).'

The imperative form of two verbs was used, in Items 2, 3, and 4. Other items were the word [ʔáywə] 'yes' and the word [wáḥdə] 'one', which can be either a noun or adjective, here used as a noun. The other item, the pronoun [ʔǽnə] 'I' was used here to mean more than self-reference; the child used it while trying to keep another child from taking a comb from her hand, indicating 'It's mine' or 'I have it'.

Semantically, the vocabulary words uttered by Child 1 were limited, like those of younger children, to references to familiar people and objects, and were quite egocentric. This child's vocabulary is too large to estimate accurately. Lenneberg's estimate of a 300- to 400-word vocabulary for a child of 27 months would seem to be upheld here; this child was about 32 months old, and was able to name many objects without hesitation. Performance in imitation and elicitation tests also indicated a good comprehension of names, directions, and sentences.

Older children were asked to name familiar animals depicted in a picture book, and they performed well. Many recognized the animals' 'house', size, food, and whether there were one, two, or more. They also knew articles of clothing and common objects such as a ball, water jug, and stick. From their conversation, it appears that these items, along with names of relatives and friends, household objects, and kinds of food are among the earliest words learned.

Adults were asked whether children, in the naming stage, frequently asked the names of objects, and how they responded to questions. Most said that children did not ask often; that they "just learned" by growing up, perhaps from other children. One mother said she does not provide the name of a new object, since the child usually asks when she already knows the name. Another said she would provide the name of the object, repeating it several times, but that she probably would not elaborate for the child on the object's use.

In the three mother-child conversations observed, each mother tended to elicit words she knew the child had learned and then expanded and corrected them, sometimes asking for a repetition. I doubt that such solicitous attention is usually given to a child, except possibly by older children.

4.3. BABY TALK

4.3.1. *Theoretical Considerations*

Much early vocabulary includes items not used in adult language, but used regularly by adults when talking to small children. This phenomenon, 'baby talk', is probably universal; at least there is no evidence yet to the contrary. It is a relatively stable, conventional part of a language. Baby talk is widely used in the Egyptian Arabic culture, and items vary little throughout the various geographical areas, or from the city to the rural areas.

Lewis has proposed general theories about what he terms "basic baby language".[37] He states that there are six archetypal nursery words throughout the world, in sound patterns broadly of these kinds: /mama/, /nana/, /papa/, /baba/, /dada/, /tata/. These have local variations and fairly well-defined ranges of meaning. The nasalized sounds often refer to urgent needs of the child–food, sleep, or mother, while the other words are likely to be uttered in times of contentment or playing. "Secondary baby language" is transitional between expressive utterances and conventional forms of the language. This includes onomatopoetic words such as English *bow-wow* and *tick-tock*, and other words substituted for adult words, such as the diminutive *horsie*.

4.3.2. *Data Obtained in This Study*

As suggested in the *Field Manual*, baby talk will be described in three broad areas: the linguistic features of baby talk, the social context in which baby talk occurs, and the belief system concerning baby talk and its use.[38]

The baby talk words obtained were the following.

Words	Gloss	Standard Adult Word
/mbū/ /ʔambú/	'water'	/máyya/
/mamm/	'food'	/ʔækl/

[37] Lewis, 1964, 33–34.
[38] Slobin, 1967, 42.

Words	Gloss	Standard Adult Word
/daḥḥ/	'defecation' (also used to indicate a sore place or wound)	–
/kuxx/	'dirty, forbidden'	/wísix/
/nínna/	'Mama'	/māma/
/naḥḥ/	'meat'	/lǽḥma/
/buff/	'bread, food'	/ʕēš/ /lúgma/
/bísbis/ /bíssa/	'cat'	/gúṭṭa/
/bōbi/	'dog'	/kælb/
/yaḥḥ/	'hot'	/suxn/
/baḥḥ/	'duck'	/baṭṭ/
/húbba/	(said when picking child up, or encouraging it to walk)	–
/diss/	'sleep!'	/nǣm/
/teh teh/	(said while clapping to get child's attention)	–
/māma/[39]	'Mama'	
/bāba/	'Papa'	

Poems, Phrases	Gloss
/hō hō nǣm nǣm/[40]	'(/hō hō/) Sleep, sleep,
/ʔaḍbáḥlak jōz ʔil-ḥamǣm/	I'll kill for you a pair of pigeons,
/ʔaḍbáḥlak jozēn kútkut/	I'll kill for you two pairs of chicks.'
/nǣm nǣm yálla yískut/[41]	'Sleep, sleep, come on, quiet,
/w ʔaḍbáḥlu jōzit il-kútkut/	And I'll kill for him a pair of chicks.'
/tēta tēta/[42]	(meaningless)
/xátti l-ʕátaba/	'Step over the threshold.
/tēta timši mēta/	(/tēta/) When will you walk?'

[39] These words are 'baby talk', but are also used in standard adult speech.

[40] The first two words in this poem, /hō hō/, are meaningless baby words, presumably for rhythm. The rest of the words are standard adult speech.

[41] This poem, said at sleeping time also, contains no special baby talk words, and is included here because it is used only for small children.

[42] The words /tēta tēta/ are meaningless rhythm words. The second line is standard adult speech. In the third line, /tēta/ is meaningless, and the rest is standard speech.

4.3.3. *Linguistic Features*

It is interesting that none of these items bears any resemblance to a corresponding adult form of these words. There is little reduplication, and the language does not provide for diminutives. Modified morphemes or words were not found. Most of the archetypal word patterns suggested by Lewis are present.

A valuable study of baby talk in the Syrian and Palestinian dialects was done by Ferguson, and several of the items are the same in this Egyptian Arabic dialect.[43] Many which differ in form at least refer to the same things. He noted that while many of the "fundamental", early-learned phonemes are present as would be expected, such as /b/, /m/, /n/, and /d/, some more difficult phonemes are also used. Among these are /ḥ/ and /x/, although /ʕ/ is not present as it was in Ferguson's data. Emphatic consonants do not occur, nor do the notoriously difficult phonemes, /r/ and /š/. Most of the phonemes are stops and nasals.

Consonant clusters are avoided, and appear in only two items, /mbū/ 'water' and /bísbis/ 'cat', the second word having an alternate form, /bíssa/, which may be learned first. The most common canonical form of words is CVC(C), with the second consonant usually doubled, or two-syllable reduplicated words of the form CVC(C)V, again with the second consonant usually doubled. These canonical forms are the same as those found by Ferguson to be typical of baby talk words in several languages.[44] Geminated consonants are extremely frequent, although they are not acquired early by children.

Baby talk words are usually spoken with a special exaggerated intonation, a higher, 'smaller' voice, and rising intonation at the end of the second syllable.

Grammatically, there are no inflections or affixes in these words. They do not have a plural form, nor any kind of marked gender. These words may be used alone, or may be incorporated into an adult sentence, with the word substituted for the standard vocabulary word.

Consistent with observations about baby talk in other languages,[45] topics and content areas referred to are related to food, body functions, kin names, basic qualities, some animals, and imperatives. However, no special words appeared referring to parts of the body.

In direct address to a child, a shift in gender may be made to express endearment. It is also common for a parent to address the child with the term /māma/ or /bāba/, the same as the child addresses that parent. For example, the mother would address her children, both male and female, as /māma/.

[43] Charles A. Ferguson, "Arabic Baby Talk", *For Roman Jakobson*, ed., Morris Halle (The Hague, Mouton, 1956) pp. 121–128.

[44] Charles A. Ferguson, "Baby Talk in Six Languages", *The Ethnography of Communication*, eds., John J. Gumperz and Dell Hymes (=Special publication of *American Anthropologist* 66.6, Part 2, (Menasha, Wisc., American Anthropological Ass'n, 1964) p. 113.

[45] Notably by Ferguson, 1964, 113.

4.3.4. *Social Context*

The adults in the village were not aware of baby talk as a standardized practice in the community, and had to be given examples before recognizing it. There is no term for baby talk; it was best conveyed as simply 'words we use with small children'.

It appears that all members of the society use baby talk. When adults were questioned they all admitted using baby talk, although the men were more hesitant than women. Most said that "everyone uses and understands these words", although one woman at first said her child's father did not.

4.3.5. *Belief System*

Discussing baby talk and providing examples were a source of embarrassment for adults, men more than women. Some men tried to avoid giving specific words, and said, for example, "Yes, we say /mbū/ for 'water', and, well, things like that." Women often gave long accounts of using baby talk, followed by a realization of what they had said, and embarrassed laughter.[46] Older children, however, readily gave examples of baby talk, and enjoyed discussing it.

Adults were asked why they used special baby talk words. Representative answers were:

> "So she would talk. It's easier."
> "At first he can't say /ya ʔabūya/, 'my father', or /ʔākul/, 'I [want to] eat', or /ʔášrab/, 'I [want to] drink'. It's easy to say /mbū/. He can say easy sounds like /ma/, /teh/, [referring to the phonemes /m/ and /t/] and /mbū/."
> "I talk that way because if the mother and father say that, he will understand and talk quickly."

Baby talk is also an expression of affection and is used with children until age 3 or 4, according to adult reports. One woman did not think baby talk words were imitations of adult speech, rather that this kind of talk "comes from them themselves". Most, however, agreed that these words are taught by adults to children.

[46] This is in contrast to the attitudes reported by Ferguson, 1964, 112. His Arab informants displayed no embarrassment in discussing baby talk, although they noted that it is more appropriate for women than for men.

5

THE DEVELOPMENT OF SYNTAX

5.1. EARLY STAGES OF SYNTACTIC DEVELOPMENT

5.1.1. *Theoretical Considerations*

Observers of child language in all linguistic communities have found that the child's first combinations of words into 'sentences' are not random combinations. Children have a grammatical system even at earliest stages, and, as in the case of phonological development, they go through stages of grammatical development, changing and adding to their 'rules' as they come closer to attaining the adult grammatical system. Although it is much simpler than the adult system, child grammar can be described in terms of generative rules and treated as a formal grammar. Menyuk has pointed out how child grammar may be described in terms of rules from which the child generates sentences, based on Chomsky's 1957 grammatical model. One may describe the phrase structure level (the underlying basic structures of sentences), the transformational level (structural changes necessary to derive other sentences from basic sentences), and the morphological level (inflectional rules required).[1]

When children first begin to acquire vocabulary items, they are making "selective reductions"[2] of adult sentences, omitting some of the words they hear. At first all words have the same syntactic function: they may be used alone as a self-sufficient utterance, and their referential range is very wide, typically referring to concrete objects or situations. These 'one-word sentences' function as full sentences for the child. Thus, *milk* may mean 'I want some milk', or *up* may mean 'Pick me up'.[3] This one-word sentence stage begins for most

[1] Paula Menyuk, "Syntactic Structures in the Language of Children", *Child Development* 34 (1963): 407–408.

[2] Roger Brown and Colin Fraser, "The Acquisition of Syntax", *The Acquisition of Language*, eds., Ursula Bellugi and Roger Brown (Lafayette, Ind., Child Development Publication of the Society for Research in Child Development, 1964) p. 78.

[3] Chao gives examples of one-word sentences for a Chinese-speaking child. Chao, 1951, 37.

children between the ages of 12 and 18 months. Lenneberg suggests that at this primitive stage, the following notation can be used to describe the child's syntax:

$$S \rightarrow \mathrm{W}$$

where a sentence S is formed by the use of any word that belongs to the class W, and all the child's words belong to it.[4]

At about 18 to 24 months, the child begins to combine words in a single utterance and this marks the beginning of syntactic development. The initial category W is split up into functionally different categories. This two-word sentence stage overlaps with the one-word sentence stage for some months, but by age $2\frac{1}{2}$, two- and three-word sentences are the most common.[5] The combinations of words are systematic, productive (i.e., not imitations), tend to be regular, and do not always correspond to adult structures. Their grammatical form changes with age and development, at first slowly, and then accelerating.

Early syntax may be characterized as "telegraphic",[6] in which 'reference' words essential for the meaning of the sentence are kept, such as nouns, verbs, and adjectives, while 'function' words such as articles, prepositions, and auxiliaries are omitted. Words omitted are usually those which are unstressed in adult speech. The omissions may also be due to the limited memory span of the child; it eliminates words of low cognitive content to economize on length of the sentence.[7] The increase in memory with age is probably a correlate in the increase in mastery of grammatical structure, as well as the development of certain perceptual and cognitive processes.[8]

While research on early syntactic development has been carried out for several other languages,[9] the most extensive research has been done in English. Based on findings in English and other languages, certain 'universal' charac-

[4] Lenneberg, 1967, 292.

[5] Weir, 1962, 85. McCarthy, 1954, 550. There is also evidence from the data of the child studied by Miller and Ervin, 1964, 14.

[6] Term used by Brown and Fraser, 1964, 72.

[7] McNeill, 1966a, 19.

[8] Jean Piaget, *The Psychology of Intelligence* (London, Routledge and Kegan Paul, Ltd., 1950) pp. 123–129.

[9] For example, studies in Russian by Gvozdev, cited by Slobin (Dan I. Slobin, "The Acquisition of Russian as a Native Language", *The Genisis of Language*, eds., Frank Smith and George A. Miller (Cambridge, MIT Press, 1966) p. 333); Dan I. Slobin, *Grammatical Development in Russian- Speaking Children* (→Center for Human Growth and Development Report No. 8) (Ann Arbor, University of Michigan, 1965). Studies in French by Antoine Gregoire, *L'Apprentissage du langage*, 2. vols. (Paris, Droz, 1937, 1947). A study in Chinese by Chao (1951). Studies in Spanish by Daniel P. Dato, *The Child's Acquisition of Spanish Syntax in the Foreign Environment*, (Washington, D.C., U.S. Office of Education, 1969); Samuel Gili y Gaya, *Funciones Grammaticales en el Habla Enfantil* (=*Publicaciones Pedagogicas*, Serie II, No. XXIV) (Rio Piedras, P.R., Univ. de Puerto

teristic stages of syntactic development have been postulated. Earliest word combinations have been analyzed into two word classes or categories, which seem to recur regardless of the language being acquired. Word order is quite inflexible in early stages of syntactic development.[10]

All researchers agree that the two-word combinations in English are composed of "Pivot" *P* class words and "Open" *O* class words.[11] In data such as the following collected by Brown and Fraser from children ages 25 to 28 months, a functional distinction of words is emerging:[12]

come here	*that bird*
now here	*that book*
here allgone[13]	*see boy*
here flowers	*see Mummy*

Words are classified on the basis of distribution. Thus, some words such as *here*, *that*, and *see* occur more frequently in the child's speech and in the same position; these are pivot words. The membership of this class is stable and fairly fixed; it expands by only a few words each month. The *P* class resembles function words in adult speech. An item in the *P* class may come first or second, but its position will be quite fixed for each type of construction. The other words appear to come from a large pool of lexical items, and this *O* class includes all other words not in the *P* class. This class has a large, rapidly-increasing membership. The *O* class resembles content words in adult speech. *O* words also occur as single-word utterances, whereas not all *P* words do. Usually any *P* word can be combined with any *O* word. Braine notes that the language grows structurally by adding new pivot words, and grows in vocabulary by adding to the open class.[14] He found that about 70% of the two-word utterances he recorded for children 19–20 months old were of the P–O form.

Rico, 1960); Keith Kernan and B. G. Blount, "The Acquisition of Spanish Grammar by Mexican Children", *Anthropological Linguistics* 8.9 (1966), 1–14. A study in Tzeltal by Brian Stross, *Language Acquisition by Tenejapa Tzeltal Children* (=Working Paper No. 20, Language-Behavior Research Laboratory (Berkeley, Univ. of California, 1969).

[10] At least in languages so far studied, notably English and Russian.

[11] The terminology used is that of Braine, (Martin D. S. Braine, "The Ontogeny of English Phrase Structure: The First Phase", *Language* 39 (1963): 1–13). Miller and Ervin refer to "operators" and "nonoperators"; Brown and Fraser refer to "C_1" and "C_2" classes. Two-word sentences are also of the *P–O* type in Russian language acquisition (Dan I. Slobin, *Psycholinguistic Similarities in the Acquisition of English and Russian as Native Languages* [Washington, D. C., U.S. Office of Education, 1965]).

[12] Brown and Fraser, 1964, 56–57.

[13] At this stage, no distinction can be made between *word* and *morpheme*. Items like *ice cream* and *all gone* are treated by the child as one word, since neither component of such words occurs alone. Braine, 1963, 3.

[14] Braine, 1963, 13.

The number of different two-word combinations found by Braine in successive months for a child 18 months old was: 14, 24, 54, 89, 350, 1400, 2500+.[15] The fact that many sentences of this type do not look like adult utterances and are not likely to be reduced imitations supports the assumption that the child has actually acquired productive grammatical rules. Examples of sentences which are hard to characterize in terms of adult grammar are:[16]

allgone sticky	(said after washing hands)
more page	'Don't stop reading.'
this do	'Do this.'

A little later, two words in the *O* class may be combined, and then their position is not fixed. Examples are:[17]

man car	'The man is in the car.'
car bridge	'The car is under the bridge.'

Two words of the *P* class are never combined to form an utterance.[18] It should be noted that membership in the *P* and *O* classes does not correspond to any particular form classes in adult language; in Braine's data, adjectives, verbs, and pronouns all occurred in the *P* class.

In the two-word sentence stage, a sentence *S* may consist of one word *O* or two words *P–O*. McNeill writes the earliest sentence as:[19]

Rule 1: $S \rightarrow (P) + O$

This rule allows for both single-word and two-word utterances. At this point, exocentric constructions are more common than endocentric (head-modifier) constructions.[20]

From this point the child begins to differentiate the *P* and *O* classes, resulting in the development of the endocentric noun phrase *(NP)*. Brown and Bellugi followed the development of differentiations in the *P* class in one child over a period of five months.[21] At first, all non-open words were classed together as Pivot_1, which could be combined with a noun. The *P* class was then differentiated into articles, demonstratives, and Pivot_2 (all other *P* words), and finally the *P* class consisted of articles, demonstratives, adjectives, possessives, and Pivot_3. Rather than being interpreted as three different rules, this may be

[15] Braine, 1963, 2.
[16] Braine, 1963, 10.
[17] Braine, 1963, 10.
[18] McNeill, 1966a, 21.
[19] McNeill, 1966a, 23.
[20] Miller and Ervin, 1964, 23.
[21] Brown and Bellugi, 1964. Based on summary by McNeill, 1966a, 26–28.

treated as the basic rule operating with different grammatical classes at different times.[22] Different privileges of occurrence of word categories also developed; the construction $O + P$ was no longer possible.

Rules for the further development of the NP have been postulated by McNeill, based on the same data from Brown and Bellugi.[23] Besides constructions of the P–O type, children also have sentences of the O–O type, of which some of the words are nouns; thus:

Rule 2: $S \rightarrow N + N$

This rule is very productive, and generates such sentences as:

Adam car
Mommy soup

The next rules are hierarchical in structure:

Rule 3: $S \rightarrow (P) + NP$

$$NP \rightarrow \begin{Bmatrix} (P) + N \\ N + N \end{Bmatrix}$$

Rule 4: $S \rightarrow Pred\ P$

$$Pred\ P \rightarrow (V) + NP$$

$$NP \rightarrow \begin{Bmatrix} (P) + N \\ N + N \end{Bmatrix}$$

Rule 3 would generate a sentence such as *that my coat*, and Rule 4 a sentence such as *want my coat*. Whereas Rules 1 and 2 generated sentences of the sequential type, the last two are clearly hierarchical constructions, consisting of two words that form a unit, combined with a third word to form a sentence. Most three-word sentences at this stage followed Rule 4. While the development of grammatical classes was changing rapidly, the grammatical rules remained more or less constant.

Lenneberg has analyzed sentences of three words or more in terms of immediate constituents. Based on utterances such as:

here two sock
more nice milk
poor Kitty there

he characterizes the structure of these sentences by postulating the splitting

[22] McNeill, 1966a, 40.
[23] McNeill, 1966a, 40–45.

of the *O* category into two, Modifier *(Mod)* and Noun *(N)*, represented by the tree diagram.[24]

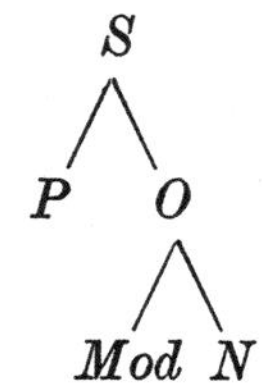

Braine suggests that in a three-word sentence, a *P* phrase replaces one of the *O* class words in an *O—O* sentence:[25]

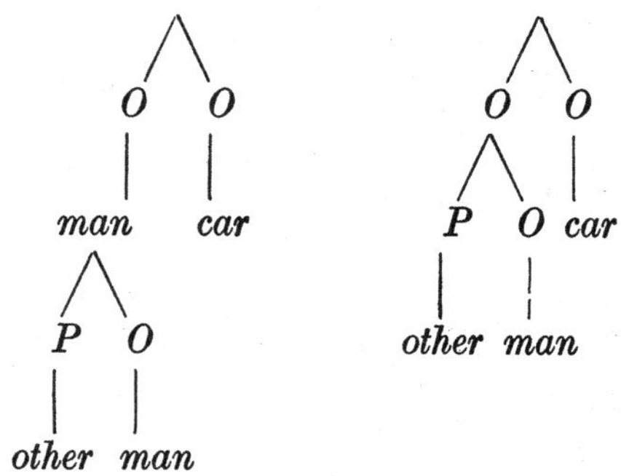

The result is a three-word sentence, *other man car,* which probably means 'The other man is in the car'. If the *P* phrase replaced the word *car,* it would result in the sentence *man other car,* meaning 'The man is in the other car'.

The *NP* is definitely a psychological reality for the child; *N* and *NP* have the same privileges of occurrence, as may be seen in the following sentences:[26]

Positions for Single *N*	Positions for *NP*
that (flower)	*that (a blue flower)*
where (ball) go?	*where (the puzzle) go?*
put (hat) on	*put (the red hat) on*

Hesitations also reveal that the *NP* is a unit, since a hesitation in a sentence comes either before or after it.[27] The child also may substitute *it* for the whole *NP*.[28]

The above rules do not generate well-formed adult sentences, although they are major constituents of well-formed sentences. The basic paradigm for adults is *NP* + *Pred P*, and the child still lacks the device of combining these into

[24] Lenneberg, 1967, 294.

[25] Braine, 1963, 11. Diagrammed by Slobin in Slobin, ed., 1967, 108.

[26] Brown and Bellugi, 1964, 158.

[27] Brown and Bellugi, 1964, 159.

[28] Brown and Bellugi, 1964, 159.

one sentence.[29] Instead, the first grammar still yields one half or the other; 'complete' sentences are not often formed.

On the transformational level, the most studied have been the development of the negative and interrogative transformations.[30]

In English and Russian, it has been shown that the earliest form of negation consists of the patterns:[31]

Neg + *S*
S + *Neg*

where a negative word or words (*Neg*) (represented by *no* or *not* in English) is simply attached to the child's sentence (*S*). The first three-word sentence in Russian is simple negation, which involves placing a negative element at the beginning of a sentence.[32]

Klima and Bellugi postulate three stages in the acquisition of negation in English, which is complex because it involves inversion and auxiliary verbs.[33] The children studied were 18–27 months old. Stage I was the pattern above, with such examples as:

no sit there
wear mitten no
no fall
not fit

Stage II, which appeared 3 to 6 months after Stage I, still had the earlier negative constructions and new forms *can't* and *don't*, with such examples as:

I can't see you.
Don't leave me.
Why not he eat?

Auxiliary verbs were used only in the negative. Double negatives and negative imperatives also occurred.

In Stage III, the *Neg* + *S* pattern disappeared. Auxiliary verbs were used separately from the negative element, but inversion still did not occur sometimes, and the copular verb was usually omitted.

[29] McNeill, 1966a, 44.

[30] Some studies on the development of negation are: Ursula Bellugi, "The Acquisition of Negation", Unpublished Ph. D. dissertation (Harvard Univ., 1967); E. S. Klima and Ursula Bellugi, "Syntactic Regularities in the Speech of Children", *Psycholinguistic Papers*, eds., J. Lyons and R. J. Wales (Edinburgh, Edinburgh Univ. Press, 1966) pp. 183–219; Menyuk, 1963a: 407–422; McNeill, 1966a, 15–84; Ervin, 1964, 163–189.

[31] Slobin, 1966a, 133.

[32] Slobin, 1966a, 134.

[33] Klima and Bellugi, 1966. Also, Bellugi's earlier studies are discussed by Slobin in Slobin, ed., 1967, 112–115, in which four stages of negation were postulated.

For example:

Why the kitty can't stand up?
I not crying.
You didn't caught me.

The development of the interrogative transformation has also been investigated, mainly in English.[34] It may be universal that children's earliest form of interrogation is marked by some form of intonation signal used with a declarative sentence.[35] There are usually two types of interrogatives to be learned–questions involving 'question words' such as *who*, *what*, and *where*, and questions requiring a *yes* or *no* answer.

Interrogation in English is complex because it also involves inversion and the use of auxiliary verbs such as *do*. Klima and Bellugi have postulated three stages in the development of the interrogative transformation in English, based on data from the same children, age 18–27 months.[36]

In Stage I, three types of interrogatives were found:

1. Yes-No Question

Sentence + Question intonation
I ride train?

2. Question Words

What + Sentence
Who + Sentence
Why
Who that?
What cowboy doing?
Why?

3. Where

Where + Sentence
Where milk go?

[34] Some studies on the development of interrogation are: Ursula Bellugi, "The Development of Interrogative Structures in Children's Speech", *The Development of Language Functions*, ed., K. F. Riegel (=Center for Human Growth and Development Report No. 8) (Ann Arbor, Univ. of Michigan, 1965) pp. 103–137; Klima and Bellugi, 1966; Menyuk, 1963a; Daniel P. Dato, "Development of Spanish Interrogatives in Children's Second Language Learning", Memorial volume for Ruth Weir, eds., M. J. Hardman-de-Bautista and V. Honsa, forthcoming.

[35] Brown and Fraser, 1964, 67. Miller and Ervin, 1964, 29. Ervin, 1964, 184. Postulated as a possible universal by Slobin in Slobin, ed., 1967, 119.

[36] Klima and Bellugi, 1966.

In Stage II, there was some development of the superficial structures like pronouns, articles and modifiers. Some inflections also occurred. The same form of questioning was continued as in Stage I. The *Why* question was more differentiated:

Why (not) (V_{neg}) + Sentence
Why you smiling?
Why not me drink it?
Why not me can't dance?

In Stage III, there were several developments: use of some auxiliary verbs, inversion with some verbs (though not all), new inflections, and embedding of clauses:

Is Mommy talking?
What did you doed?
Where I should put it?

Syntactic transformations are usually acquired relatively late, although Menyuk found that by age 3, children had incorporated "most basic generative rules" while still modifying some transformations.[37] McNeill observed that by age 3, English-speaking children had almost everything that could be included in a grammar of competence,[38] and their "linguistic development" is complete by age 4.[39] Gvozdev also found that by age 3 almost all of the complex and complex-subordinate sentence types of Russian were present and the child knows all the generic grammatical categories.[40] Russian children have acquired basic grammar by age 4 or 5.[41]

5.1.2. *The One-Word Stage*

There is clear evidence that children in this linguistic community begin communicating in one-word 'sentences'. In data collected from Child E, Zakiya, and Child F, Suʕād, who were ages 1.11 and 2.3, almost 100% of the utterances were single-word sentences.

[37] Paula Menyuk, "A Preliminary Evaluation of Grammatical Capacity in Children", *Journal of Verbal Learning and Verbal Behavior* 2 (1963): 438. Miller and Ervin report that in English, "transformations are not found in earliest linguistic systems"; Miller and Ervin, 1964, 34.

[38] McNeill, 1966a, 102.

[39] David McNeill, "The Creation of Language by Children", *Psycholinguistic Papers*, eds., J. Lyons and R. J. Wales (Edinburgh, Univ. of Edinburgh Press, 1966), p. 115.

[40] Cited by Slobin, 1966a, 135.

[41] Frank Smith and George A. Miller, eds., (no author), "General Discussion, McNeill and Slobin Presentations", *The Genesis of Language*, (Cambridge, MIT Press, 1966) p. 103.

Child E's one multi-word utterance, [hūs ə bɪt] 'make the girl go away' is very likely an imitation of a sentence which is treated as a single item by the child.

Child F's apparent multi-word utterances are also doubtful. One of her utterances was the repetition of the same word [hǣti hǣti] 'give me, give me' and could as well be described as a single-word utterance repeated twice. Other utterances were imitations of expressions often heard by the child:

[xælt æmīna]	'my aunt Amina'
[bába dɪh]	'Papa came'
[máma dæt]	'Mama came'

These constructions are most likely treated as units by the child. They were frequently said by adults. The other four utterances were reported by the older sister, of which three were of the form *N* (vocative particle) + Name:

[bɪzzə māma]	'the breast, Mama'
[yaḥ ya māma]	'It's hot, Mama'
[lɔz ya bābə]	'rice, Papa'

The fourth, if it was actually said by the child, would be the only real example of putting words together, although elliptically: [ʔænə buyə biyə] 'I, father, a dress'. The structure of the other utterances, however, makes it appear doubtful that this was reported accurately.

I believe the evidence is strong that both children were still in the one-word stage. Child F was just at the point where she would begin combining words together. Her vocabulary was surprisingly large for her not to have begun developing syntactic constructions.

The utterances of both Children E and F included imitations, usually of short, simple sentences or phrases which the children 'reduced' to one word. Examples of model sentences and the children's reductions are presented in Tables 6 and 7.

5.1.3. *The Multi-Word Stages*

There is evidence in the data, although in small quantity, that children begin to combine words into two- and three-word sentences as the next stage in syntactic development.

Child 1, Manāl, was in the two-word stage, although even at her age, 2.8, there were almost as many single-word as multi-word sentences. Some of her utterances have been presented previously; others were gathered in conversations with older children. She was recorded on six occasions during a three-month period.

Table 6
Imitations produced by child E

Model Utterance	Child's Imitation	Gloss for Model	Gloss for Imitation
/di bíḥḥa/ /šūfi l-bíḥḥa/	[bíha]	'This is a duck. See the duck.'	'duck'
/gūli di bitǽʕti/	[táti]	'Say: "This is mine"'.	'mine'
/nrūḥ bárra/	[bǽyə]	'(Shall) we go outside?'	'outside'
/ʕáyza ḥalǣwa/	[həwə́wə]	'(Do you) want sweets?'	'sweets'

Table 7
Imitations produced by child F

Model Utterance	Child's Imitation	Gloss for Model	Gloss for Imitation
/šūfi l-bísbis/ /fēn il-bíssa/ /bissa ḥílwa/	[bísə]	'See the cat. Where is the cat? Is it a nice cat?'	'cat'
/ʔǽna saʕdíya/ /ʔúxtik saʕdíya/	[díyə]	'I am Saʕdiya. Your sister Saʕdiya.'	'Saʕdiya'
/tákli ʔēh/ /ʕáyza tákli baṭāṭis/	[tāte]	'What do you want to eat? (Do you) want potatoes?'	'potatoes'

Table 8
Imitations produced by Manāl

Model Utterance	Child's Imitation	Gloss for Model	Gloss for Imitation
1. /ʔinta rāyiḥ fēn/	/rāḥ fēn/	'Where are you going?'	'Where going'
2. /ḥa-nḥuṭṭu fēn/	/ḥuṭṭu fēn/	'Where will we put it?'	'Where put it'
3. /kælna jibna w zaytūn/	/kælna jibna/	'We ate cheese and olives.'	'We ate cheese.'
4. /huwa lǣbis jakitta/	/huwa jakitta/	'He (is) wearing a jacket.'	'He jacket'
5. /ʔabūya fil-ɣēṭ/	/ʔabūya ɣēṭ/	'My father (is) in the field.'	'My father field'
6. /ʔummi miš ʔabūya ʔilli fil-bēt/	/ʔabūya bēt/	'My mother not my father who (is) in the house.'	'My father house'
7. /huwa rāḥ ʔil-ɣēṭ/	/huwa ɣēṭ/	'He went to the field.'	'He field'
8. /šuft ʕasfūra/	/šuft ʕasfūra/	'I saw a bird.'	'I saw a bird.'
9. /šuft ʕasfura suɣayyara ḥilwa fis-sajara/	/sajara ḥilwa/	'I saw a small pretty bird in the tree.'	'Tree pretty'
10. /ʕin-nǣs ʕamyišrabu šǣy kull yōm/	/yišrab šǣy/	'People drink tea every day.'	'Drink tea'

Child 2, Wafā, a girl age 3.0, was also in the earliest stages of syntactic development. She was recorded both on tape and in transcription during play and conversations with other children, in three one-month intervals.

Child 4, Sanā, a girl age 3.6, was more advanced than the other two children. Her utterances were gathered mainly in conversation with her aunt (age 8½) and the investigator, over a period of three months.

Since no individual child could be followed for the length of time necessary to trace stages of syntactic development, the records of these children will be juxtaposed in the hope of putting together some sort of continuous picture.

All utterances produced by children will be presented in regularized phonemic transcription in this and the next chapter, unless a particular mispronunciation of a word is relevant to the analysis of syntactic or morphological development (such as the omission of the definite article or certain inflections). In general, words will be presented here in adult form, so that easier comparisons with adult syntax can be made.

5.1.3.1. *Early Stage*

The mean utterance length for Manāl was about 1.75 words; about 70% of her utterances were more than one word.[42] Her mean utterance length did not change over the period she was observed. Since the mean utterance length for Wafā was about 2.5 words, her utterances will be considered with those of Manāl as the 'early stage'.

We may begin by looking closely at the children's imitations of adult utterances. The imitations of models in the imitation tests have already been discussed regarding phonological analysis. Samples of Manāal's imitations of more than one word are presented in Table 8; there were 16 such utterances altogether. Samples from Wafā's 24 imitations of more than one word are presented in Table 9.

These imitations are similar to those for children at this stage reported by Brown and Bellugi. The imitations are 'reductions' of model sentences, and tend to preserve word order, which suggests that the model sentence is processed by the child as a total construction rather than as a list of words.[43] Also, as model sentences increase in length, there is not a corresponding increase in the imitation. Most imitations stay in the range of 2–4 words. Brown and Bellugi suggest that the constraint is a limitation on the length of utterance the children are able to program or plan.[44] Slobin and Welsh found that a

[42] It should be noted that one 'word' in Arabic often contains bound morphemes which are expressed as two words in English, for example, /ḥissu/ 'his voice'.

[43] Brown and Bellugi, 1964, 136.

[44] Brown and Bellugi, 1964, 136. The development of children's memory span is also discussed briefly by Brown and Fraser, 1964, 77.

Table 9

Imitations produced by Wafā

Model Utterance	Child's Imitation	Gloss for Model	Gloss for Imitation
1. /ʔæna šuftu/	/ʔæna šuftu,	'I saw him.'	'I saw him.'
2. /ʔæna ma-šuftuh-š/	/ʔæna ma-šuftuh-š/	'I did not see him.'	'I did not see him.'
3. /ḥa-nḥuṭṭu fēn/	/nḥuṭṭu fēn/	'Where will we put it?'	'Where we put it'
4. /hiya ṭawīla jiddan/	/hiya jiddan ṭawīla/	'She (is) very tall.'	'She (is) tall very.'
5. /ʔil-qurʔān ʔil-kærīm/	/ʔil-kærīm ʔil-qurʔān/	'The Holy Koran'	'The Koran Holy'
6. /kælna jibna w zaytūn/	/kælna jibna w zaytūn/	'We ate cheese and olives.'	'We ate cheese and olives.'
7. /huwa lǣbis jakitta/	/lǣbis jakitta	'He (is) wearing a jacket.'	'Wearing a jacket'
8. /ʔil-mayya suxna/	/mayya suxna/	'The water (is) hot.'	'Water hot'
9. /ʔabūya fil-ɤēṭ/	/ʔabūya fil-ɤēṭ/	'My father (is) in the field.'	'My father (is) in the field.'
10. /huwa ʕam-yiʕraf yiktib ʕašǣn ʕam-yrūḥ il-mædrasa/	/ʕam-ʔiktib rūḥ il-mædrasa/	'He knows how to write because (he) goes to school.'	'Write go to school'
11. /ʔummi miš ʔabūya ʔilli fil-bēt/	/miš ʔabūya fil-bēt/	'My mother not my father who (is) in the house.'	'Not my father in the house.'
12. /ʔiš-šuɤl miš sæhl/	/miš sæhl ʔiš-šuɤl/	'The work (is) not easy.'	'Not easy the work.'
13. /šuft ʕasfūra/	/šuft ʕasfūra/	'I saw a bird.'	'I saw a bird.'
14. /šuft ʕasfūra suɤayyara ḥilwa fis-sajara/	/šuft ḥilwa w sajara ʔil-ḥilwa/	'I saw a small pretty bird in the tree.'	'I saw pretty and tree the pretty (one)'
15. /ʔin-nǣs ʕam-yišrabu šǣy kull yōm/	/ʔin-nǣs yišrabu kull yōm šǣy/	'People drink tea every day.'	'People drink every day tea.'

child would reduce a model sentence only if it is beyond the child's normal sentence processing span and is not anomalous; this is of more importance than the number of words in the sentence.[45]

As expected, the children omitted some words, most of them 'function words' and non-reference words. Manāl omitted the definite article (Items 5, 7, 9), optional pronoun (Item 1), preposition (Item 5), future and progressive markers of the verb (Items 2, 10), a participle (Item 4), and a verb (Item 7). Item 8 was a correct and complete imitation. Items 6, 9 and 10 were too long for her to imitate more than two stressed words in each. Many inflections were also omitted.

Wafā also omitted the same types of words, although not as often. Her imitations were, on the whole, more complete and accurate. Her omissions were the definite article (Item 8), the optional pronoun (Items 7, 10), the future and progressive markers of the verb (Items 3, 10), the linking word *because* (Item 10), and the subject noun (Item 11). Some inflections were omitted, but they were fewer. Wafā inverted word order in several sentences (Items 4, 5, 12, 14, 15).[46] Items 1, 2, 6, 9, and 13 were correct and complete imitations. Some sentences were too long for her to repeat successfully (Items 10 and 14), although Item 24 was long and was repeated quite successfully.

It has been noted that Ervin found no evidence of imitation being a significant source of grammatical progress, when imitated utterances were compared with spontaneous ones. Models were reduced to the grammatical level of the children.[47] In the spontaneous conversation of these children, however, sentences were never heard which were as long or as complex as those produced in imitations.

The word combinations produced by Manāl and Wafā were usually not more than two words. The word combinations produced are presented in Table 10. The presumed Pivot and Open classes are labeled. The basis for classifying groups of words together as *P* or *O* is distributional.

The most striking characteristic of these constructions is that most of them are also complete, well-formed sentences in adult language, which is not the case with *P–O* constructions produced by English-speaking children. This is because Arabic syntax is much simpler than English. Because a copular verb is not required in an equational sentence and the use of the subject pronoun is optional, many of the utterances which would be considered 'primitive' in English (e.g., *this mine, want this)* are complete sentences in Arabic. Perhaps it would be more accurate to say that many constructions in the adult language can also be analyzed as *P–O* and *O–O* constructions. The first noun of an *O–O*

[45] Slobin and Welsh, 1968, 3.

[46] Slobin and Welsh report that inversion of word order is common in imitations. Slobin and Welsh, 1968, 8.

[47] Ervin, 1964, 172.

Table 10

Multi-word utterances produced by Manāl and Wafā

Pivotal Constructions

Utterance	Gloss
(P) (O)	
/*ʕayza ḥalǣwa/[a]	'I want sweets.'
/*ʕayza di/	'I want this (one).'
/*ʕayza ʔarawwaḥ/	'I want to go home.'
/*ʕayza mbū (ya māma)/	'I want water, (Mama).'
(P) (O)	
/*ma-fī-š talǣta/	'There are not three.'
/*ma-fī-š tǣni /	'There is no more.'
/*ma-fī-š ḥadd/	'There is nobody.'
(O) (P)	
/ḥalǣwa tǣni/	'Sweets again.'
/*ʔæna tǣni/	'I again.' (i.e., 'Let me do it again.')
(O) (O)	
/*hǣt di/	'Give (me) this.'
/*hǣt il-ḥǣja/	'Give (me) the thing.'
(P) (O)	
/*miš di/	'Not this (one).'
/miš yaḷḷa/	'Not "let's go".'
/*miš huwa/	'Not him.'
(O) (P)	
/bit kæbīra/	'Big girl'
(O) (P)	
/*bit ʔahe/	'(A) girl here.'
(O) (P) (P)	
/bissa di ʔahe/	'(A) cat, this, here.' (i.e., 'This is a cat here.')
(P) (O) (P)	
/ʔahe bit di/	'Here (a) girl, this.' (i.e., 'This is a girl here.')

Open-Open Constructions

Utterance	Gloss
(O) (O)	
/ʔæna di/	'I (want) this.'
/ʔæna ḥalǣwa/	'I (want) sweets.'
/ʔæna ʔil-bēt/	'I (want to go) home.'
(O) (O)	
/*di bissa/	'This (is) a cat.'
/*di bit/	'This (is) a girl.'
/*di bitæʕti/	'This (is) mine.'
(O) (O)	
/*ʔēh da/	'What (is) that?'
/ʔēh hina/	'What (is) here?'

[a] (*) indicates that the utterance is a complete and correct sentence in adult language.

(Table 10–continued)

Other Utterances

Utterances	Gloss
/*ma-ʕamælt-iš ḥǣja/	'I didn't do anything.'
/*yjibli sandal/	'He gets me sandals.'
/*kælt naḥḥ/	'I ate meat.'
/*kælt ṭabīx/	'I ate cooked food.'
/*yaḷḷa sanǣʔ/	'Let's go, Sanā.'
/*tiddīni di/	'(Will you) give me this?'
/*ʔāxud di/	'(May) I take this?'
/*ʔaḥuṭṭu hina/	'(May) I put it here?'
/*šūfi s-sitt/	'(Do you) see the woman?'
/*taxdi di/	'(Do you want to) take this?'
/*ʔiddīni waḥda/	'Give me one.'
/*xudi ya bit/	'Take it, girl.'
/*buṣṣi l-wād/	'Look at the boy.'

construction must, however, be definite (or a pronoun), or the construction will be a noun phrase.

Word order is more flexible in Arabic than in English. It may be noted that the pivot word /di/ 'this' appears in both the *P* and *O* slots, both before and after nouns. In the adult language, /di/ preceding a noun or occurring alone is a demonstrative pronoun 'this (one)', and following a noun is usually an adjective 'this'. /ʔahe/ 'here'[48] also may occur in first or second position in free variation, so the position of the *P* and *O* words in a particular construction is not as fixed as was found in data for English-speaking children.[49] Nevertheless, most *P* and *O* words show enough consistency in their recurrence in certain positions that this may be interpreted as evidence of contextual generalization on the part of the children.

There appear to be fewer words used as pivots in Arabic than were found in English. One of the reasons may be that there are no 'two-word verbs' in Arabic, so the range of utterances like *sweater on* and *shoe off* is not produced. Arabic is, in general, more inflected and has fewer function words on the syntactic level than does English.

All words placed in the *O* class can also occur alone. Most words in the *P* class were also heard as single-word utterances; they can also be used alone in adult language. The pivot words which may occur alone are: /ʕayza/ '(I) want', /ma-fī-š/ 'there isn't (any)', /tǣni/ 'again, another', /hǣt/ 'give (me)', /ʔahe/ 'here'.

[48] This word is used like *voici* is used in French.

[49] As reported by McNeill, 1966a, 21.

All but one of the irregular constructions were irregular only because they were elliptical. The exception, /miš yaḷḷa/, produced by Wafā, is the only real example of a child's overgeneralization on the level of syntax, a combination of *P* and *O* words which is incorrect in adult language. The child heard /yaḷḷa/ 'let's go, hurry' and attempted to express her objection to leaving by adding the negative word /miš/, which cannot be used with this type of expression in a negated statement.

Words used as *P* words are several parts of speech in adult language:

/ʕayza/	active participle
/ma-fī-š/	negated verb
/tǣni/	adverb
/hǣt/	imperative verb
/miš/	negative particle
/kæbīra/	descriptive adjective
/ʔahe/	locative particle
/di/	demonstrative adjective

The parts of speech of words appearing in the *O* class in *P–O* constructions were:

/ḥalǣwa; mbū; talǣta; tǣni; bit; bissa/	noun
/di; ḥadd; ʔæna; huwa/	pronoun
/ʔarawwaḥ/	verb
/yaḷḷa/	interjection

One word, /tǣni/, appears in both the *P* and *O* class in different constructions. It may function as a noun or an adverb in adult language. In the case of /ma-fī-š tǣni/ 'There is no more', it is a noun; in /ḥalǣwa tǣni/ 'sweets again', it is an adverb, so this does not imply that the first construction could be interpreted as a $P + P$ construction.[50]

Since nouns occur only in the *O* class and are the words most easily acquired as a child increases its vocabulary, it seems probable that this *O* class will expand in membership much more rapidly than the *P* class.

[50] Etymologically, this word is related to the ordinal number, *second*, and thus could mean 'second one' or 'second time'.

The generative phrase structure rule for S at this stage may be written:

1. $$S \rightarrow \left\{ \begin{array}{l} \left(\left\{ \begin{array}{l} P \\ O \end{array} \right\} \right) \quad + O \\ \left(\left\{ \begin{array}{l} O \\ (O + P) \end{array} \right\} \right) \quad + P \\ P + (O + P) \end{array} \right\}$$

2. $(O + P) \rightarrow NP$
3. $NP \rightarrow \quad N + Mod$
4. $P \rightarrow$ /ʕayza, ma-fī-š, . . . /
5. $O \rightarrow$ /ḥalǣwa, di, tǣni, . . . /
6. $N \rightarrow$ /bit, bissa, . . . /
7. $Mod \rightarrow$ /kæbīra, ʔahe, di, . . . /

This conflates the following rules which are possible patterns for S:

$$S \rightarrow \left\{ \begin{array}{l} P + O \\ O + O \\ O \\ O + P \\ O + P + P \\ P \\ P + O + P \end{array} \right\}$$

Since constructions without copular verbs are sentences in the language, combinations which might be analyzed as NP ($Mod + N$) were more likely intended as sentences by the child. For example, it is debatable whether a construction such as /ḥalǣwa tǣni/ should be interpreted as, literally, 'Sweets again' (a sentence) or 'sweets more' (a NP of the pattern $N + Mod$). The only two constructions produced which are definitely NP's were:

Utterance	Gloss
/(ʔahe) bit di/	'here this girl'
/bit kæbīra/	'big girl'

The generative phrase structure rule for the NP at this stage may be written:

1. $NP \rightarrow N + Mod$
2. $N \rightarrow$ /bit/
3. $Mod \rightarrow Adj_{desc}, Adj_{dem}$
4. $Adj_{desc} \rightarrow$ /kæbīra/
5. $Adj_{dem} \rightarrow$ /di/

The pattern in adult language for most adjectives is to follow the noun. It is to be expected that this pattern will be very productive in later stages of the children's development. No other examples of endocentric *NP*'s were obtained from these two children.

It is interesting to note that most of the constructions are semantically similar to those found in English. Some semantic pairs are presented in Table 11.[51]

Table 11

Semantic similarities in Arabic and English P–O constructions

Arabic Utterances	Gloss	English Utterances
/ʕayza ḥalǣwa/	'I want sweets.'	*want baby*
/ʕayza ʔarawwaḥ/	'I want to go home'.	*want do*
		want up
/ma-fī-š tǣni/	'There is no more'.	*allgone shoe*
/ma-fī-š ḥadd/	'There is nobody'.	*allgone egg*
/ḥalǣwa tǣni/	'Sweets again.'	*more bread*
/ʔæna tǣni/	'I again.'	*more walk*
/miš di/	'Not this.'	*no bed*
/miš yaḷḷa/	'Not "let's go".'	*no down*
		no mama
/bit kæbīra/	'Big girl'	*big boat*
/bit ʔahe/	'(A) girl here.'	*here bed*
/bissa di ʔahe/	'This cat here.'	*here doll*

5.1.3.2. *Later Stage*

The utterances recorded from Sanā's speech will be considered as the next stage in the development of syntactic constructions. The mean utterance length for Sanā was 3.5 at the beginning of the study, and was close to 3.75 after three months.

Structurally, most of Sanā's imitations were complete. Some which were reduced are presented in Table 12.

Besides some inflections, Sanā's omissions were minor ones, the definite article (Items 1, 2, 3, 5), a preposition (Item 3), the progressive marker of the

[51] English data are from Braine, 1963.

McNeill compared the grammatical classes of P and O words in the utterances of an English-speaking and a Japanese-speaking child, which overlapped wherever the structure of the two languages allowed it; McNeill, 1966, 112. Chao reports that in Chinese, some (presumably) *P* words which were consistently used at the beginning of two-word constructions are semantically 'this . . .', 'want more . . .', and 'not . . .', the latter being used to negate whole sentences; some *O* words used only in second position were '. . . is here' and '. . . finished'; Chao, 1951, 36.

Slobin has presented a table of examples of semantically similar *P* and *O* utterances in six languages. Dan I. Slobin, *Universals of Grammatical Development in Children* (=Working Paper No. 22, Language-Behavior Research Laboratory) (Berkeley, Univ. of California, 1969) p. 5.

Table 12

Imitations produced by Sanā

Model Utterance	Child's Imitation	Gloss for Model	Gloss for Imitation
1. /ʔil-qurʔān ʔil-kærīm/	[qurʔān kærīm]	'The Holy Koran'	'Holy Koran'
2. /ʔil-wǣd ʕa-yḥibb ʔis-sukkar/	[ʔil-wǣd ḥibb sukkar]	'The boy likes sugar.'	'The boy like sugar.'
3. /ʔabūya fil-ɣēṭ/	[ʔabūya ɣēṭ]	'My father (is) in the field.'	'My father field'
4. /ʔummi miš ʔabūya ʔilli fil-bēt/	[miš ʔabūya ʔilli fil-bēt]	'My mother not my father who (is) in the house.'	'Not my father who (is) in the house.'
5. /ʔin-nǣs ʕam-yišrabu šǣy kull yōm/	[nǣs kull yōm ʕam-yišrabu šǣy]	'People drink tea every day.'	'People every day drink tea.'

verb (Item 2), and one noun (Item 4). She produced some long sentences and in general, her imitations were much more accurate than those of Manāl and Wafā. In sentences where her only 'error' was inverted word order (Item 5 and others not listed here), the resulting sentence was still acceptable grammatically.

Some word combinations produced by Sanā in conversation are presented in Table 13. Again, words are divided into *P* and *O* classes.

Table 13

Multi-word utterances produced by Sanā

Pivotal Constructions

Utterance				Gloss
(P)	*(O)*			
/*ma-fī-š	tǣni/[a]			'There is no more.'
/ma-fī-š	māma/			'There is no Mama.' (i.e., 'Mama is not here.')
(O)	*(P)*	*(O)*	*(P)*	
/*humma	dōl	kulluhum	ʔaha/[b]	'They, those, all of them (are) here.'
/*ʔitnēn	ʔaha/			'Two (are) here.'
(O)	*(P)*[c]			
/kūra	di/			'This ball'
/firǣx	dōl/			'These chickens'
(P)	*(O)*[d]			
/talǣta	dīk/			'Three roosters'
/ʔitnēn	bitǣʕ/			'Two things'
(O)	*(P)*	*(P)*		
/*ʔid-dīk	da	kæbīr/		'The rooster, that, (is) big.'
/*huwa	da	kæbīr/		'He, that, (is) big.'
(O)	*(P)*	*(P)*		
/da	guṭṭa	kætīr/		'That cat many' (i.e., 'Those are many cats.')
(O)	*(P)*			
/warda	ḥilwa/			'Pretty flower'
(P)	*(O)*			
/*hǣti	māma/			'Give (it to me), Mama.'
/*hǣti	mæha/			'Give (it to me), Maha.'
/*hǣti	ʔil-ʕarūsa/			'Give (me) the doll.'
(O)	*(P)*			
/*mæha	hǣti/			'Maha, give (it to me).'

[a] (*) indicates that the utterance is a complete and correct sentence in adult language.
[b] This will be treated as two *O* + *P* constructions together.
[c] These utterances could also be analyzed as *O* + *O* constructions and complete sentences. 'This (is) ball' and 'These (are) chickens', although if this was the intended meaning, word order is usually reversed.
[d] These utterances are correct syntactically, but neither noun is inflected correctly for number.

(Table 13–continued)

Open-Open Constructions

Utterance			Gloss
(O)		(O)	
/*dōl	(kulluhum)	dīk/	'Those (all of them) (are) roosters.'
(O)	(O)		
/*di	guṭṭa/		'This (is a) cat.'
/*da	bōbi/		'This (is a) dog.'
/humma	kæbīr/		'They (are) big.'

Other Utterances

Utterance	Gloss
/*miš hina/	'Not here.'
/*bæss ya māma/	'Enough, Mama.'
/*hina kida/	'Here like this.'
/yaxdu ɣēṭ/	'(He) takes it (to the) field.'
/*ʔiwʕi ʔinti/	'Look out, you !'
/ʔarbaʕ xæmsa/[e]	'Four, five'
/*ʔæna ʕawza ʔarawwaḥ/	'I want to go home.'

In these data also, the position of *P* and *O* words is not fixed. Any variations of word order which occur, however, are also acceptable in the adult language.

The only irregular construction was /ma-fī-š māma/ 'There is no Mama', an unacceptable combination in adult language, because this negative word can be used only with indefinite nouns.

The parts of speech for words in the *P* class were:

/ma-fī-š/	negated verb
/ʔaha/	locative particle
/di; da; dōl/	demonstrative pronoun
/talǣta; ʔitnēn/	cardinal numeral (here adjective)
/kæbīr/	descriptive adjective
/hǣti/	imperative verb

The parts of speech for words in the *O* class in *P–O* constructions were:

/tǣni; kūra; firǣx; (ʔid-) dīk; bitǣʕ/	noun
/māma; mæha/	proper noun
/kulluhum; huwa/	pronoun
/ʔitnēn/	cardinal numeral (here noun)

There were no new *P–O* construction patterns in Sanā's utterances.

Sanā produced more noun phrases than did the other children, and more types of modifiers were used. Some *NP*'s are constituents in larger sentences.

[e] Said when playing with several objects, trying to count them.

Most were elicited from pictures in a book. Her endocentric *NP* constructions are presented in Table 14.

Table 14

Noun phrase constructions produced by Sanā

Utterance	Gloss	Pattern
/humma dōl (kulluhum ʔaha)/	'They, those, (all of them here).'	$Pron+Adj_{dem}$
/huwa da (kæbīr)/	'He, that, (is big).'	$Pron+Adj_{dem}$
/kūra di/	'This ball'	$N+Adj_{dem}$
/firǣx dōl/	'These chickens'	$N+Adj_{dem}$
/ʔid-dīk da (kæbīr)/	'The rooster, that, (is big).'	$N+Adj_{dem}$
/(da) guṭṭa kætīr/	'(That), cat many'	$N+Adj_{quant}$
/warda ḥilwa/	'Pretty flower'	$N+Adj_{desc}$
/talǣta dīk/	'Three roosters'	$Num+N$
/ʔitnēn bitǣʕ/	'Two things'	$Num+N$

In some of the constructions above the adjectives were not properly inflected, but all are syntactically correct. All follow the pattern *Head* + *Mod* except the two phrases using cardinal numerals, which precede the noun in adult language. Descriptive, quantifying and demonstrative adjectives follow the noun. The definite article is prefixed to the noun, and will not be considered on the syntactic level.

When the child combined several modifiers in a sentence, they were in correct order, for example:

/ʔid-dīk da kæbīr/ 'The rooster, that, (is) big.'

The pattern is:

$$H + Adj_{dem} + Adj_{desc}$$

The order of modifiers is quite flexible in adult language; the positions of the two adjectives could be interchanged. Similarly, the word order of the first utterance is correct:

/humma dōl kulluhum ʔaha/ 'They those, all of them (are) here.'

The pattern is:

$$Pron + Adj_{dem} + Adj\ P + Loc\ Part$$

The order of the demonstrative adjective and adjective phrase could be interchanged, however, and still be correct. Arabic does not have the complex and rigid order of pre- or post-modifiers of nouns that is found in English. Gamal-Eldin has expressed the modified *NP* with the formula:[52]

$$NP = Adj_{quant}, Num + \begin{Bmatrix} n \\ N_{def} \end{Bmatrix} + Adj$$

Where n = indefinite noun
N_{def} = definite noun (including *NP* and pronouns)

Sanā has made the required distinctions as to position of modifiers which have definite privileges of occurrence–the numerals and the adjectives. She did not use other quantifying modifiers which also precede the noun, so her mastery of this could not be determined.

The hierarchy of Sanā's three-word utterances could be represented in the tree diagram:

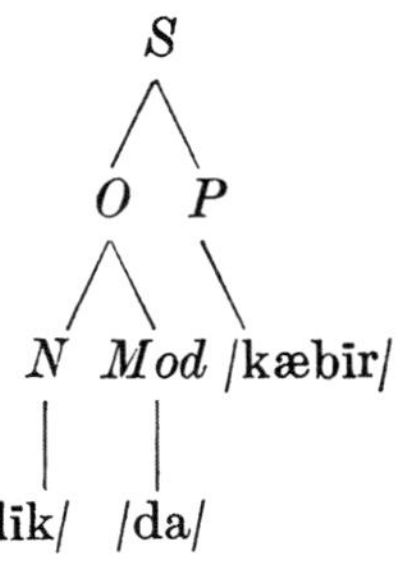

'The rooster, that, (is) big.'

The generative phrase structure rule for her *NP* constructions at this more advanced stage may be written as follows. Demonstrative and descriptive adjectives agree with the Head word in gender and number.

1. $NP \rightarrow \begin{Bmatrix} H + Mod_1 \\ Mod_2 + N_{indef} \end{Bmatrix}$
2. $H \rightarrow$ *Pron, N*
3. $Mod_1 \rightarrow Adj_{desc}, Adj_{dem}, Adj_{quant}$
4. $Mod_2 \rightarrow Num$
5. N_{indef} /dīk, bitæʕ/
6. $Pron \rightarrow$ /humma, huwa/
7. $N \rightarrow$ /kūra, firǣx, ʔid-dīk, guṭṭa, warda/
8. $Adj_{desc} \rightarrow$ /ḥilwa/
9. $Adj_{dem} \rightarrow$ /dōl, di, da/
10. $Adj_{quant} \rightarrow$ /kætīr/
11. $Num \rightarrow$ /ʔitnēn, talǣta/

[52] Saad M. Gamal-Eldin, *A Syntactic Study of Egyptian Colloquial Arabic* (The Hague, Mouton, 1967) p. 54. A discussion of the maximum expansion of head-modifier positional relations is found in Khalafallah, 1961, 117–118.

In conclusion, it may be stated that the children observed appear to be developing a mastery of syntax by going through the same types of stages as children observed learning English.

Children in this study were, however, considerably older than their linguistic peers learning English. While the English-speaking children began making two-word sentences at age 18–24 months, children in this community appear to begin at about age 2½ and do not progress much beyond this stage until age 3 or as late as 3½. One boy observed (Jamāl, Child 3) was 3½ and produced almost no utterances longer than two words. It seems unlikely, too, that these children had vocabularies as extensive as those estimated for the English-speaking children.

5.2. THE ACQUISITION OF THE NEGATIVE

5.2.1. *Rules for Negation in Adult Language*

The ways of expressing negation in this dialect of Arabic will be described,[53] considering facts which are relevant to the early stages of language acquisition. There are some types of negation which did not occur in early stages; these will not be discussed.[54]

There are two morphemes used for negation:

1. The free form {læʔ}, with the alternative form ᵃ/lǣ/. This particle is equivalent to English 'no'; it is the opposite of /ʔaywa/ 'yes'.
2. The morpheme {m . . . š}, with two allomorphic realizations, the free allomorph ᵃ/miš/, and the bound allomorph ᵃ/ma- . . . -š/.[55] /miš/ is used in the following environments:

(a) In equational sentences in pre-predicate position, without restriction as to type of predicate.

$$T\ opt\ N_{1a}:$$
$$Subj + Pred \Rightarrow Subj + /\text{miš}/ + Pred$$
$$Pred \rightarrow \begin{Bmatrix} N \\ Pron \\ NP \\ Adj \\ Partic \\ Prep\ P \\ Loc\ Part \end{Bmatrix}$$

[53] Based on descriptions by Khalafallah 1961, 127–130, but adapting his rules to northern Saʕīdi dialect. Also, Lehn and Abboud, 1965; Gamal-Eldin, 1967, 51–52, 85–87.

[54] For example, /la . . . wala/ 'neither . . . nor', /wala/ 'not a . . .'.

[55] Negation with /ma- . . . -š/ actually operates on the morphological level, but it will be discussed here with the other forms of negation which are on the syntactic level.

/ʔir-rājul mudarris/ →	/ʔir-rājul miš mudarris/
'The man (is) a teacher.'	'The man (is) not a teacher.'
'huwa mudarris il-walad/ →	/huwa miš mudarris il-walad/
'He is the teacher of the boy.'	'He is not the teacher of the boy.'
/huwa kæbīr/ →	/huwa miš kæbīr/
'He (is) big.'	'He (is) not big.'
/huwa rāyiḥ/ →	/huwa miš rāyiḥ/
'He is going.' (lit., 'is a goer')	'He is not going.'

(b) In nominal and verbal sentences in pre-verbal position, when the verb is prefixed with /ḥa-/, future marker, or /ʕam-/, progressive marker.

T opt N_{1b}:

$$\begin{Bmatrix} /\text{ḥa-}/ \\ /\text{ʕam}/ \end{Bmatrix} V \Rightarrow /\text{miš}/ + \begin{Bmatrix} /\text{ḥa}/ \\ /\text{ʕam}/ \end{Bmatrix} V$$

/ʔir-rājul ḥa-yrūḥ/ →	/ʔir-rājul miš ḥa-yrūḥ/
'The man will go.'	'The man will not go.'
/ʕam-yištaɣal/ →	/miš ʕam-yištaɣal/
'(He) is working.'	'(He) is not working.'

(c) In pre-modal position in verb phrases.

T opt N_{1c}:

$$Modal + V \Rightarrow /\text{miš}/ + Modal + V$$

/ʔir-rājul lǣzim yrūḥ/ →	/ʔir-rājul miš lǣzim yrūḥ/
'The man must go.'	'The man does not have to go.'

3. The bound allomorph /ma- . . . -š/ is used in the following environments:

(a) In equational sentences:

(1) Negating the predicate, where the predicate is a prepositional phrase + object, or a participle.[56]

T opt N_{2a}:

$$Subj + Pred \Rightarrow Subj + X + Pred$$

$$X \rightarrow /\text{ma- . . . -š}/$$

$$Pred \rightarrow \begin{Bmatrix} Pred\ P + Obj \\ Part \end{Bmatrix}$$

/ʔir-rājul ʕindu kitǣb/ →	/ʔir-rājul ma-ʕinduh-š kitǣb/
'The man has a book.' (lit., 'with him a book')	'The man does not have a book.'
/huwa rāyiḥ/ →	/huwa ma-rayiḥ-š/
'He is going.'	'He is not going.'

[56] This is an alternative way of negating the participle. In the rule given above in *T opt* N_{1a}, it was shown that the participle could also be negated with /miš/ preceding it in an equational sentence.

(2) Negating the subject, where the subject is a personal or indefinite pronoun.[57]

T opt N_{2b}:

$$Subj + Pred \Rightarrow X + Subj + Pred$$
$$X \rightarrow /\text{ma-} \ldots \text{-š}/$$
$$Subj \rightarrow \begin{Bmatrix} Pron_{pers} \\ Pron_{indef} \end{Bmatrix}$$

/huwa kæbīr/ →	/ma-huwā-š kæbīr/
'He (is) big.'	'He (is) not big.'
/ḥadd hina/ →	/ma-ḥadd-iš hina/
'Someone (is) here.'	'Nobody (is) here.'

(b) In nominal and verbal sentences:

(1) Negating any verb form other than the affixed forms which are negated with /miš/, including a verb with a bound object.

T opt N_{2c}:

$$V \Rightarrow X + V$$
$$X \rightarrow /\text{ma-} \ldots \text{-š}/$$

/kætab il-jawæb/ →	/ma-kætab-š il-jawǣb/
'He wrote the letter.'	'He did not write the letter.'
/fī ḥadd hina/ →	/ma-fī-š ḥadd hina/
'There is someone here.'	'There is not anyone here.'
/huwa ḍarabha/ →	/huwa ma-ḍarabhā-š/
'He hit her.'	'He did not hit her.'

(2) Negating the first constituent of a verb phrase, where the modifier is a "time marker".[58]

T opt N_{2d}:

$$Mod + V \Rightarrow X + Mod + V$$
$$X \rightarrow /\text{ma-} \ldots \text{-š}/$$
$$Mod \rightarrow \text{time marker}$$

/huwa kǣn ḥa-yrūḥ/ →	/huwa ma-kæn-š ḥa-yrūḥ/
'He was going to go.'	'He was not going to go.'

[57] Usually, if the negated word ends in a vowel, the final vowel is lengthened and major stress is shifted to it. This is an alternative way of negating these sentences. In the rule given above in *T opt* N_{1a}, it was shown that the equational sentence could also be negated with /miš/ in pre-predicate position, which negated only the predicate. Here, the whole sentence is negated. There is a change in meaning.

[58] This distinction between three types of verbal modifiers, "time markers", modals, and auxiliaries, is made by Hanna. Hanna M. Hanna, "The Phrase Structure of Egyptian Colloquial Arabic", Unpublished Ph. D. dissertation (Cornell Univ., 1962) p. 19.

(3) Negating the second consituent of a verb phrase, where the modifier is a modal.[59]

T opt N_{2e}:

$$Mod + V \Rightarrow Mod + X + V$$
$$X \rightarrow \text{/ma- . . . -š/}$$
$$Mod \rightarrow Modal$$

/huwa lǣzim yrūḥ/ →	/huwa lǣzim ma-yruḥ-š/
'He must go.'	'He must not go.'

(4) Negating the first or second constituent of a verb phrase, where the modifier is an auxiliary.[60]

T opt N_{2f}:

$$Mod + V \Rightarrow \begin{Bmatrix} X + Mod + V \\ Mod + X + V \end{Bmatrix}$$
$$X \rightarrow \text{/ma- . . . -š/}$$
$$Mod \rightarrow Aux$$

/huwa ḥǣwil yrūḥ/ →	/huwa ma-ḥawil-š yrūḥ/
'He tried to go.'	'He did not try to go.'
	/huwa ḥǣwil ma-yruḥ-š/
	'He tried not to go.'

T opt N_{2g}:

$$V_{imper} \Rightarrow X + V_{pres}$$
$$X \rightarrow \text{/ma- . . . -š/}$$

/ʔiktib/	/ma-tiktib-š/
'Write!' (m.sing.)	'Don't write!' (m.sing.)
/ʔiktibi/	/ma-tiktibī-š/
'Write!' (f.sing.)	'Don't write!' (f.sing.)

5.2.2. *The Negation Test*

A negation test was administered to all children in the study who were able to comprehend its purpose. The test consisted of 11 affirmative sentences of various types which each child was asked to repeat in negated form. The explanation and directions given to the child were approximately: "If 1 say, 'The girl is playing' and you know she isn't, you will say 'No . . . what?'". Usually two or three examples were required before a child understood the directions well enough to proceed with the test.

[59] This is an alternative way of negating these sentences. In the rule given above in *T opt* N_{1c}, it was shown that the sentence could also be negated with /miš/ in pre-modal position, where the negative would be an immediate constituent (IC) of the whole verb phrase; here, it is an IC of the verb only. There is a change in meaning.

[60] Depending on which constituent is negated, there is a difference in meaning.

The results of the negation test are presented by item. For each sentence, the cue sentence is presented. The 'negative model' sentence is what would be expected in adult speech to negate the cue sentence; any optional words or phrases are enclosed in parentheses. For each sentence, the standard adult form of negation was confirmed by using the responses of Child 31, age 15, as the model. Sometimes a child repeated the cue sentence instead of giving a negated sentence as a response, so there are 'gaps' in the data. Children 1–4 did not take the test because they did not understand its purpose. Child 2 responded with a negative sentence in Item 2 only.

The Negation Test

1. Cue Sentence. /ʔil-bit ʕam-tʕ ayyaṭ/
'The girl is crying.'
Negative Model. /(ʔil-bit) miš ʕam-tʕ ayyaṭ/
'(The girl) is not crying.'

This item tested negation of the verb form prefixed with /ʕam-/, progressive marker. Children 5 and 24 repeated the sentence with the present tense, unaffixed form of the verb, /ma-tʕ ayyaṭ-š/, and their negation of that form was correct. Child 8 inexplicably changed the sentence to 'The girl is not good'; the negation is correct.

2. Cue Sentence. /huwa rāḥ il-ɣēṭ/
'He went to the field.'
Negative Model. /(huwa) ma-rāḥ-š (ʔil-ɣēṭ)/
'(He) did not go (to the field).'

This item tested negation of the past tense form of the verb, third person singular. Child 2 used a very primitive form of negation, adding the free form /læʔ/ to the end of the affirmative sentence. Her utterance was /ʔil-ɣēṭ læʔ/ 'The field, no.' The other children who gave non-standard answers were Children 15, 17, 25, and 26; all used the free allomorph /miš/ instead of bound /ma- . . .-š/.

3. Cue Sentence. /humma kælu šwayyit ʕēš/
'They ate a little bread.'
Negative Model. /(humma) ma-kælū-š (šwayyit ʕēš)/
'(They) didn't eat (any bread).'

This item also tested negation of the past tense form of the verb, third person plural. Children 5 and 8 repeated the sentence with a third person singular subject; their negation of the verb was correct. Child 15 responded in the same way as in the previous item, using /miš/ instead of /ma- . . . -š/. Other responses were correct.

4. Cue Sentence. /ʔis-sitt šæfitna/
'The woman saw us.'
Negative Model. /(ʔis-sitt) ma-šæfitnǣ-š/
'(The woman) did not see us.'

This item tested negation of the past tense form of the verb with a bound pronoun object. Only Children 13 and 25 used the free /miš/ form of negation incorrectly.[61]

5. Cue Sentence. /ʔil-bit-di ʔuxtak (ʔuxtik)/
'(Is) this girl your (m. f.) sister?'
Negative Model. /(ʔil-bit-di) miš ʔuxti/
'(This girl is) not my sister.'

This item tested negation of an equational sentence with a noun as predicate. It was negated correctly by all children.

6. Cue Sentence. /ʔir-rādyu-da bitǣʕak (bitǣʕik)/
'(Is) that radio yours (m.f.)?' (lit., 'belonging to you')
Negative Model. /(ʔir-rādyu-da) miš bitǣʕi)
'(That radio) is not mine.' (lit., 'belonging to me')

This item tested negation of an equational sentence with a prepositional phrase as predicate. Children 11, 17, and 24 negated the sentence correctly, but replaced the *Noun* + *Prep* phrase construction (lit., 'the radio belonging to me') with the *Noun* + bound possessive pronoun suffix, resulting in one word, /radwiya/ 'my radio'.

7. Cue Sentence. /huwa rāyiḥ il-fikriya/
'He is going to Fikriya [a nearby town].'
Negative Model. (a) /(huwa) miš rāyiḥ (ʔil-fikriya)/
'(He) is not going (to Fikriya).'
(b) /(huwa) may-rayiḥ-š (ʔil-fikriya)/
'(He) is not going (to Fikriya).'

This item tested negation of the present participle of the verb. Two alternative forms of negation for this sentence are acceptable. Child 9 used the right

[61] When responding to a different cue sentence (outside the test), Child 28 said /miš ḍarabitna ʔil-bit/ 'The girl did not hit us' using the /miš/ form of negation which is incorrect.

negative, /miš/, but placed it incorrectly before /huwa/. Children 13, 15, 18, 19, and 21–30 negated the sentence like model (a); Children 11 and 16 negated it like model (b). The other children who gave deviant responses changed the verb form to past tense, 'He did not go to Fikriya', in which case it was negated correctly.

8. Cue Sentence. /huwa ḥa-yirkab ṭayyāra/
'He will ride an airplane.'
Negative Model. /(huwa) miš ḥa-yirkab (ṭayyāra)/
'(He) will not ride (an airplane).'

This item tested negation of the verb form prefixed with /ḥa-/, future marker. The only deviant responses were by Children 11, 14, 17, 23, and 24, who repeated the present tense form of the verb, /huwa ma-yirkab-š/ 'He does not ride', in which case it was negated correctly.

9. Cue Sentence. /huwa ḍarabu/
'He hit him.'
Negative Model. /(huwa) ma-ḍarabuh-š/
'(He) did not hit him.'

This item tested negation of the past tense form of the verb with a bound object. Children 13, 25, and 30 erred in the form of negation of the sentence, saying /miš ḍarabu/. Child 5 changed the verb form to present tense, /ma-yiḍrab-š/, which was correctly negated. Children 11, 20, 24, and 28 changed the verb form to passive (consequently implying a different subject), /ma-itḍarab-š/ 'He was not hit', in which case the /ma- . . . -š/ form of negation was correct.

10. Cue Sentence. /ʔugʕud hina/[62]
'Sit here (m.sing.).'
Negative Model. /ma-tugʕud-š (hina)/
'Don't sit (here).'

This item tested negation of the imperative form of the verb, which requires not only a negative morpheme but also the addition of the second person affix to the affirmative stem form. No child erred in negating the form without adding the required affix. Children 8 and 12 made a different sentence, 'I don't

[62] The cue was "When I say to a boy, 'Sit here' and you don't want him to sit, what would you say to him?"

want him to sit' and 'I don't want you to sit'. The response form Child 26 was negation of a non-existent form of this verb, /ma-guʕud-š/; perhaps this was intended to be the affirmative form without the required affixation.

11. Cue Sentence. /fī kælb hina/
'There is a dog here.'
Negative Model. /ma-fī-š (kælb hina)/
'There is not (a dog here).'

This item tested negation of the stative verb /fī/ 'there is (are)'. It was negated correctly by all children. This is probably related to the fact that this word is an early pivot word.

5.2.3. *Child Syntactical Rules and Stages for Negation*

In Arabic, the negative transformations are not as complicated as in English, and it is to be expected that they will be fully acquired in fewer stages. The use of the negative allomorph /miš/ is quite simple; using the allomorph /ma- . . . -š/ with the morphophonemic variations which accompany it is more complex. Responses to Items 15 and 24 in the comprehension test indicate that the youngest children comprehend negated sentences.

Based on data from the negation test and from a few examples collected in spontaneous speech of younger children, rules may be formulated to describe the probable stages of development by which the children acquire negation. The aim is to find basic regularities which may be interpreted as reflecting the competence of the children.

5.2.3.1. *Stage 1*

The earliest and simplest form of negation heard from children was the free form /læʔ/ 'no', pronounced [læ]. They probably comprehend this form first; it is used to warn the child against doing something forbidden, much like *no no* in English. On one occasion observed, Child 1 (age 2.8) responded to another child trying to take something from her with the utterance /læʔ læʔ bitæʕti/ 'No, no, mine', spoken with some vehemence. She also responded to direct questions such as 'Do you want to go home?' with /læʔ/.

Child 2 (age 3.0) negated a sentence with /læʔ/ (Item 2), which is impossible in adult language. Her negation of the sentence 'He went to the field' was /ʔil-ɣēṭ læʔ/ 'The field no'. She used the same construction when answering questions put to her by the investigator:

Question	Response
/ʔil-bit-di ḍarabitik/	/hiya læʔ/
'(Did) this girl hit you?'	'She no.'
/ʔummik hina/	/ʔummi læʔ/ /hina læʔ/
'(Is) your mother here?'	'My mother no.' 'Here no.'

Child 4 (age 3.6) was also asked direct questions, and some of her responses are presented.

Question	Response
/ʔil-bit-di ḍarabitik/	/læʔ/ /hiya ḍarabitni læʔ/
'(Did) this girl hit you?'	'No.' 'She hit me no.'
/di farrūja/	/læʔ di wizza/
'(Is) this a chicken?'	'No, this (is) a goose.'

In the first instance, she used the same construction used by Child 2, preceding it with what was apparently intended as the free form. In the second response, the sentence is correct, the free form followed by an affirmative sentence.

The children appear to have established a pattern of negating sentences, simply:

T opt N_3:

$$S \Rightarrow S + /\text{læʔ}/$$

This type of negation was never heard from children older than Child 4. Based on this limited evidence, this pattern will be postulated as Stage I in negation. It is used until about age 3½, thus overlapping for some time with the types of negation described in Stages II and III.

5.2.3.2. *Stage II*

The other type of negation observed in the youngest children's speech is found in the following sentences, gathered from the speech of Children 1, 2, and 4.

/miš di/	'not this'
/miš yaḷḷa/	'not let's go'
/miš huwa/	'not him'
/miš hina/	'not here'

This pattern is also simple:

T opt N_1:

$$S \Rightarrow /\text{miš}/ + S$$

It is not clear whether this pattern of negation actually develops after the pattern postulated as Stage I; it is just as simple and certainly strongly recurrent in young children's speech. Children younger than Child 1, who might be expected to use one pattern before the other, did not produce negatives in the conversations observed.

Since this pattern continues to be used at later ages even in place of the other negation pattern, while the /læʔ/ form is dropped, it will be treated here as a later, more advanced stage.

Data from the negation test show many instances in which children used the /miš/ form of negation when /ma- . . . -š/ should have been used. Examples are:

	Utterance	Correct Negation
(Item 2)	/huwa miš rāḥ/ 'He did not go.'	/huwa ma-rāḥ-š/
(Item 3)	/ḥumma miš kælu/ 'They did not eat.'	/humma ma-kælū-š/
(Item 4)	/ʔis-sitt miš šæfitna/ 'The woman did not see us.'	/ʔis-sitt ma-šæfitnǣ-š/
(Item 9)	/huwa miš ḍarabu/ 'He did not hit him.'	/huwa ma-ḍarabuh-š/

These errors were made by children as old as age 10 and 11, although they tended to be repeated by the same children each time.

5.2.3.3. *Stage III*

The acquisition of the /ma- . . . -š/ form of negation will be considered as Stage III. Smaller children were not heard using this form of negation;[63] it was first heard in the speech of Child 4 (age 3.6), in response to a question in the comprehension test (Item 17):

Question	Response
/fēn il-bit illi ḥa-tišrab/	/ʔahe/ /ma-tišrab-š/
'Where is the girl who will drink?'	'Here. (She) is not drinking.'

The /ma- . . . -š/ type of negation involves the complexity of affixing both a prefix and suffix to the negated word, and the word may undergo complex morphophonemic changes, such as a change in vowel length or shift in major stress. In the negation test, the /ma- . . . -š/ form of negation was never substituted for the simpler /miš/ pattern.

[63] Children 1, 2, and 3 did, however, imitate a word negated with /ma- . . . -š/ in Item 1 of the imitation test.

Child 5 used the /ma- . . . -š/ form of negation with the present and past tense forms of the verb, and with the prepositional phrase /ʕindi/ 'with me', so he appears to have definitely mastered it. He did not respond to all items in the test, for example, the item with the imperative form, so it is not certain if he could use this negation in all contexts.

Most of the older children had mastered the two forms of negation well; few errors were made throughout the test. The errors made by some of the younger children taking the test (Children 9, 11, and 12, ages 5 and 6) did not show consistent areas of poor mastery of negation; most often they erred by using the /miš/ form where /ma- . . . -š/ was required, or placed /miš/ in the wrong position in the sentence.

No pattern emerges as to the order in which various types of constructions are learned to be negated with /ma- . . . -š/, since the children ages 4 to 6 already used it with all constructions elicited.

One final comment should be made about the negated stative verb /ma-fī-š/ 'there isn't (aren't)'. This item is used by even the youngest children in the two-word stage. Since it is used as an early pivot word before it is contrasted with the affirmative /fī/ 'there is (are)', I think this is strong evidence that this item is first learned as a unit. The word /fī/ was the only item in the negation test requiring /ma- . . . -š/ which was negated correctly by all children who took the test (Item 11). Child 3 answered a question with /ma-ḥadd-iš/ 'nobody'; this may also be learned early as a vocabulary item.

The above stages should be considered as a first attempt at characterizing the development of negation, based on the limited data available. Certainly additional data are needed to determine with more certainty the order in which the general negation patterns are acquired, to what extent their use overlaps at different linguistic ages, and how negation is learned for the various type of sentences, phrases, and words in the language.

5.3. THE ACQUISITION OF THE INTERROGATIVE

5.3.1. *Rules for Interrogation in Adult Language*

The forms of interrogation in this dialect will be described,[64] considering facts which are relevant to early language acquisition.[65]

There are two types of interrogatives, questions requiring *yes* or *no* as an answer ('yes-no' questions), and questions using 'question words'.

[64] Adapted from descriptions by Khalafallah, 1961, 131–132; Lehn and Abboud, 1963; Gamal-Eldin, 1967, 52–53, 80–82, 87–88.

[65] 'Question tags' such as /miš kida/ 'Isn't that so?' and indirect questions will not be discussed.

1. Yes-no questions for all types of sentences differ from statements (declarative sentences) only in intonation.

T opt Q_1:

S 231 # ⇒ *S 233* / /

2 3 1	*2 3 3*
/huwa hina #/ →	/huwa hina / / /
'He (is) here'.	'(Is) he here?'
2 3 1	*2 3*
/rāḥ il-ɣēṭ #/ →	/rāḥ il-ɣēṭ / / /
'(He) went to the field.'	'Did (he) go to the field?'

2. The question words *(QW)* are:

1. /ʔeh/	'what'
2. /mīn/	'who'
3. /kǣm/ /gadd ʔēh/	'how much (how many)'
4. /fēn/	'where'
5. /minēn/[66]	'from where'
6. /lē/[67]	'why'
7. /mēta/	'when'
8. /ʔizzǣy/ /kīf/	'how'

They occur in the following environments:

(a) Question words 1–5 occur in non-verbal sentences, in initial or final position.

T opt Q_{2a}:

$$X \Rightarrow \begin{Bmatrix} QW + X \\ X + QW \end{Bmatrix}$$

$$X \rightarrow \begin{Bmatrix} N \\ pron \\ NP \end{Bmatrix}$$

/da ʔēh/	'What (is) that?'
/ʔēh da/	
/ʔis-sitt-di mīn/	'Who (is) this woman?'
/mīn is-sitt-di/	
/dōl kǣm/	'How many (are) these?'
/kǣm dōl/	
/huwa fēn/	'Where (is) he?'
/fēn huwa/	
/ʔir-rājul minēn/	'Where (is) the man from?'
/minēn ir-rājul/	

[66] This is a contraction of /min fēn/ 'from where'.
[67] This is a contraction of /li ʔēh/ 'for what'.

(b) All question words occur in verbal sentences, in initial, post-verbal, or final position (subject or object position), although post-verbal position is preferred stylistically. Question words 1 and 2 require a clause preceded by the relative pronoun /ʔilli/ when they occur in subject position.

T opt Q_{2b}:

$$X(Y) \Rightarrow \left\{\begin{matrix} QW + X(Y) \\ X + QW(Y) \\ X(Y) + QW \end{matrix}\right\}$$

$$X \rightarrow \left\{\begin{matrix} V \\ VP \end{matrix}\right\}$$

$$Y \rightarrow \left\{\begin{matrix} \text{Locative} \\ \text{Time} \\ \textit{Prep P} \text{ (etc.)} \end{matrix}\right\}$$

$$QW_1 + X(Y) \Rightarrow QW_1 + /\text{ʔilli}/ + X(Y)$$

$$QW_1 \rightarrow /\text{ʔēh, mīn}/$$

/ʔištarēt ʔēh/	'What did you buy?' (lit., 'You bought what?')
/ʔēh illi ištarētu/	(lit., 'What that you bought it?')
/šuft mīn fis-sūg/	'Who did you see in the market?' (lit., 'You saw who in the market?')
/mīn illi šuftu fis-sūg/	(lit., 'Who that you saw him in the market?')
/huwa jæh minēn/	'Where did he come from?'
/rāḥ lē/	'Why did he go?'

(c) Some question words may occur in combination with certain prepositions, and become phrases *(Prep + QW)*. They usually occur in final position in a sentence. Some combinations are presented here.

(1) /ʔēh/

/da li ʔēh/	'What is this for?' (lit., 'for what')
/da ʕašǣn ʔēh/	'What is this for?' (lit., 'because what')
/huwa ɣalṭān fi ʔēh/	'In what [way] is he mistaken?'

(2) /mīn/

/ʔil-kitǣb li mīn/	'Who is the book for?' (lit., 'for who')
/huwa ʕind mīn/	'Whose house is he at?' (lit., 'with who')

(3) /kǣm/

/dōl bi kǣm/	'How much do these cost?' (lit., 'for how much')
/fi kǣm yōm ḥa-txallaṣ/	'In how many days will you finish?'

(4) /fēn/

/humma min fēn/[68]	'Where are they from?' (lit., 'from where')
/ḥa-trūḥ ʕala fēn/	'Where will you go?' (lit., 'to where')

(5) /mēta/

/ʔinta jēt min mēta/	'When did you come?' (lit., 'from when')

(d) /kǣm/ 'how many' may function as the pre-modifier of a noun, and occur in medial sentence position.

/hina kǣm wāḥid/	'How many are here?' (lit., 'here how many one')

5.3.2. *The Interrogation Test*

The interrogation test was administered to all children who could comprehend its purpose. It consisted of six declarative sentences of various structural types. To elicit the interrogative, the child was told, for example, "Ask the girl what she wants to eat". In Arabic, however, the transformation from this sentence to an interrogative sentence does not involve auxiliary words or inversion of word order; literally, the corresponding interrogative sentence would be "What you want to eat?". The sentence is identical in structure with the last part of the eliciting sentence, with the only required change being that of person, in the personal pronoun (which is optional in the sentence) and the corresponding verb inflection. For this reason, it was difficult to assess the children's competence in forming interrogatives, since interrogatives could not be elicited without giving the sentence structure as a model in the cue statement.

Only sentences with question words were used, because the other type of interrogation ('yes-no' questions) involves no grammatical changes.

The results of the interrogation test are presented by item. Again, the utterances of Child 31, age 15, were used as the adult model. The cue sentence is presented, and then the 'model' interrogative sentence which would be expected in adult speech. It was not uncommon for children to 'answer' the cue sentence instead of forming an interrogative, for example:

Cue	Response
'Ask her what the soap is for.'	'It's for washing.'

In these cases, the answer could not be counted.

Children 1 and 2 did not take the test.

[68] This is used in free variation with the contracted form /minēn/.

The Interrogation Test

Introductory Phrases.	/ʔisʔæl il-bit . . ./
	'Ask the girl . . .'
	/ʔisʔæl il-ʕarūsa . . ./
	'Ask the doll . . .'
1. Cue Sentence.	/hiya ʕayza tākul ʔēh/
	'. . . what she wants to eat.'
Interrogative Model.	/(ʔinti) (ʕayza) takli ʔēh/
	'What do (you want) to eat?'

This item elicited interrogation for a sentence in which the question word was the object of the verb. All children who formed interrogative sentences from the cue sentence did it correctly.

2. Cue Sentence.	/hiya ḥaṭṭit il-ḥælla fēn/
	'. . . where she put the cooking pot.'
Interrogative Model.	/(ʔinti) ḥaṭṭēti l-ḥælla fēn/
	'Where did (you) put the cooking pot?'

Child 3 repeated the question word, /fēn/, only. Child 14 produced a correct interrogative sentence, but the verb was inflected for second person singular masculine, /ḥaṭṭēt/, instead of feminine, /ḥaṭṭēti/. All other responses were correct.

3. Cue Sentence.	/lē hiya miš ʕam-tsaʕdak fiš-šuɣl/
	'. . . why she doesn't help you in the work.'
Interrogative Model.	(a) /lē (ʔinti) miš ʕam-tsaʕdīni fiš-šuɣl/
	(b) /(ʔinti) miš ʕam-tsaʕdīni fiš-šuɣl lē/
	'Why don't (you) help me in the work?'

This sentence was longer. There were two acceptable alternative interrogative sentences possible. Responses were approximately equally divided as to placement of the question word.

Children 3 and 8 repeated only one word of the cue sentence; younger children did not respond. The other deviant sentences produced by Children 12, 16, and 30 contained the question word /lē/ in medial position; this is not incorrect, but is poor style.

4. Cue Sentence.	/ʔis-sabōn illi maʕāha ʕašǣn ʔēh/
	'. . . what the soap which she has is for.'
Interrogative Model.	/ʔis-sabōn illi maʕāki ʕašǣn ʔēh/
	'What is the soap which you have for?' (lit., 'because what')

This sentence was long and fairly complex, and contained a Preposition + Question Word construction. Many children 'answered' the cue sentence instead of making it interrogative. Some children changed the prepositional phrase /maʕāki/ 'with you' to /ʕindik/, which has approximately the same meaning. Child 11 repeated the word /ʔēh/ without the accompanying preposition, which is incomplete. Children 13, 14, and 26 changed the sentence, using the question word /fēn/ 'where' and Child 28 used the question word /lē/ 'why'; the sentences are correct. Children 25 and 30 changed the sentence, 'What do you do with the soap you have?'; their sentences are correct. Child 29 placed the question word phrase in medial position in the sentence; it is not incorrect, but is poor style.

5. Cue Sentence. /ʔēh illi hiya šæfitu/
'. . . what she saw.'
Interrogative Model. (a) /ʔēh illi (ʔinti) šuftī/
(b) /(ʔinti) šufti ʔēh/
'What did (you) see?'

The cue sentence elicited interrogation where the question word /ʔēh/ 'what' was used as the subject in a verbal sentence. This sentence could be made interrogative using the word as subject (type a) or changing its position to object of the verb (lit., 'You saw what?', type b, the more common pattern), so the two alternative sentences are acceptable. All the children's responses were correct. Responses by older children tended to be closer to the structure of the cue sentence; more of them used type (a).

6. Cue Sentence. /hiya ḥa-trūḥ fēn il-wakt/
'. . . where she will go now.'
Interrogative Model. /(ʔinti) ḥa-trūḥi fēn (ʔil-wakt)/
'Where will (you) go (now)?'

There were no errors in making this sentence interrogative; several children changed the verb to second person plural instead of second person singular feminine.

5.3.3. *Child Syntactical Rules and Stages for Interrogation*

In Arabic the formation of the interrogative is very simple. The 'yes-no' type of interrogation does not involve syntactic transformations and is acquired early, apparently without errors or stages of development. Question words have relative freedom of occurrence and do not require inversion of word order, so little difficulty would be expected in learning them.

Based on data from the interrogation test and from examples observed in spontaneous speech of younger children, the developmental stages in acquiring the interrogative will be described.

5.3.3.1. *Stage I*

The earliest form of interrogation is the declarative sentence spoken with rising intonation *(233 / /)*. This is so simple that it is probably acquired by age 2 or before, during the one-word stage. Child F, age 2.3, did not produce interrogative utterances, but showed evidence of understanding them, as when

2 3

her sister asked her /takli buff / / / 'Do you want to eat bread?', and she responded /mm/ 'yes'. Child 1, age 2.8, also responded to many questions, such as in the conversation with her mother, presented in Chapter 4. Some interrogative utterances heard in the speech of Child 1 during free conversation were:

2 3
/tiddini di / / / — '(Will you) give me this?'

2 3
/ʔāxud di / / / — '(May I) take this?'

Child 2, age 3.0, also produced a few 'yes-no' interrogative utterances:

2 3 3
/ʔaḥuṭṭu hina / / / — '(May) I put it here?'

3
/di / / / — 'This (one)?'

2 3
/šūfi s-sitt / / / — '(Do you) see the woman?'

2 3
/taxdi di / / / — '(Do you want to) take this?'

The 'yes-no' interrogative sentences develop in length and complexity corresponding to the development of the declarative sentences. This pattern of interrogation may be written like the adult pattern:

T opt Q_1*:*

$$S\ 231\ \# \Rightarrow S\ 233\ /\ /$$

5.3.3.2. *Stage II*

Interrogatives with question words are also acquired early, but slightly later than the 'yes-no' type of interrogation. One of the first question words learned is /ʔēh/ 'what', which is used to ask the names of objects, usually in a sentence like /ʔēh da/ 'What is that?'. The child also hears the question word /mīn/ 'who' when being asked to identify persons. At first, question words are not used with prepositions. They may be used alone, or tend to occur at the beginning of a *P–O* construction. The following examples of early question word sentences were observed in the speech of Children 1, 2, and 3:

/*ʔeh* da (di)/	'What (is) this (m.,f.)?'
/*ʔeh* hina/	'What (is) here?'
/*mīn* da/	'Who (is) that?'
/*fēn* il-kūra/ (*fēn* huwa/	'Where (is) the ball?'
	'Where (is) it?'
/*lē* ma-fī-š/	'Why isn't there any?'

The structure of question word interrogative sentences at this stage may be written:

T opt Q_2:

$$S \Rightarrow QW + S$$

In the interrogation test, Child 3, age 3.6, produced the following utterances:

/takli ʔēh/	'What do (you want) to eat?'
/fēn/	'Where?'
/lē/	'Why?'
/šufti ʔēh/	'What did (you) see?'
/rūḥu fēn/	'Where will (you) go?'

Here, question words tended to come at the end of the sentence.

5.3.3.3. *Stage III*

Further development in the use of question words includes learning the stylistic placement of the words in various positions in the sentence, and using them with prepositions.

Data from the interrogation test reveal some of the characteristics of this stage for younger children. For the most part, the question word interrogative seems to be well mastered by age 5 (as seen in the responses of Children 8 and 9). There were so few errors in the interrogation test that not much insight is provided into the stages of development; perhaps few errors are made by children. It should be taken into consideration also that the similarity of structure in the cue sentences and elicited interrogatives may have reduced potential errors which may have been found in spontaneous speech.

In the interrogation test, the only 'errors' made were in placement of the question word in the sentence, and this could not be considered grammatically unacceptable. Some children showed a preference for simplifying

Prep + *QW* phrases, as in Item 4, where /ʕašǣn ʔēh/ 'because what' was replaced with /lē/ 'why' or a different expression, and the word /ʕašǣn/ was omitted by one child.

Data regarding interrogatives for children between the ages of 3.6 (Children 3 and 4) and 5 (Children 8 and 9) are not available, so although children at age 5 have surely mastered the use of interrogatives, they are probably learned before that age. Child 3 was already able to understand and produce many types of question word constructions. Stage III will be considered mastery of the adult usage of the question word type of interrogation.

This outline of the stages of development of the interrogative is necessarily simple, since the formation of the interrogative itself is simple in this language. In the absence of more data, it must be considered only a general description of the developmental stages.

5.4. SUMMARY

Some systematic aspects observed in the children's speech in the gradual approximation to adult syntax were:

1. The speech of children in the early stages of syntactic development consisted primarily of one-, two-, and three-word sentences, and some words had particular functions in the sentences. Word order was more free than that observed for some languages, but was still quite rigid.
2. In the earliest stage of development, the non-negative and non-interrogative sentences were kept as intact as possible, with the negative or interrogative elements attached to them, not incorporated into them.
3. At first the negative word /miš/ and the interrogative question words were combined with whatever part of speech constituted the child's 'sentence', and usually preceded the sentence.
4. Optional elements which alter the form of the sentence or introduce other accompanying elements were acquired later, such as the /ma-. . .-š/ form of negation or question words which occur in prepositional phrases.
5. There was an early preference to use simple, affirmative, declarative sentences ('kernel sentences' in transformational terms). The children tended to omit function words and words or constructions not essential to the meaning of the sentence. They used mainly nouns and action verbs.
6. Word order was relatively free in the children's utterances.
7. Compared to a language like English, syntactic errors were few, reflecting the syntactic simplicity of the language.

6

THE DEVELOPMENT OF MORPHOLOGY

6.1. EARLY STAGES OF MORPHOLOGICAL DEVELOPMENT

6.1.1. *Theoretical Considerations*

In observations of child language thus far, it has been found that morphology is the last aspect of a language to be mastered.[1] The age at which a child can be said to have mastered the morphological system is apparently affected by the complexity of the native language, as well as factors of individual development. English-speaking children learn the basic morphology by about age 4 or 5;[2] in a language with a more complex inflectional system such as the Russian system of cases or Spanish verb inflections, morphology is not fully mastered until age 7 or 8.[3] This is probably also due in part to the fact that in the languages observed, the morphological system of inflections and derivations is not as essential to the conveyence of meaning as are the phonological and syntactic systems in the language.

One of the most widely observed characteristics of early morphological development is that children begin to use words without any sort of inflection; the use of words in "unmarked strings" is probably a universal characteristic in early language acquisition.[4] For example, the verbal contrasts of tense, voice, and agreement in adult language were found to be expressed by one invariable verb form in "stage -i" of development for children learning English, French, and German.[5]

[1] Ervin and Miller, 1963, 127. Slobin, 1966a, 134. Observations made thus far, however, have dealt with languages where syntax has a more important role in communication than morphology; in a language where morphology is more important, it is theorerically possible that the order of acquisition would be reversed.

[2] Jean Berko, "The Child's Learning of English Morphology", *Psycholinguistics, A Book of Readings*, ed., Sol Saporta (New York, Holt, Rinehart and Winston, 1961) pp. 359–375. Some allomorphs of the inflections are learned later.

[3] Reported by Slobin 1965a, 8, and by Kernan and Blount, 1966.

[4] Slobin, 1966a, 134–135. Ervin and Miller, 1963, 25. Leopold, 1961, 357.

[5] Kahane, Kahane and Saporta, 1958.

The 'unmarked' grammatical system becomes 'marked', i.e., words are identified not only in terms of order, but also by markers.[6] For example, nouns occur before the plural suffix, and verbs occur before {-ing}. When inflections begin to be acquired, children tend to 'overregularize' or 'overgeneralize' the inflections, using the regular ones in adult language. This, too, is probably universal.[7] They are attempting to impose an 'order' on the language system. Some examples of the "strange regularities" of children's utterances and thought are reported by Chukovsky.[8]

Some detailed investigations have been made into children's stages of acquisition of certain morphological patterns, since this is a relatively easy aspect of language development to test.

In English, it has been observed that children may, for example, inflect irregular verbs for past tense in the same manner as the regular verbs, saying 'comed', 'breaked', or 'goed'. It has been found, however, that at first the irregular forms such as *came* or *went* are learned and used correctly as semantic units, but after the child links semantic 'pastness' with past tense inflections, he replaces these correct forms with the incorrect overgeneralized forms.[9] Although the correct irregular form may be practicd for some months, it is driven out of the child's speech by overregularization for some time.[10]

The acquisition of plurals of nouns in English has been investigated, notably by Berko and by Ervin and Miller. The same process of overregularization was found. Ervin and Miller found that two children, ages 2 and 3, gave as the plural of *foo*t the forms 'foots', 'feets', 'footez', and 'footses'.[11] This indicates that the children are producing new plurals, not imitating adult speech. Ervin concludes that "even highly practiced, familiar plurals may be temporarily changed in form by overgeneralization of new patterns".[12]

In the now-classic test devised by Berko, the development of morphological inflections in English was investigated: the plural and possessive {-s} endings of nouns, the {-s} suffix for third person singular verbs, progressive {-ing} and past tense {-d} endings of verbs, and comparison endings {-er} and {-est} of adjectives.[13] Nonsense forms were used for the test, to avoid the possibility

[6] Ervin and Miller, 1963, 122.

[7] Slobin, ed., 1967, 111. Slobin gives examples in Russian in his 1966a article "The Acquisition of Russian,"; examples in French are given by Guillaume, cited by Brown and Fraser, 1964, 45; examples in English are presented in works cited below.

[8] Kornei I. Chukovsky, *From Two to Five*, trans., Miriam Morton (Berkeley, Univ. of California Press, 1963).

[9] Lenneberg, 1967, 304.

[10] Slobin, ed., 1967, 111. This is also the case in Russian language acquisition, reported by Slobin, 1965a, 7–8.

[11] Ervin and Miller, 1963, 33.

[12] Ervin, 1964, 177.

[13] Berko, 1961.

that correct answers would be imitations of adult speech, and to obtain an insight into how children inflected words they had not heard before. The children's responses were compared with those of adults. The inflections given for nonsense forms showed that children did have productive rules for extending inflectional patterns to new words. It was found that mastery of inflections, with their allomorphic variations, increased with age, but there was no significant difference between the performance of boys and girls.[14] Similar results were found by Kernan and Blount in a test of this kind with nonsense words given to Spanish-speaking children in Mexico.[15]

In English, the earliest inflections to be learned are to plural {-s}, possessive {-s}, progressive marker {-ing}, and past tense marker {-d}, at about age 2 or 2½.[16] It was found that for a Russian-speaking child, inflections for number and diminuitive of nouns, and the imperative mood of verbs were acquired first, by about age 2.[17] In Spanish, children appear to master the plural, possessive, and past tense inflections first; there was no significant difference found in their use between younger and older children in Kernan and Blount's data.[18] Apparently once the principle of inflection is acquired, it is immediately applied over a wide range of types,[19] but the use of markers learned is still optional and inconsistent for some time. Child speech does not advance abruptly from the total absence of inflections to the invariably correct use of them; the percentage of use shows a gradual increase with age.[20]

Morphological classes whose reference is clearly concrete energe first; classes based on relational criteria such as cases, tenses, and persons of the verb are later.[21] Gvozdev's evidence in Russian indicates that when grammatical complexity is held constant, semantic difficulty is related to the age of acquisition of certain patterns.[22] The distinctions learned last are those with few semantic correlates. Suffixes are seldom used with the wrong lexical class, such as when a two-year-old child said "stand up-ed".[23]

Children seem to have no difficulty discovering morpheme boundaries; inflections are used with word stems from the beginning, so the stem and its inflections are apparently psychologically real units.[24]

[14] Berko, 1961, 364.

[15] Kernan and Blount, 1966.

[16] Ervin and Miller, 1963, 26, 32. Weir, 1962, 143.

[17] Slobin, 1966a, 141.

[18] Kernan and Blount, 1966, 12.

[19] Slobin, 1966a, 136. Velten found the acquisition of past, plural, and possessive suffixes in his child's speech in a span of three months; Velten, 1943.

[20] Smith and Miller, eds., (no author) 1966, 99.

[21] Slobin, 1966a, 141.

[22] Cited by Ervin, 1964, 164.

[23] Ervin and Miller, 1963, 26.

[24] Slobin, 1966a, 137.

Mastery of agreement between syntactic classes probably begins at about age 3. Berko found that for the inflection {-s} of the third person singular verb, four-year-old children performed as well as older children, and more than half of them used the inflection with nonsense items.[25] Slobin reports that gender agreement for adjectives and verbs is mastered in Russian at age 2.10 or 3, although children still may not distinguish the gender inflections of nouns.[26] Gili y Gaya found that four-year-olds learning Spanish made few mistakes in concordance of nouns, adjectives, and pronouns.[27] Kahane, Kahane and Saporta report that their analysis of data in English, French, and German revealed that children had acquired inflections for verbal categories by the end of the third year.[28]

6.1.2. *Some Characteristics of Early Morphological Development*

The children in this study appear to develop their mastery of morphological inflections in much the same manner as that observed for children learning other languages.[29]

6.1.2.1. *Children E and F*

An examination of the spontaneous utterances of Children E and F reveals that their words were morphologically quite simple, with few inflections. Where inflections occurred, they were usually correct and were of certain types.

All nouns in the speech of Child E (age 1.11) were singular. There were no nouns used which contrasted masculine and feminine forms (to indicate an awareness of gender) nor abstract nouns (which may have gender markers). The only verb occurring in her speech was [ḥūs], the imperative form of the verb *to hold back*, which is the uninflected stem form /ḥūš/ in adult language.

Child F (age 2.3) also used only singular nouns. She used one noun with the possessive ending [búya] (/ʔabūya/) 'my father', although this is probably used as a form of address rather than being a truly inflected noun.[30] Her verbs showed inflection:

[25] Berko, 1961, 368.

[26] Slobin, 1966a, 137–138.

[27] Gili y Gaya, 1970, 17.

[28] Kahane, Kahane and Saporta, 1958, 2.

[29] Although the language has a few derivations, only inflections will be considered here. Rules for some inflections of nouns and adjectives are presented in the following sections.

[30] Parents are addressed as /ʔummi/ 'my mother' and /ʔabūya/ 'my father' as commonly as with the terms /māma/ and /bāba/. Other members of the family are also addressed in this way, e.g., /sīdi/ 'my grandfather', /sitti/ 'my grandmother', /ʔaxūya/ 'my brother'.

Utterance	Adult Form	Gloss
[hǣti]	/hǣti/	'give me (f.sing.)'
[bāba dɪh]	/bāba jih/	'Papa came.'
[māma dæt]	/māma jæt/	'Mama came.'

Again, there is doubt as to the extent the forms reflect the child's competence in using inflections. The last two utterances are frequently said by older siblings to the child when one of the parents enters the home. The first utterance, the imperative inflected for feminine singular, is more likely to be an inflected form (masculine imperative would be unmarked /hǣt/); it also could be merely an imitation of the imperative form used in addressing this child, thus being the form most often heard by her.

The only other inflected word in the speech of Child F was [ʕāk] 'with you (m.sing.)', which is /maʕāk/ in adult language (consisting of the preposition /maʕa/ 'with' plus the suffix /-k/ 'you (m.sing.)'). This was used in addressing her father; use of the contrasting feminine form /maʕāki/ was not observed, but it seems very possible that this is an example of true inflection.

Some spontaneous and imitated utterances which reveal the morphological development of Children 1–4 will be considered (others are discussed in the following sections referring to the development of specific inflections).

The words uttered which require inflection were usually inflected, even in the speech of Child 1, who was only five months older than Child F. It appears from the speech of Children 1 and 2 that by the time children have reached the multi-word stage in syntax (about age 2 or 2½), they have already begun using most basic inflections; no inflectionally 'unmarked strings' were found. Whatever items were missing in early sentences were more often function words such as articles and prepositions, rather than inflections.

When the children did omit inflections (or pronounce the words unclearly–it is not always easy to determine which is the case), they were usually inflections used with verb forms. Plural nouns were not often produced in the spontaneous speech observed; adjectives usually were inflected correctly to agree with the noun or referent in number and gender. Errors in inflection and agrrement were mostly due to omissions, not to the use of the wrong form. More inflections were omitted in imitation than in spontaneous speech.

In the presentation of utterances, inflectional affixes and their corresponding glosses are italicized.

6.1.2.2. *Child 1*

All the inflected words in the spontaneous speech of Child 1 (age 2.8) were correct (the utterances are phonemically regularized here). For example, she used the first person possessive suffix with nouns and a possessive word:[31]

Utterance	Gloss
/xǣl*i*/	'*my* uncle'
/sīd*i*/	'*my* grandfather'
/ʔuxt*i*/	'*my* sister'
/bitæʕt*i*/	'belonging to *me*'

She used the first person ending also with verbs, and inflected imperatives correctly for the feminine:

Utterance	Gloss
/ʕamæl*t*/	'*I* did'
/kæl*t*/	'*I* ate'
/xud*i*/	'Take (it) (f.sing.)'
/hǣt*i*/	'Give (it to me) (f.sing.)'

She also used a verb phrase correctly:

/yjib*li*/	'He gets *for me*'

In her imitations, all the forms in which inflections were omitted were verbs, for example:[32]

Model Utterance	Child's Utterance	Gloss
/*n*ḥuṭṭu/	/ḥuṭṭu/	'*we* put it'
/ʕa, -*y*ḥibb/	/ḥibb/	'*he* likes'
/ʕam-*y*ṣīd/	/ṣīd/	'*he* is fishing'
/ʕam-*y*išrab*u*/	/yišrab/	'*they* drink'

6.1.2.3. *Child 2*

Child 2 (age 3.0) omitted one inflection in her spontaneous speech, when the verb was not inflected for gender:

Utterance	Gloss
/hǣt bit/	'Give (m.sing.) (it to me), girl.'

[31] The first words are 'names' also, but she produced the forms in response to a question like /sīdik ʔismu ʔēh/ 'Your grandfather, what is his name?', thus changing the inflection correctly for the answer.

[32] This may be due to the fact that the child is simply imitating only the stressed syllables of the model words.

This is the masculine form of the imperative, and should have been suffixed with the feminine marker /-i/. Otherwise, Child 2 produced a variety of correctly inflected forms, including other imperatives inflected for feminine, for example:

Utterance	Gloss
/bit kæbīr*a*/	'a big *(f.)* girl'
/xud*i* ya bit/	'Take *(*f.sing.*)* (it), girl.'
/šūf*i* s-sitt/	'See *(*f.sing.*)* the woman?'
/ʔ*a*ḥuṭṭu hina/	'(Shall) *I* put it here?'

In her imitations, Child 2 omitted only inflections for verbs, and added an unnecessary inflection for one adjective which modified a masculine noun, /šuɤl/.

Model Utterance	Child's Utterance	Gloss
/ʕam-*y*ḥibb/	/ḥibb/	'*He* likes.'
/ʕam-*y*rūḥ/	/rūḥ/	'*He* goes.'
/ʕam-*y*iktib/	/ʕam-iktib/	'*He* writes.'
/sæhl/	/sæhl*a*/	'easy (m.)'
		'easy (f.)'

6.1.2.4. *Child 3*

Child 3 (age 3.6) did not speak very clearly, so whether he actually omitted inflections could not always be determined with certainty. In spontaneous speech, he omitted the inflections for two verbs:

Adult Form	Child's Utterance	Gloss
/ʕam-*t*naḍḍaf/	[naṭṭaf]	'*She* is cleaning.'
/*y*isgī/	[ski]	'*He* waters [animals].'

He produced other correctly inflected words:

Utterance	Gloss
/ʔisma*ha*/	'*her* name'
/ʔism*i*/	'*my* name'
/zarʕit*na*/[33]	'*our* field'
/bēt*u*/	'*his* house'
/*n*isgī/	'*We* water [animals].'
/kæl*t*/	'*I* ate.'

[33] Feminine nouns like /zarʕa/ which end in /-a/ undergo an allomorphic change in which the /-a/ is replaced by /-it/ before suffixes. This has also been mastered by this child.

In imitations, Child 3 omitted inflections for several verbs, an adjective, and a prepositional phrase:

Model Utterance	Child's Utterance	Gloss
/ʕam-*y*ḥibb/	/ḥibb/	'*He* likes'
/ʕam-*y*itḍarab/	/ḍarab/	'*He* is being hit.'
/ʕam-*y*išrab*u*/	/ʔišrab/	'*They* drink.'
/suxn*a*/	/sux/	'hot (f.)'
/ʕalē*k*/	/ʕalē/	'on you *(m.sing.)*'

6.1.2.5. *Child 4*

Child 4 (age 3.6) had a better mastery of inflections than Child 3, who was her age. She spoke much more, and in spontaneous speech produced several examples of non-agreement of words:

Utterance	Gloss
/hǣt ya bit/	'Give (m.sing.) (it to me), girl.'
/da guṭṭa kætīr/	'That (m.) (are) many (m.sing.) cats.' (lit., 'cat many')
/humma kæbīr/	'They (are) big (m.sing.).'

In the first utterance, the imperative verb should have been inflected with /-i/ for feminine. The other two utterances contained adjectives in the 'stem' masculine form which were not inflected for plural, and the second utterance also contained a singular noun which was not pluralized. Child 4 produced a large number of other correctly inflected utterances (including the correctly inflected imperative), for example:

Utterance	Gloss
/hǣt*i* māma/	'Give *(f.sing.)* (it to me), Mama.'
/ʕam-*n*ilʕab/	'*We* are playing.'
/ʔæna ʕawz*a* ʔ*a*rawwaḥ/	'*I* want to go home.' (lit., '*I* want *I* go home.')
/ruḥ*t* maʕā*ki*/	'*I* went with you *(f.sing.)*.'
/warda ḥilwa/	'a pretty (*f.sing.*) flower'
/ʕam-*y*ilʕab bī*ha* l-kūra/[34]	'*He* is playing with the ball.' (lit., 'with it *(f.sing.)* the ball')

Child 4 omitted very few inflections in imitations. The three omitted were verb forms:

[34] Elicited in the comprehension test.

Model Utterance	Child's Utterance	Gloss
/*n*ḥuṭṭu/	/ḥuṭṭu/	'*We* put it.'
/ʕam-*y*ḥibb/	/ḥibb/	'*He* likes.'
/ʕam-*y*itḍarab/	/ʔitḍarab/	'*He* is being hit.'

The development of specific inflections for nouns and adjectives will be investigated in the following sections, analyzing the children's speech from Child 1 through those who have mastered adult forms.

6.2. THE ACQUISITION OF INFLECTIONAL AFFIXES FOR NOUN PLURALS

6.2.1. *Rules for Pluralizing Nouns in Adult Language*

6.2.1.1. *Noun Inflections for Number*

Nouns which can be counted are inflected for singular, dual, and plural number.

6.2.1.1.1. *The Singular Form*

Singularity of the noun is usually expressed by the noun alone; the word /wāḥid/ (fem., /waḥda/) 'one' may follow the noun as a modifier.

/kitæb/	'a book, one book'
/kitæb wāḥid/	'one book'

A special class of nouns, which usually refer to a unit of measurement, may occur with the number *one* preceding it in a noun phrase construction.[35]

/kīlo/	'a kilo, one kilo'
/wāḥid kīlo/	'one kilo'
/kīlo wāḥid/	
/jinē/	'a pound, one pound [unit of money]'
/wāḥid jinē/	'one pound'
/jinē wāḥid/	

The singular form of the noun is the 'base' form and is the stem to which dual and plural affixes (suffixes or infixes) are added. The addition of these affixes will be expressed in terms of morphophonemic rules (M-Rules).

[35] This "special class" of nouns is discussed in detail by Abdel-Malek. Zaki N. Abdel-Malek, "Numerals in Colloquial Egyptian Arabic", Unpublished Masters's thesis (Georgetown Univ. 1965) pp. 25–26.

6.2.1.1.2. *The Dual Inflection*

The inflection for dual, *two* is the suffix /-ēn/, added to the noun stem. This inflection is regular. Suffixed noun stems may have morphophonemic alternations. If a feminine noun ends in /-a/, the /-a/ is usually replaced by /-(i)t/ before the suffix. A long vowel in a stem may be shortened before the suffix, and primary stress is shifted to the suffix. For some nouns, /w/ or /y/ may be added before the dual suffix.

Opt Rule Dual:

$$Ns \Rightarrow Ns + Af$$
$$Af \rightarrow \text{/-ēn/}$$

/rājul/	'a man, one man'
/rajulēn/	'two men'
/kitǣb/	'a book, one book'
/kitæbēn/	'two books'
/warda/	'a flower, one flower'
/warditēn/	'two flowers'
/rādyu/	'a radio, one radio'
/radyuwēn/	'two radios'

Most count nouns may be inflected for dual. Exceptions are the 'special class' of nouns, and certain unpredictable items, which are dualized with the number *two* preceding the noun in a noun phrase.

/ʔitnēn kīlo/	'two kilos'
/ʔitnēn ǰinē/	'two pounds'
/ʔitnēn fellaḥīn/	'two farmers'

6.2.1.1.3. *The Plural Inflections*

The types of inflections which are allomorphic variations of the plural morpheme of nouns are many, complex, and often unpredictable. There are two types of plural inflections for nouns, 'regular' and 'irregular'.

1. Regular plurals are suffixes, /-īn/ for masculine nouns and /-āt/ (with the allomorphic variation /-ǣt/) for feminine nouns.

Opt Rule Pl_1:

$$\begin{bmatrix} N_{fs} \\ \\ N_{ms} \end{bmatrix} \Rightarrow \begin{bmatrix} N_{fs} \\ \\ N_{ms} \end{bmatrix} + \begin{bmatrix} Af_1 \\ \\ Af_2 \end{bmatrix}$$
$$Af_1 \rightarrow \text{/-āt/}$$
$$Af_2 \rightarrow \text{/-īn/}$$

Certain types of nouns are more likely to have regular plural affixes. Feminine nouns ending in /-a/ or referring to female persons usually take the regular feminine plural suffix /-āt/. (Some other nouns may also take this plural.) A noun stem may undergo minor morphophonemic changes when suffixed. Primary stress is shifted to the long vowel of the suffix.

/mudarrisa/	'teacher (f.)'
/mudarrisǣt/	'teachers (f.)'
/sitt/	'lady'
/sittǣt/	'ladies'
/sajara/	'tree'
/sajarāt/	'trees'

Masculine nouns beginning with /m-/ and referring to persons usually take the regular masculine plural suffix /-īn/.

/mudarris/	'teacher (m.)'
/mudarrisīn/	'teachers (m.,f.)'
/maṣri/	'Egyptian (m.)'
/maṣriyīn/	'Egyptians (m.,f.)'

2. Some nouns have both a counted plural form and a collective plural form. They usually end in /-a/, which is dropped for the collective plural. The counted plural is the regular feminine plural suffix.

Opt Rule Pl_2:

$$Ns + X \Rightarrow Ns$$

$$X \rightarrow \text{/-a/}$$

/sajara/	'tree'
/sajarāt/	'trees' (counted)
/sajar/	'trees' (collective)
/bēḍa/	'egg'
/beḍāt/	'eggs' (counted)
/bēḍ/	'eggs' (collective)

3. Most nouns have irregular plurals. In this form of plural, the root consonants of the noun are rearranged with new vowels, consonantal elements may be added, and feminine endings are lost. The irregular allomorphic patterns of the plural are of certain types, and sometimes the pattern of the plural can be predicted with some degree of certainty from the pattern of the singular noun. There are, however, many exceptions. Morphophonemic variations of the noun stem are common, and vary with the pattern of the noun and the plural.

Irregular plural patterns are so numerous (sometimes represented by only one or two nouns in the language) that only the major ones, those heard in children's speech, and those tested will be discussed here.[36]

Opt Rule Pl_3:

$X + Y \Rightarrow X + Z$
$X \rightarrow$ Consonantal root
$Y \rightarrow$ Singular vowel pattern
$Z \rightarrow$ Irregular plural vowel patterns

(a) Some nouns which end in /-a/ may be pluralized by inversion of the /-a/ and the consonant preceding it.

/guṭṭa/	'cat'
/gúṭaṭ/	'cats'
/kūra/	'ball'
/kúwar/	'balls'

(b) Some nouns which end in /-a/ and begin with /m-/ may take an irregular plural of a different pattern.

/muškila/	'problem'
/mašǣkil/	'problems'
/masʔæla/	'issue'
/masǣʔil/	'issues'

(c) Nouns which consist of two reduplicated syllables may take the same special pattern for the plural.

/bulbul/	'nightingale'
/balǣbil/	'nightingales'
/filfil/	'pepper'
/falǣfil/	'peppers'

(d) Many nouns have an unpredictable form of plural. However, the plurals tend to be of recurring canonical patterns, and the canonical form of the singular noun limits to some extent which type of plural it is likely to have. Following are a few examples of singular nouns with various canonical patterns and their plural forms.

[36] Khalafallah 1961, 55–65, has analyzed the correspondences between nouns and their plurals on the basis of canonical form of the singular and plural patterns. He found six general classes of nouns based on the type of plural they have and, for example, 23 singular-plural patterns for one of the noun classes, with as many as eight vocalic "sub-patterns" within a pattern group.

/kælb/	'dog'
/kilǣb/	'dogs'
/wād/	'boy'
/wilǣd/[37]	'boys'
/ʔīd/	'hand'
/ʔayǣdi/[38]	'hands'
/ṣubāʕ/	'finger'
/ṣawābiʕ/	'fingers'
/ɣēṭ/	'field'
/ɣeṭān/	'fields'
/sirr/	'secret'
/ʔasrār/	'secrets'
/bēt/	'house'
/buyūt/	'houses'

(e) Some plural patterns are less common, found in only a few words in the language.

/rājul/	'man'
/rijjǣla/	'men'
/kitǣb/	'book'
/kutub/	'books'
/sæna/	'year'
/sinīn/	'years'

6.2.1.2. *The Use of Cardinal Numerals with Nouns*[39]

When the noun is counted (except for the dual form), the cardinal numeral precedes the noun in the noun phrase. Numerals 3 through 10 are followed by a noun inflected for plural. Numerals 11 and above are followed by the noun in the singular.

Opt Rule Num:

$$N_{sg} \Rightarrow \begin{bmatrix} Num_1 \\ Num_2 \end{bmatrix} + \begin{bmatrix} N_{pl} \\ N_{sing} \end{bmatrix}$$

$$Num_1 \rightarrow \text{Numerals 3–10}$$
$$Num_2 \rightarrow \text{Numerals 11 and above}$$

[37] In Classical Arabic and the Cairene dialect, the singular noun is /walad/.

[38] This noun, like other parts of the body which are in pairs, may also be pluralized by use of the dual form, e.g., /ʔidēn/, 'hands'.

[39] Adapted from the description in Abdel-Malek, 1965.

6.2.1.2.1. *The Numerals 3–10*

Numerals 3 to 10 have two forms, 'long' and 'short'. The long form ends in /-a/. The short form is without /-a/ and may have vocalic and stress changes.

/talǣta/ 'three'
/tǽlat/
/xǽmsa/ 'five'
/xǽmas/

The long form of the numeral is the citation form. The short form is used when in a noun phrase construction, except for nouns of the 'special class', which are preceded by the long form.

/tælat riǰǰǣla/ 'three men'
/talǣta kīlo/ 'three kilos'
/xæmas kutub/ 'five books'
/xæmsa ǰinē/ 'five pounds'

For some nouns, usually those which begin with /ʔa-/, the /ʔa-/ may be replaced with /ti-/.

/ʔayyǣm/ 'days'
/xæmas tiyyǣm/ 'five days'

6.2.1.2.2. *The Numerals 11 and Above*

Numerals 11 and 12 consist of a base which is an allomorph of the numerals 1 and 2, and the suffix /-āšar/.

/wāḥid/ 'one'
/ḥidāšar/ 'eleven'
/ʔitnēn/ 'two'
/ʔitnāšar/ 'twelve'

Numerals 13 to 19 consist of a base which is the same as the short form of the numerals 3–9, and the suffix /-tāšar/.

/talǣta/ 'three'
/tælattāšar/ 'thirteen'

The tens 30–90 consist of a base which is an allomorph of the numerals 3–9 and the suffix /-īn/. (The numeral 20 was probably originally the dualized form of the numeral 10).

/ʕašara/ 'ten'
/ʕišrīn/ 'twenty'
/talǣta/ 'three'
/tælatīn/ 'thirty'

Examples of noun phrase constructions with numbers 11 and above are:

/ḥidāšar rājul/	'eleven men' (lit., 'eleven man')
/ʕišrīn kitǣb/	'twenty books' (lit., 'twenty book')
/xæmsa w ʕišrīn kitǣb/	'twenty-five books' (lit., 'five and twenty book')
/mīt kitǣb/	'one hundred books' (lit., 'one hundred book')

6.2.2. *The Noun Plural Test*

The noun plural test was administered to all children. The test consisted of 20 items. The singular (uninflected) noun was given as the cue accompanied by a picture (nonsense words were illustrated with various geometric figures). Pictures also depicted the noun as two and more than two, thus eliciting it in dual and plural form. If the child could not count the number of objects in the picture, the numeral was given as a cue and the child provided the form of the noun.

Items in the noun plural test were of the following general types: (a) real, familiar nouns with both regular and irregular plurals, (b) real, but uncommon, nouns, (c) real nouns in a noun phrase construction with an adjective, and (d) nonsense forms with the same singular pattern as some nouns elicited in the test.

The results of the noun plural test are presented by item. For each item the noun and adult form of dual and plural are given.

The Noun Plural Test.

1.	Cue Word.	Dual.	Plural.	Plural.
	/kælb/ 'dog'	/kælbēn/ 'two dogs'	/tælat kilǣb/ 'three dogs'	/ḥidāšar kælb/ 'eleven dogs' (singular noun)

This is a very familiar word with an irregular plural, /kilǣb/, and most children knew the plural, using it after the numeral 3. About half of the children, of all ages, used the plural form after the numeral 11, incorrectly. Only the six oldest children and Children 5 and 13 used the correct dual suffix /-ēn/; some repeated the numeral 2 with the plural and some used the plural form alone. Some younger children tended to use the uninflected singular form exclusively.

2.	Cue Word.	Dual.	Plural.
	/dælb/ (/mælb/) (nonsense)	/dælbēn/ (/mælbēn/) 'two__________'	/tæman________/ 'eight________'

This was a nonsense word with the same singular pattern as the preceding word /kælb/. The form /mælb/ was first used, which proved a poor choice because of its similarity to the word /mælban/, a kind of candy, and several children gave plural forms for this word. The form was changed to /dælb/ for most children taking the test.

Child 1 repeated the form as /kælb/ and kept it in the singular form, as she had done with the previous item; Child 14 also produced the plural form for /kælb/. Only Children 14, 20, 25, and 31 produced the irregular plural form /dilǣb/ on the pattern of /kilǣb/. Others either did not inflect the singular form or pluralized it with the regular feminine plural suffix /-āt/. Children who understood the cue words as /mælban/ usually pluralized it with the/-āt/ suffix. Even fewer children produced the dualized form with the suffix.

3.	Cue Word.	Dual.	Plural.
	/guṭṭa/	/guṭṭitēn/	/xæmas gúṭat/
	'cat'	'two cats'	'five cats'

This was a very familiar word with an irregular plural, /gúṭat/. Most of the younger children missed the plural form, giving a great variety of plurals, both the suffix /-āt/ and irregular vowel patterns. For example, Children 7, 8, 12, and 20 gave such inventive plural forms as /guṭṭatīl/ (not a plural pattern in the language), /guṭāṭa/, and /guṭūt/. Child 5 apparently added the suffix /-āt/ to a stem formed from the dual, which resulted in /guṭṭatǣt/. Most children, including older ones, missed the dual form.

4.	Cue Word.	Dual.	Plural.	Plural.
	/fuṭṭa/	/fuṭṭitēn/	/tælat______/	/ʔitnāšar fuṭṭa/
	(nonsense)	'two______'	'three______'	'twelve______'

This was a nonsense word with the same singular pattern as the preceding word /guṭṭa/. Children who produced the dual form all replaced the final syllable /-a/ with /-it/ for the word /fuṭṭitēn/, which is required for nouns ending in /-a/ before the dual suffix /-ēn/ in adult language.

Most children did not pluralize the noun after the numeral 3. Some used the suffix /-āt/; some used an irregular vowel pattern /fúṭat/, like the one for the preceding word, /gúṭat/. Children 17 and 25 changed the word to a real one, /fūta/ 'towel', but did not pluralize it.

Most children used the singular form correctly after the numeral 12.

5.	Cue Word.	Dual.	Plural.
	/warda ṣafra/	/warditēn ṣufr/	/ʔarbaʕ wardǣt ṣufr/
	'yellow flower'	'two yellow flowers'	'four yellow flowers'

This was a noun phrase consisting of a familiar feminine noun followed by a feminine adjective. The noun has the regular feminine plural with /-āt/; the adjective has the regular plural for adjectives of color, and must be inflected for plural after the dual and plural noun.

This proved to be a difficult item and younger children could not repeat the whole phrase. Children 9 and 10 repeated it uninflected for number. Several older children used the correct dual form; about the same number used the numeral 2, sometimes repeating the adjective only.

Most children knew the regular plural forms of the noun and adjective. Children 23 and 27 used an irregular vowel pattern for the noun plural, /wírad/ and /wárad/ respectively. Children 14 and 24 incorrectly used the collective form of the plural, and without the correctly inflected adjective to modify it. Child 5 attempted to dualize the adjective as a response for the plural, saying /ʔarbaʕ ṣafritēn/.

6.	Cue Word.	Dual.	Plural.
	/ṣēda/	/ṣedtēn/	/tisaʕ———/
	(nonsense)	'two'———	'nine———'

This was a nonsense word with a singular pattern like a familiar noun, /bēḍa/ 'egg', which would have both the collective plural /bēḍ/ and the counted plural /beḍāt/. Few children dualized the word; those who did correctly inserted the /-t/ before the dual suffix, saying /ṣedtēn/. Most children, including older ones, did not pluralize the word after the numeral 9. Plural forms given were usually the suffix /-āt/, and a few gave irregular vowel pattern plurals such as /ṣayǣda/ or /ṣiyād/. Child 8 repeated the dualized form with the numeral, saying /tisaʕ ṣedtēn/.

7.	Cue Word.	Dual.	Plural.
	/ṣubāʕ/	/ṣubaʕēn/	/ʔarbaʕ ṣawābiʕ/
	'finger'	'two fingers'	'four fingers'

This was a familiar noun with a difficult irregular plural which only Children 16, 17, 18, 19, and 30 knew. Most children pluralized the word with the suffix /-āt/ or left it uninflected. Among incorrect plural patterns given were inventive ones like /ʔiṣbaʕ/ (/tiṣbaʕ/ following the numeral), which was quite common among older children, and Child 24 gave /ṣaʕíba/. Few children inflected the noun for dual; most used the numeral 2 with the uninflected form.

8.	Cue Word.	Dual.	Plural.	Plural.
	/wād ʔasmar/	/wadēn sumr/	/tælat wilǣd sumr/	/ḥidāšar wād ʔasmar/
	'a dark boy'	'two dark boys'	'three dark boys'	'eleven dark boys'

This was a familiar masculine noun modified by an adjective of color in a noun phrase construction. The noun has an irregular plural /wilǣd/; the adjective has the regular plural for adjectives of color and is inflected for plural after the dual and plural noun. Again, younger children could not repeat the phrase and did not inflect the words.

Dualized forms given were usually correct, but Child 8 inserted /-t/ before the suffix as though it were a feminine noun, saying /wadtēn/. Children 9 and 13 changed the word to /ʕayil/ 'child' and dualized it correctly.

For the plural form, several children changed the word to /ʕayil/ and gave the correct irregular plural, /ʕayǣl/; Children 12 and 14 used the word /ṣubyān/ 'boys', also inflected correctly for plural. Incorrect plurals were almost all irregular vowel types; apparently the semantic content of the word inhibited use of the regular feminine suffix /-āt/, which is the common regularizing form. It was used by Children 16 and 17 only, and none used the regular masculine plural suffix. Some incorrect plurals given were /wilǣda/, /widǣn/; and /wilída/. All children inflected the adjective correctly for plural.

After the numeral 11, both words in the phrase should have been in singular form. Most children, including older ones, pluralized both words, and many used the singular noun but left the adjective plural. This lack of agreement between a counted noun and its adjective is also common in adult usage, probably because of the semantic content, which overrides the agreement rule. Perhaps it should not be analyzed as an 'error'.

9.	Cue Word.	Dual.	Plural.		
	/sajara/	/sajartēn/	/tælat sajarāt/	/sajarāt kubār/	/sajarāt ṣuɣayyarīn/
	'tree'	'two trees'	'three trees'	'big trees'	'small trees'

This was a familiar feminine noun with the regular feminine plural /-āt/. It was elicited for dual and plural, and in noun phrases modified by adjectives with regular and irregular plurals. (The use of the adjectives will be discussed later in this chapter.)

Many children produced the correct dualized inflection for this word and added /-t/ before the suffix, saying /sajartēn/. For the plural form, a few children gave the collective plural, /sajar/ (incorrect), but almost all gave the regular counted plural form, except for the incorrect plural /sudilla/ given by Child 24.

10.	Cue Word.	Dual.	Plural.
	/dælb/	/dælbēn/	/tæman______/
	(nonsense)	'two______'	'eight______'

This item is a repetition of the word given in Item 2. It was repeated here to see whether there would be any change in the children's responses when the word was not immediately preceded by a familiar noun of the same pattern. There was no significant difference in the responses.

11.	Cue Word.	Dual.	Plural.
	/bēt/	/betēn/	/ʕašar buyūt/
	'house'	'two houses'	'ten houses'

This was a familiar noun with an irregular plural, /buyūt/. About half of the children inflected the word correctly for dual. Smaller children did not inflect it for plural after the numeral 10; Child 8 used the dualized form after the numeral. Plurals given for the noun were all the correct irregular form, if the noun was pluralized.

12.	Cue Word.	Plural.
	/ʔil-ɣēṭ/	/tælat ɣeṭān/
	'the field'	'three fields'

This was a familiar noun of the same singular vowel pattern as the preceding word. The singular form is usually used with the definite article. It has the irregular plural /ɣeṭān/. Younger children did not inflect the noun for plural. Plural forms given by older children were all correct, except for Children 22 and 26, who used the suffix /-āt/. Child 28 also used this suffix and then corrected himself, using the correct plural. Child 26 invented the plural /ɣeyāṭ/.

13.	Cue Word.	Dual.	Plural.
	/wēt/	/wetēn/	/sæbaʕ______/
	(nonsense)	'two______'	'seven______'

This was a nonsense word with the same singular vowel pattern as the two preceding words. Only eight children inflected this word for dual, as compared with twelve who did so for the noun /bēt/.

Plural forms given were not patterned after the irregular plurals of either preceding word; most children used the suffix /-āt/. Child 15 gave /witǣn/ as the plural, like the word /geṭān/. Unusual plural forms were given by Child 22 who gave /wǣt/ and /wāt/, and Child 27, who gave /weyǣt/. Younger children did not inflect the word.

14.	Cue Word.	Dual.	Plural.
	/ʔīd/	/ʔidēn/	/tælat ʔayǣdi/ (/ʔidēn/)
	'hand'	'two hands'	'three hands'

This was a familiar noun with an irregular plural which is seldom used. The dual form is the most common form, which may be used as plural in adult language.

Most older children inflected the noun for dual correctly, except Child 13, who inserted /-t/ before the suffix as though the noun ended in /-a/ (it is feminine); his utterance was /ʔidtēn/. Most used the dualized form of the noun for the plural. Child 14 pluralized it with the suffix /-āt/ and Children 15, 16, and 22 used the suffix /-ān/. Child 23 used an irregular vowel pattern /ʔiyād/ for the plural, similar to the irregular plural form in adult language.

15.	Cue Word.	Dual.	Plural.	Plural.
	/fuṭṭa/	/fuṭṭitēn/	/tælat_____/	/ʔitnāšar fuṭṭa/
	(nonsense)	'two_____'	'three_____'	'twelve_____'

This was a repetition of the nonsense word given in Item 4. It was repeated here to see whether there would be any change in the children's responses. The only significant difference in the responses was that fewer children used an irregular pattern the second time (whereas the first time, many patterned an irregular plural like the preceding word /guṭṭa/). More used the /-āt/ suffix plural.

16.	Cue Word.	Dual.	Plural.	Plural.
	/kūra ḥamra/	/kurtēn ḥumr/	/ʔarbaʕ kuwar ḥumr/	/sittāšar kūra ḥamra/
	'a red ball'	'two red balls'	'four red balls'	'sixteen red balls'

This was a familiar feminine noun modified in a noun phrase by an adjective of color. The noun has an irregular plural /kuwar/, and the adjective has the regular plural for adjectives of color. The adjective is inflected for plural after the dual and plural noun.

Children who inflected the noun for dual correctly inserted the /-t/ before the dual suffix, but most used the numeral 2 with the uninflected noun. Children 5, 22, and 23 used the numeral with a form of plural noun, leaving the adjective uninflected. Children 14 and 18 used the plural noun and changed the adjective form to masculine singular, /ʔaḥmar/.

Most children gave the correct form of irregular plural with the numeral 4, followed by the plural adjective. Several used the /-āt/ suffix for plural. Child 3 used the numeral 4 with the dualized form of the noun.

After the numeral 16, the noun phrase should be singular. Most children used the plural noun after this number, often not inflecting the adjective to agree with the noun.

The adjective was not in agreement with the noun in many responses for this item.

17.	Cue Word.	Dual.	Plural.
	/mūra/	/murtēn/	/xæmas____/
	(nonsense)	'two____'	'five_______'

This was a nonsense word with the same singular vowel pattern as the preceding word /kūra/. Fewer children inflected this noun for dual than the previous one, and fewer repeated the numeral 2 with a plural. For both the dual and plural, more children tended to repeat the form uninflected.

Only Children 23 and 29 patterned the plural after the irregular plural /kuwar/ of the preceding word. Most used the suffix /-āt/. Child 3 used the dualized form after the numeral; Child 27 invented a plural form /múrad/.

18.	Cue Word.	Dual.	Plural.
	/bulbul/	/bulbulēn/	/ʔarbaʕ balǣbil/
	'nightingale'	'two nightingales'	'four nightingales'

This was a fairly unfamiliar noun with two reduplicated syllables which has an irregular plural. Few children inflected it for dual; some inserted /-t/ before the dual suffix although the noun does not end in /-a/, saying /bulbultēn/. Many left the noun uninflected in both the dual (or after the numeral 2), and after the numeral 4.

Younger children did not inflect the noun for plural. Older ones who did often used the suffix /-āt/; only a few knew the irregular plural form. Child 22 invented a plural form /bulalǣb/.

19.	Cue Word.	Dual.	Plural.
	/rājul laṭīf/	/rajulēn luṭāf/	/sitt rijjǣla luṭāf/
	'a nice man'	'two nice men'	'six nice men'

This item was a familiar masculine noun modified by a familiar adjective in a noun phrase. Both the noun and the adjective have irregular plurals. The adjective is inflected for plural after the noun in dual and plural form.

Several older children inflected the noun for dual. Some inexplicably substituted the phoneme /g/ for /j/ in the dual form (which is the Cairene pronunciation of this word), saying /raglēn/. Many did not inflect the adjective for plural, whether it followed a dualized noun or one inflected for plural after the numeral 2.

For the plural, younger children did not inflect the noun. Older children used the correct irregular plural. Six children did not inflect the adjective for plural.

20.	Cue Word.	Dual.	Plural.
	/wēt/	/wetēn/	/sæbaʕ______/
	(nonsense)	'two______'	'seven______'

This nonsense word was given before in Item 13. More children created irregular plural patterns in this elicitation than in the first.

6.2.3. *Child Rules and Stages for Noun Pluralization*

It can readily be seen that the inflections for noun plurals are complex, and it is to be expected that children will experience difficulty in acquiring irregular plurals, probably overregularizing them for some time. In fact, this is the most difficult and latest aspect of the language structure to be mastered; older children in this study erred in pluralizing even familiar nouns. Responses to both real and nonsense nouns indicate a strong tendency to use the suffix /-āt/ to regularize irregular plurals or create plurals for new words. Children also tended to dualize nouns on the pattern of counting other nouns with numerals, i.e., to use the numeral 2 followed by the plural noun, and to use the plural noun after numerals 11 and above.

Based on data in the noun plural test, characteristics of acquisition of the pluralizing inflection for nouns and the use of nouns with numerals will be discussed.

6.2.3.1. *Noun Inflections for Plural*

6.2.3.1.1. *Quantitative Results of the Test*

Quantitative results of the test are presented in Tables 15 and 16, showing the relative number of types of plurals given for each noun. In the calculations, if a child gave both a correct and an incorrect response to an item, the correct response is counted. The emphasis is on determining the children's competence, rather than merely reporting their performance.

Referring to Table 15, the relative number of correct plurals given for real nouns varied greatly according to item. The more familiar nouns and the two with the regular plural /-āt/ were pluralized correctly by the highest percentage of children. The items /kælb/ 'dog', /rājul/ 'man', /guṭṭa/ 'cat', and /bēt/ 'house' were pluralized correctly by 65–75% of the children. The two regular items /warda/ 'flower' and /sajara/ 'tree', were correct for 60% and 50% respectively, and even the 'irregular' plurals given for these items were usually collective plurals, not invented forms; including the collective plurals as 'correct' would raise the percentages for these two nouns to about 75%.

Table 15

Number of children using correct noun plurals, real nouns

Noun	Total Responses (31 children)	Correct	Plural: Incorrect /-āt/	Plural: Incorrect[a] Irregular Pattern	Plural: Not Pluralized
kælb (kilǣb)/	31	24	0	1	6
guṭṭa (gúṭat)/	31	21	1	5	4
warda (wardāt)/	25	15	–	5	5
ṣubāʕ (ṣawābiʕ)/	31	5	5	6	15
wād (wilǣd)/	20	8	1	4	7
sajara (sajarāt)/	29	14	–	8	7
bēt (buyūt)/	30	19	0	1	10
ʔil-ɣēṭ (ɣeṭān)/	30	15	2	0	13
ʔīd (ʔidēn; ʔayǣdi)/	26	12	1	4	9
kūra (kuwar)/	28	15	6	2	5
bulbul (balǣbil)/	27	4	5	2	16
rájul (rijjǣla)/	28	21	0	0	7

[a] Including collective plurals and dualized forms used for plural.

Two nouns, /ṣubāʕ/ 'finger' and /bulbul/ 'nightingale' were pluralized correctly by only about 15% of the children. Other nouns were pluralized correctly by about 40–50% of the children.

For the incorrect plurals, there was no tendency to use either the /-āt/ plural or an irregular vowel form more often. Results varied with the item. For the most familiar nouns (/kælb/, /rājul/, /ʔil-ɣēṭ/, /bēt/), there was little inventing of new plurals; if not pluralized correctly, the noun was usually left uninflected. An exception was the familiar noun, /guṭṭa/ 'cat', for which several children gave invented plurals. The nouns /kūra/, /ṣubāʕ/ and /bulbul/ were the only nouns often pluralized with the regular /-āt/ suffix, the first probably because it ends in /-a/, and the others because their plurals are unfamiliar.

For most nouns, in only about 25% of the responses was the noun uninflected for plural. The two most difficult nouns, however, /ṣubāʕ/ and /bulbul/, were uninflected in about 50% and 60% of the responses respectively.

Referring to Table 16, there is no 'correct' plural form for nonsense nouns, although certain plural patterns may be more likely to be used intuitively with certain singular patterns.

The percentages of responses given for both types of plural and leaving the noun uninflected are about the same for all the nouns.

In the first elicitation of each noun, about 25–30% of the responses were pluralizations with the suffix /-āt/; in the second elicitation, this increased to 40–50%. This is compared to only about 3–8% for most real nouns, and 20%

for the most difficult ones. Nonsense nouns ending in /-a/ were pluralized with /-āt/ a larger percentage of the time than other nouns. Fewer irregular plural patterns were given for nonsense nouns than for real nouns (many included here were dual forms).

Table 16

Number of children using plural patterns, nonsense nouns

Noun	Total Responses (31 children)	Plural with /-āt/	Plural with Irregular Pattern	Not Pluralized
/dælb (mælb)/ (1)	31	7	5	19
/dælb (mælb)/ (2)	27	7	5	15
/fuṭṭa/ (1)	29	5	7	17
/fuṭṭa/ (2)	27	9	1	17
/ṣēda/	29	9	5	15
/wēt/ (1)	26	9	2	15
/wēt/ (2)	26	6	8	12
/mūra/	29	11	4	14

There are significant differences in number of responses with irregular plurals for two items. The word /fuṭṭa/ was pluralized with the irregular pattern /fúṭat/ four times in the first elicitation, when it followed the noun /guṭṭa/, which has this plural pattern. In the second elicitation, only one child used this pattern for plural and more used the /-āt/ type of plural. The word /wēt/ was pluralized with an irregular vowel pattern more often in the second elicitation.

For all nonsense nouns, about 50–60% of the responses were with the noun uninflected, as compared to about 25% for most real nouns.

6.2.3.1.2. *Development of the Use of Plurals*

The youngest children did not inflect the noun for plural. Examples from the responses of Children 1 and 2 on the test are:

Child 1,2	Cue	Child's Response	Gloss for Cue	Gloss for Child
	/ʔitnēn ʔēh/	/kælb/	'two what?'	'dog'
	/talǣta ʔēh/	/kælb/	'three what?'	'dog'
	/ḥidāšar ʔēh/	/kælb/	'eleven what?'	'dog'
	Cue	Child's Response	Gloss for Cue	Gloss for Child
Child 2	/xæmsa ʔēh/	/guṭṭa/	'five what?'	'cat'
	/ʔarbaʕa ʔēh/	/kulluhum ṣubāʕ/	'four what?'	'All of them (are) finger.'

Child 1,2	/talǣta ʔēh/	/kullu sajara/	'three what?'	'It's all tree.'
	/talǣta ʔēh/	/kulluhum bēt/	'three what?'	'All of them (are) house.'
Child 1	/ʔarbaʕa ʔēh/	/kulluhum kūra/	'four what?'	'All of them (are) ball.'
Child 1,2	/dōl ʔēh/	/dōl bulbul/	'those (are) what?'	'Those (are) nightingale.'

This can be called Stage I, and the rule for pluralization at this stage may be written:

Stage I:

$$T\ opt\ Pl$$
$$N_{sing} \Rightarrow (Pron) + N_{sing}$$

Older children often used this pattern. Its use tended to be correlated with the age of the child and lack of familiarity with the item. Older children used this pattern more often with unfamiliar and nonsense nouns.

It may be speculated whether responses to nonsense words were more often of this pattern because children may have been treating some as mass nouns, which cannot be pluralized. However, if the child was attentive to the pictures illustrating numerous items, and since cue numerals were sometimes given, this is not likely.

It was common for small children to express plurality by repeating the noun, such as Child 4 in Item 3, who responded /di guṭṭa w di guṭṭa/ 'This is a cat and this is a cat'.[40]

This is evidence that children learning Arabic tend to prefer use of the 'unmarked' form before learning the 'marked' forms of words, which is consistent with observations of child speech in other languages.

After the concept of plural is acquired, which may be considered Stage II, the child must learn which type of plural is required for each noun, and must differentiate between the general types, regular and irregular. If these children master irregular morphological inflections in the same manner as those observed in other languages, one would except to find overgeneralization of the regular forms (the suffixes /-āt/ and /-īn/) for irregular plurals, including replacement of some irregular plurals which may have been learned correctly as separate items earlier.

This overgeneralization of regular plural forms does occur, but there is not a clear 'stage' or time of development when all plurals are generalized in the same way. The regularized plural was invariably the /-āt/ feminine suffix, never the masculine one. This is probably because the regular masculine suffix is

[40] Chao reported the same type of pluralization in Chinese. Chao, 1951, 37.

reserved for reference to persons, whereas the regular feminine suffix is used much more widely, for feminine nouns (animate or inanimate) and even for a few masculine nouns.

Younger children who have a strong tendency to overgeneralize plurals with this /-āt/ suffix at the same time use certain familiar nouns with the correct irregular plural from the beginning and do not appear to 'backslide' into overgeneralizing these irregular forms once they are learned. Noun plurals like /kilǣb/ 'dogs', /buyūt/ 'houses', and /rijjǣla/ 'men', were never heard with the /-āt/ suffix. Either children used the correct irregular plural (as young as age 3.6) or the dual, or did not pluralize the noun at all. The rule for pluralization in Stage II may be written:

Stage II:

$$\begin{aligned} &T\ opt\ Pl \\ &N_{sing} \Rightarrow (Pron) + N_{pl1,2} \\ &\qquad N_{pl1} \rightarrow Ns + /\text{-āt}/ \\ &\qquad N_{pl2} \rightarrow non\text{-}/\text{-āt}/ \text{ plurals} \end{aligned}$$

Other types of plurals are grouped as one plural form, as opposed to the regular /-āt/ suffix plural, because they are not used for overgeneralization with unfamiliar words.

While no time of exclusive use of the /-āt/ suffix plural was observed, there is certainly a correspondence between the frequency of its use and the age of the children using it. It was most commonly used by children between ages 3½ and 6 (Child 3 to Children 13 and 14) in the test, and older children used it incorrectly less and less. This may be seen in Items 7 and 20. Although older children more often 'experimented' with plurals, sometimes inventing new ones with irregular patterns, the /-āt/ suffix form was strongly preferred for pluralizing nonsense nouns by children of all ages. Two items with real nouns elicited overgeneralization by most children regardless of age, the nouns /ṣubāʕ/ 'finger' and /bulbul/ 'nightingale', both of which have the same CVCV̄CVC pattern for plural, /ṣawābiʕ/ and /balǣbil/.

The overgeneralized use of the /-āt/ plural continues in the speech of some older children indefinitely, since even the oldest child in the study, age 15, incorrectly pluralized the noun /kūra/ 'ball' (Item 16) as /kurāt/, while several younger children knew the irregular plural. Instances of children correcting themselves from using the /-āt/ suffix to the irregular suffix were common enough to provide evidence that it is a strong and lasting impulse even after the child has learned the irregular form (Child 16 in Item 16; Child 22 in Item 18).[41]

[41] Ervin and Miller note that six-year-old children learning English may use an irregular and a regular inflection interchangeably, such as *buyed* and *bought*, where the pattern has been learned but is not established as a firm habit. Ervin and Miller, 1963, 125.

In spite of the diversity of responses among the children in their choice of plurals, individual children did not often change their response when an item was elicited a second time.

A stage of further development cannot be proposed as such, since the recognition and use of other irregular plural forms is gradual and apparently continues into adolescence.[42] Correct plurals are acquired item by item, just as singular vocabulary words are.[43]

6.2.3.2. *Noun Inflection for Dual*

6.2.3.2.1. *Quantitative Results of the Test*

Quantitative results regarding use of the dual inflection are presented in Table 17.

For real nouns, the percent of responses with the correct form of dualization varied by item. It was about 40% for most nouns. The noun /kælb/ was correctly dualized by only 31%, possibly because it was the first item in the test, and children tended to increase the use of the dual suffix with more 'practice' in the test. Regular nouns /warda/ and /sajara/ were correctly dualized 55–60% of the time, and, as expected, the noun /ʔīd/ 'hand', which has the dual form as the usual plural was correct in the highest percentage of responses, about 65%.

Nonsense nouns were correctly dualized only about 30–35% of the time; the noun /wēt/ was dualizeda larger percentage of the time in the second elicitation.

While nonsense nouns were dualized correctly less often, they were correspondingly left uninflected much more often and used with the numeral 2. About 50–70% of the responses for nonsense nouns were with the uninflected form, compared to 25–30% for real nouns. (The two difficult real nouns /ṣubāʕ/ and /bulbul/ were uninflected about 55% of the time, treated more like the nonsense nouns.)

Most real nouns were used in the plural with the numeral 2 in about 25–30% of the responses (with notable exceptions for the two difficult nouns and the noun /ʔīd/). Nonsense nouns were used in the plural with the numeral 2 only in about 4–8% of the responses (probably because a plural was never heard for these 'new' words).

[42] Adults said that they sometimes make errors in pluralizing nouns as "slips of the tongue". It is not uncommon for adults to disagree about plurals of unusual or rare words.

[43] These stages of development may be compared to those found by Ervin and Miller in English. Their conclusion was: "In sum, the acquisition of the plural contrast followed a simple pattern in most children from noncontrast to acquisition of particular instances of contrast, generalization several months after acquisition of particular instances, and finally, differentiation of irregular forms." Ervin and Miller, 1963, 34.

Table 17

Number of children using the dual inflection

Noun[a]		Total Responses (31 children)	Dual Correct Inflection	2 + Sing. (Uninflected)	2 + Plural
/kælb (kælbēn)/		29	9	8	12
/*dælb (dælbēn)/	(1)	29	10	18	1
/*dælb (dælbēn)/	(2)	25	8	14	3
/guṭṭa (guṭṭitēn)/		31	13	8	10
/*fuṭṭa (fuṭṭitēn)/	(1)	30	9	19	2
/*fuṭṭa (fuṭṭitēn)/	(2)	27	9	17	1
/warda (warditēn)/		22	13	6	3
/*ṣēda (ṣedtēn)/		31	9	19	3
/ṣubāʕ (ṣubaʕēn)/		29	12	17	0
/wād (wadēn)/		22	12	7	3
/sajara (sajartēn)/		30	17	5	8
/bēt (betēn)/		29	12	10	7
/*wēt (wetēn)/	(1)	29	8	21	0
/*wēt (wetēn)/	(2)	25	10	14	1
/ʔid (ʔidēn)/		28	18	10	0
/kūra (kurtēn)/		28	13	7	8
/*mūra (murtēn)/		28	9	18	1
/bulbul (bulbulēn)/		28	11	15	2
/rājul (rajulēn)/		28	13	8	7

[a] Nonsense nouns are marked with (*).

6.2.3.2.2. *Development of the Use of the Dual*

The earliest form of dualization observed, which may be considered Stage I, was the use of the numeral 2 followed by the uninflected, singular noun. Some examples from the test are:

Child 4, 6	/ʔitnēn kælb/	'two dog'
Child 6	/ʔitnēn guṭṭa/	'two cat'
Child 5, 6	/ʔitnēn fuṭṭa/	'two /fuṭṭa/'
Child 6	/ʔitnēn warda/	'two flower'
Child 9	/ʔitnēn warda ṣafra/	'two yellow flower'
Child 6, 9	/ʔitnēn ṣubāʕ/	'two finger'
Child 5, 6, 9	/ʔitnēn sajara/	'two tree'
Child 5, 6, 9	/ʔitnēn bulbul/	'two nightingale'

The rule for dualization at this stage may be written:

Stage 1:

T Opt Dual

$N_{sing} \Rightarrow$ /ʔitnēn/ + N_{sing}

Some children tended to use this pattern more than others, especially at about ages 4 and 5 (Children 5, 6, and 9).

The next stage, Stage II, is the use of the pluralized noun with the numeral 2, generalizing the pattern for numerals 3–10 (or for some children, for all numerals at this time). Examples are:

Child 3, 8, 9, 12, 14, 17	/ʔitnēn kilæ̅b/	'two dogs'
Child 3, 15, 18	/ʔitnēn guṭat/	'two cats'
Child 5	/ʔitnēn ṣedāt/	'two /ṣēda/s'
Child 9, 18	/ʔitnēn ʕayæ̅l sumr/	'two dark children'
Child 8	/ʔitnēn kurāt ḥumr/	'two red balls'
Child 20	/ʔitnēn kuwar ḥumr/	'two red balls'
Child 9, 14, 18, 23	/ʔitnēn rijjæ̅la/	'two men'

The rule for dualization at this stage may be written:

Stage II: *T Opt Dual*

$N_{sing} \Rightarrow$ /ʔitnēn/ $+ N_{pl}$

This pattern was commonly used by children age 5 (Children 8 and 9). It was also used by children considerably younger and older than this, and thus overlaps with Stage I.

The data show that the dualization suffix /-ēn/ was acquired relatively late for most children. It did not appear consistently in responses until about age 5 and 6 (beginning with responses from Children 8, 11, and 12) and older. Individual differences in age of mastery are evident; for example, Children 3 and 8, ages 3½ and 5, used the dualizing suffix for several nouns, while some older children like Children 10, 22, and 30, ages 5½, 8½ and 14, almost never used it. Most children older than age 6½ (beginning with Children 14 and 15) used the dual in alternation with the construction of numeral 2 + Noun, tending to dualize real, familiar nouns more often than unfamiliar and nonsense nouns.

Use of the dualization suffix was accurate, once acquired, even including the morphophonemic rule of adding /-t/ to nouns ending in /-a/ before the suffix. This is Stage III, mastery of the adult form of dualization, and the rule is the same:

Stage III:

T Opt Dual

$Ns \Rightarrow Ns + Af$

$Af \rightarrow$ /-ēn/

All children, regardless of age, used the Numeral + Noun construction for some dualized items, so the correct rule, once learned, was not strongly productive as would be expected in adult speech. All children gave evidence of understanding dualized nouns if the form was given after the child's incorrect response; if a child did not dualize the first few noun items in the test, the investigator sometimes 'reminded' him of dualization by dualizing the noun in question. The children usually readily repeated the form and some dualized other items thereafter.

It is possible that the testing situation inhibited use of the dual to some extent. Sometimes the numeral 2 was given as a cue with the picture ("This is a tree. These are two. Two what?") and the children may have been motivated to use the numeral in imitation of the cue numeral. Some children did, in fact, make redundant constructions like /ʔitnēn warditēn/ 'two flowers (dualized)' (Children 8 and 20, Item 5; Child 12, Item 11; Children 8, 14, 30, Item 14). Use of this cue numeral was avoided when possible, but was necessarily used when small children could not, or did not, count items in the illustrations.

6.2.3.3. *The Use of Nouns with Numerals*

6.2.3.3.1. *Quantitative Results of the Test*

Quantitative results regarding the use of nouns with numerals are presented in Table 18.

Real nouns were used in plural form after numerals 3–10 in about 65–70% of the responses, compared with 40–45% for nonsense nouns.

There were variations by item for both types of nouns. Familiar nouns (/kælb/, /guṭṭa/, /kūra/) were used in the plural more often, in about 80–85% of the responses; the two regular nouns /warda/ and /sajara/ were used in the plural more often, in about 75% of the responses. The two difficult nouns /ṣubāʕ/ and /bulbul/ were used in the plural only in 50% and 40% of the responses respectively. For nonsense nouns, the two ending in /-a/ (presumably easier to pluralize) were used in the plural in 50–55% of the responses.

Use of nouns in the singular after numerals above 10 was common but, as noted, this may be too high considering that some children who responded with singular (uninflected) nouns never used inflections at all. Real nouns were used in singular form in 50–60% of the responses, while the nonsense noun /fuṭṭa/ was used 75–80% of the time in the singular. This is probably because children had never heard a plural for this word.

6.2.3.3.2. *Development of the Use of Nouns with Numerals*

Data already presented for the younger children (Children 1 and 2) have shown that when the children are still using the singular form of the noun for plural, they do this even when it occurs after numerals. Usually the younger children did not repeat the numeral but on a few occasions it was repeated, forming a noun phrase. Examples are:

	Cue	Child's Response	Gloss for Cue	Gloss for Child
Child 1	/ʕašara ʔēh/	/ʕašara bēt/	'ten what?'	'ten house'
Child 3	/talǣta ʔēh/	/talǣta fuṭṭa/	'three what?'	'three /fuṭṭa/'
Child 6	/talǣta ʔēh/	/talǣta kælb/	'three what?'	'three dog'
Child 6	/xæmsa ʔēh/	/xæmsa guṭṭa/	'five what?'	'five cat'

The rule for noun pluralization which was given as Stage I should now be expanded to read:

$$N_{sing} \Rightarrow \left(\begin{Bmatrix} Pron \\ Num \end{Bmatrix}\right) + N_{sing}$$

Older children did not often use this pattern after the numerals 3–10 unless the noun was unfamiliar. For example, Child 30, age 14, used the uninflected nouns /mælb/, /wēt/, /fuṭṭa/, /mūra/, /bulbul/, and /ṣēda/ after numerals below 10, of which all but one are nonsense forms, and /bulbul/ is one of the difficult real nouns.

Table 18

Number of children using the correct noun form with numerals

Noun[a]	Total Responses (31 children)	Numbers 3–10[b] (plural)	Total Responses (31 children)	Numbers over 10[c] (singular)
/kælb/	31	25	26	16
/*dælb/ (1)	31	12	–	–
/*dælb/ (2)	27	12	–	–
/guṭṭa/	31	27	–	–
/*fuṭṭa/ (1)	29	12	26	19
/*fuṭṭa/ (2)	27	10	25	21
/warda/	25	20	–	–
/*ṣēda/	29	14	–	–
/ṣubāʕ/	31	16	–	–
/wād/	27	20	19	10
/sajara/	29	22	–	–
/bēt/	30	20	–	–
/ʔil-ɣēṭ/	30	17	–	–
/*wēt/ (1)	26	11	–	–
/*wēt/ (2)	26	14	–	–
/ʔīd/	26	17	–	–
/kura/	28	23	24	12
/*mūra/	29	15	–	–
/bulbul/	27	11	–	–
/rājul/	28	21	–	–

[a] Nonsense nouns are marked with (*).
[b] Both correct and incorrect plurals are counted.
[c] Many smaller children who used the singular noun here were probably in Stage I of noun pluralization and used only the singular noun in their speech (such as Children 1, 2, 4, 6, 7), so in evaluating the number of 'correct' singular responses here, at least 5 should be subtracted from the total.

It seems probable that besides the 'universal' tendency noted for smaller children to omit noun plural inflections, another factor which may contribute to omission of the plural inflection is the fact that children hear nouns used in the singular form in adult language after numerals above 10, and the 'special class' of nouns in the singular form after all numerals. This may reinforce the tendency to use a singular noun after a numeral. Most children used singular nouns after numerals in most items until about age 5 (Children 9 and 10). But individual differences were apparent; for example, Child 3, age 3½, used plural forms more often than did Children 6 and 7, ages 4 and 4½.

Corresponding with Stage II in the development of noun plurals, when the plural form is used, it is also used after numerals. Overgeneralizing from the adult pattern of using a plural noun after numerals 3–10, however, the children tended to use the plural noun with **all** numerals, including 2 (as was seen in Stage II for acquisition of the dual) and numerals above 10.

The rule given in Stage II of noun pluralization should be expanded to read:

$$N_{sing} \Rightarrow \left(\begin{Bmatrix} Pron \\ Num \end{Bmatrix}\right) + N_{\mathrm{pl}_{1,2}}$$

It is not surprising that for a time after learning the plural, children use it with all numerals including those above 10 which should be followed by a singular noun. This rule in adult language is counter-intuitive and data in the test showed that in many items, older children still did not differentiate between using a singular or plural noun after numerals above and below 10. Examples of responses are:

Item 1	Child 12, 15, 17, 18, 20, 23	/talǣta kilǣb/	'three dogs'
		/ḥidāšar kilǣb/	'eleven dogs'
Item 4	Child 15,21	/talǣta fuṭat/	'three /fuṭṭa/s'
		/ʔitnāšar fuṭat/	'twelve /fuṭṭa/s'
Item 8	Child 25, 28	/talǣta wilǣd sumr/	'three dark boys'
		/ḥidāšar wilǣd sumr/	'eleven dark boys'
Item 16	Child 12, 24, 29	/ʔarbaʕ kuwar ḥumr/	'four red balls'
		/sittāšar kuwar ḥumr/	'sixteen red balls'

It is assumed that eventually all children will learn the consistent use of plural nouns with numerals 3–10 and singular nouns with larger numerals, since this is the rule in adult speech and errors were never heard from adults. Mastery of the rule for the enumeration transformation in adult speech would be considered Stage III. No approximate age of mastery can be determined from the data, since correct and incorrect responses were made frequently by all age groups above age 5 (Children 8, 9, and above), and individual children were not consistent in their distinctions of numeral and noun agreement.

6.3. THE ACQUISITION OF INFLECTIONAL AFFIXES AND AGREEMENT FOR ADJECTIVES

6.3.1. *Rules for Adjective Inflection and Agreement in Adult Language*

6.3.1.1. *Adjective Inflections for Gender and Number*

Adjectives are inflected for gender and number.[44]

The masculine singular form of the adjective is the 'base' form and is the stem to which feminine and plural affixes are added. There is no dual inflection for adjectives. A few types of adjectives do not follow the general rules of inflection; only the major exceptional forms and those tested will be discussed here, and expressed as morphophonemic rules.

Participles are inflected like descriptive adjectives and will be discussed with adjectives.

6.3.1.1.1. *Adjective Inflections for Gender*

The suffix /-a/ is added to the stem form of the adjective to make it feminine singular; adjectives are not inflected for gender in the plural. In the present participle, the short vowel may be dropped.

Opt Rule F_1:

$$Adj\ s \Rightarrow Adj\ s + Af$$
$$Af \rightarrow /\text{-a}/$$

/kæbīr/	'big (m.sing.)'
/kæbīra/	'big (f.sing.)'
/rāyiḥ/	'going (m.sing.)' (active participle)
/rayḥa/	'going (f.sing.)'
/mabsūṭ/	'happy (m.sing.)' (passive participle)
/mabsūṭa/	'happy (f.sing.)'

Adjectives of color which have the regular masculine pattern are inflected for feminine gender with a special pattern (which is slightly changed if the word contains /y/ or /w/):

Opt Rule F_2:

$$Adj\ s_1 \Rightarrow X + Y$$
$$X + Y \Rightarrow X \times Z$$
$$X \rightarrow \text{Consonantal root}$$
$$Y \rightarrow \text{Masculine vowel pattern}$$
$$Z \rightarrow \text{Feminine vowel pattern CáCCa}$$

[44] Not including comparative adjectives and some special forms.

/ʔaḥmar/	'red (m.sing.)'
/ḥamra/	'red (f.sing.)'
/ʔasmar/	'dark, brown (m.sing.)'
/samra/	'dark, brown (f.sing.)'
/ʔabyaḍ/	'white (m.sing.)'
/bēḍa/	'white (f.sing.)'

Some adjectives of color are not inflected for gender:

/ḍæhabi/	'golden'
/bunni/	'brown'

6.3.1.1.2. *Adjective Inflections for Plural*

There are two types of plural inflections for adjectives, regular and irregular.

1. The regular plural suffix for adjectives is /-īn/. The adjective stem may undergo minor morphophonemic changes when suffixed. Primary stress is shifted to the long vowel of the suffix.

Past participles usually have the regular plural suffix. Present participles have the regular plural; the short vowel is dropped and the long vowel is shortened with a shift in primary stress.

Opt Rule Pl_1:

$$Adj\ s \Rightarrow Adj\ s + Af$$
$$Af \rightarrow \text{/-īn/}$$

/kwayyis/	'good (m.sing.)'
/kwayyisīn/	'good (pl.)'
/ṣuɣayyar/	'small (m.sing.)'
/ṣuɣayyarīn/	'small (pl.)'
/mæftūḥ/	'opened (m.sing.)' (passive participle)
/mæftuḥīn/	'opened (pl.)'

2. Some adjectives have irregular plurals, but there are fewer patterns for adjectives than for noun plurals. The same types of morphophonemic changes may occur for adjective stems as for noun stems.

Opt Rule Pl_2:

$$X + Y \Rightarrow X + Z$$
$X \rightarrow$ Consonantal root
$Y \rightarrow$ Singular vowel pattern
$Z \rightarrow$ Irregular plural vowel patterns

One pattern of irregular plural for adjectives is the most common.

/kæbīr/	'big (m.sing.)'
/kubār/	'big (pl.)'
/ṭawīl/	'tall (m.sing.)'
/ṭuwāl/	'tall (pl.)'

Another pattern is less common for adjectives of the same singular pattern.

/fægīr/	'poor (m.sing.)'
/fúgara/	'poor (pl.)'

Some adjectives have less common or unpredictable plural forms.

/zæki/	'intelligent (m.sing.)'
/ʔazkíya/	'intelligent (pl.)'

6.3.1.2. *Inflections for Comparison*

Most adjectives are inflected for the comparative by adding /ʔa-/ to the positive stem form, which usually results in a change in vowel pattern. Adjectives ending in /w/ or /y/, and adjectives with the last two consonants the same have a slightly different pattern.

Opt Rule $Comp_1$:

$Adj\ s \rightarrow X + Y$
$X + Y \Rightarrow X + Z$
$X \rightarrow$ Consonantal root
$Y \rightarrow$ Stem vowel pattern
$Z \rightarrow$ Vowel pattern CáCCaC

/kæbīr/	'big (m.sing.)'	/huwa kæbīr/	'He is big.'
/ʔakbar/	'bigger'	/huwa ʔakbar/	'He is bigger.'
/læzīz/	'delicious (m.sing.)'	/ʔil-ʔækl læzīz/	'The food (is) delicious.'
/ʔalæzz/	'more delicious'	/ʔil-ʔækl-da ʔalæzz/	'This food (is) more delicious.'

Comparative adjectives are not inflected for gender or number.

Participles and some adjectives cannot be inflected for comparison. The passive participle or adjective may be modified with the word /ʔaktar/ 'more' or the comparative form of a different adjective may be substituted.

Opt Rule $Comp_2$

$Adj \Rightarrow Adj + X$
$X \rightarrow$ /ʔaktar/

/mabsūṭ/	'happy (m.sing.)' (passive participle)
/mabsūṭ ʔaktar/	'more happy, happier'
/kwayyis/	'good (m.sing.)'
/ʔaḥsan/[45]	'better'

The addition of the definite article /ʔil-/ to the comparative form makes it superlative.

Opt Rule Sup:

$$Adj\ s_2 \Rightarrow X + Adj\ s_2$$
$$X \rightarrow /ʔil\text{-}/$$

/ʔakbar/	'bigger'	/huwa ʔakbar/	'He (is) bigger.'
/ʔil-ʔakbar/	'biggest'	/huwa ʔil-ʔakbar/	'He (is) the biggest.'

6.3.1.3. *Agreement of Adjectives and Nouns*

Adjectives (except quantifiers) follow the noun (or nominal) they modify and agree with singular nouns in gender and number.

Adjectives modifying dual and plural nouns are inflected with one plural form regardless of the duality or gender of the noun.

Opt Rule Adj Mod₁:

$$\begin{bmatrix} N_{ms} \\ N_{fs} \\ N_{d,pl} \end{bmatrix} \Rightarrow \begin{bmatrix} N_{ms} \\ N_{fs} \\ N_{d,pl} \end{bmatrix} + \begin{bmatrix} Adj_{ms} \\ Adj_{fs} \\ Adj_{pl} \end{bmatrix}$$

/mudarris kwayyis/	'a good teacher (m.sing.)'
/mudarrisa kwayyisa/	'a good teacher (f.sing.)'
/mudarrisīn kwayyisīn/	'good teachers (m.,f.)'
/mudarrisǣt kwayyisīn/	'good teachers (f.pl.)'
/mudarrisēn kwayyisīn/	'two good teachers (m.)'

Plural nouns which refer to inanimate objects may be modified by the adjective inflected for either plural or feminine singular, in free variation.[46]

Opt Rule Adj Mod₂

$$N_{inan} \Rightarrow N_{inan} + \begin{Bmatrix} Adj_{fs} \\ Adj_{pl} \end{Bmatrix}$$

/kutub jædīda/	'new books'
/kutub judǣd/	'new books'

[45] This is from the Classical Arabic word /ḥasan/ 'good'.
[46] Harrell *et al.*, 1963, 34. Lehn and Abboud, 1965, 184.

The collective plural form of nouns is modified with the adjective in the uninflected masculine singular form.

Opt Rule Adj Mod$_3$:

$$N_{coll} \Rightarrow N_{coll} + Adj_{ms}$$

/warda ḥilwa/	'a pretty flower'
/ward ḥilw/	'pretty flowers' (collective)

Adjectives agree with the nouns they modify in a NP construction in definiteness.

Opt Rule Adj Mod$_4$:

$$\begin{bmatrix} N_{indef} \\ N_{def} \end{bmatrix} \Rightarrow \begin{bmatrix} N_{indef} \\ N_{def} \end{bmatrix} + \begin{bmatrix} Adj_{indef} \\ Adj_{def} \end{bmatrix}$$

/warda ḥilwa/	'a pretty flower'
/ʔil-warda ʔil-ḥilwa/[47]	'the pretty flower'
/bēt kæbīr/	'a big house'
/betna l-kæbīr/	'our big house'

6.3.2. *The Adjective Test*

The adjective test was administered to all but two of the children. The test consisted of nine items. All were sentences containing adjectives which modified nouns in a noun phrase construction or adjectives as the predicate of an equational sentence. The adjective occurred in one form in the cue sentence, and then alternative nouns or pronouns were given as cues to be modified by the same adjective, eliciting different inflections of agreement for gender and number.

The first seven items were familiar adjectives with varying patterns for plural; the last two items were nonsense adjectives, one with the singular pattern of most descriptive adjectives, and one with the passive participle pattern.

A few items eliciting the comparative and superlative forms of adjectives were given to some children, but it proved impossible to elicit the forms. The children did not understand the purpose of sentences such as "This girl is big and so is this one, but she is ____". In the comprehension test described in Chapter 4, there was evidence that children comprehended the use of the com-

[47] This construction may be contrasted with an equational sentence, in which the definite noun would be modified by an indefinite adjective: /ʔil-warda ḥilwa/ 'The flower (is) pretty'.

parative form of the adjective (Item 16), and some comparative adjectives were used in free conversation.

The results of the adjective test are presented by item. For each item, the cue adjective and adult forms of inflection are given. The responses of Child 31 are taken as the adult form.

The Adjective Test.

1. Cue Sentence. /ʔil-wād kæbīr/
'The boy (is) big (m.sing.).'

Cue Words.	(a) /ʔil-bit/ 'the girl'	(b) /ʔil-wadēn/ 'the two boys'	(c) /ʔil-wilǣd/ 'the boys'
Adult Forms.	(a) /kæbīra/ 'big (f.sing.)'	(b) /kubār/ 'big (pl.)'	(c) /kubār/ 'big (pl.)'

This item was a familiar adjective with an irregular plural form on a common pattern. The cue adjective was the uninflected base form. The feminine adjective was elicited with a feminine noun, and the plural adjective with a dualized noun and a plural noun.

For the feminine inflection, only Child 2 left the stem form uninflected after the feminine noun. The other children all responded correctly.

For the plural, only the youngest children attempted to regularize it with the regular suffix /-īn/, saying /kæbirīn/. All the other children knew the irregular plural form. Child 29 attempted to dualize the adjective to agree with the dualized noun, which is not done in adult language, saying /kubarēn/. After the plural noun, Children 3 and 6 left the adjective uninflected (although they had pluralized it before) and Child 12 used the feminine singular adjective (although he had pluralized it before).

2. Cue Sentence. /ʔiḥna mabsuṭīn/
'We (are) happy (pl.)'

Cue Words.	(a) /ʔæna/ 'I'	(b) /ʔinta (ʔinti)/ 'You (m.,f.)'
Adult Forms.	(a) /(ʔinti) mabsūṭa/ 'You (are) happy (f.sing.).'	(b) /(ʔæna) mabsūṭ(a)/ 'I (am) happy (m.,f.).'

This adjective was a familiar passive participle form, which has a regular plural with the suffix /-īn/. The plural was the cue form. The masculine and feminine singular forms of the adjective were elicited with pronouns. The investigator used *I*, which required the child to respond with the feminine singular adjective, and the child was then asked to modify *you*, referring to himself, either masculine or feminine.

All children inflected the adjective for feminine when refering to the investigator. All children inflected the adjective correctly for gender when referring to themselves except Child 8, who used the adjective in plural form after the pronoun *I*. The form referring to himself was elicited first, right after the cue adjective was given; he was probably imitating it.

3. Cue Sentence.	/ʔir-rājul fagīr/ 'The man (is) poor (m.sing.).'	
Cue Words.	(a) /ʔis-sitt/ 'the woman'	(b) /humma/ 'they'
Adult Forms.	(a) /fagīra/ 'poor (f.sing.)'	(b) /fúgara/ 'poor (pl.)'

This adjective was familiar, but has an irregular plural. The cue form was the uninflected masculine form, and the adjective was elicited in the feminine and plural.

All children inflected the adjective correctly for feminine.

Plural forms varied. The youngest cildren tended to regularize the plural with the suffix /-īn/; Child 9 used the regularized suffix but also changed the vowel pattern to match that of the irregular plural, saying /fugarīn/. Child 8 repeated the feminine singular form for the plural. Inventive irregular forms were given by Children 11 and 12, which included /fagūr/, /fugr/, and /fugāra/. Others either gave the correct plural, /fúgara/, or used a more common irregular pattern for the adjectives of this type, /fugār/ (like /kubār/). Children 16 and 18 used both forms for the plural.

4. Cue Sentence.	/hiya kwayyisa/ 'She (is) good (f.sing.).'	
Cue Words.	(a) /ʔaḥmad/ 'Ahmad'	(b) /ʔaḥmad w ʔuxtu/ 'Ahmad and his sister'
Adult Forms.	(a) /kwayyis/ 'good (m.sing.)'	(b) /kwayyisīn/ 'good (pl.)'

This was a familiar adjective with a regular plural. The cue form was inflected for feminine singular, and it was elicited in the masculine singular and plural.

It was expected that this would be an easy item, and this was the case. All children gave the uninflected stem form for the masculine singular. All gave the regular plural form with the /-īn/ suffix except Child 5, who used the feminine singular form (possibly a repetition of the cue adjective) and Child 12, who used an irregular form /kwayyísu/.

5. Cue Sentence.	/ʔil-mudarris ṭawīl/ 'The teacher (m.) (is) tall (m.sing.).'	
Cue Words.	(a) /ʔil-mudarrisa/ 'the teacher (f.)'	(b) /ʔil-mudarrisīn/ 'the teachers'
Adult Forms.	(a) /ṭawīla/ 'tall (f.sing.)'	(b) /ṭuwāl/ 'tall (pl.)'

This was a familiar adjective with an irregular plural. It was in the uninflected masculine form as a cue, and was elicited in the feminine and plural. The eliciting noun had a regular plural pattern with the suffix /-īn/, while the adjective did not.

All children inflected the adjective correctly for feminine.

Only Child 3 regularized the adjective plural with the suffix /-īn/, saying /ṭawilīn/, and Child 9 used the regularized suffix and changed the vowel pattern as well. Children 5, 6, and 27 used the feminine singular form of the adjective with the plural noun (Child 27 corrected this to the plural form) and Children 8 and 24 used the uninflected masculine form. All other plurals were the correct irregular form /ṭuwāl/, except for the response of Child 23, who used an irregular pattern /ṭúwala/ (like /fúgara/).

6. Cue Sentence. /ʔil-bēt kæbīr/
'The house (is) big (m.sing.).'
Cue Word. /ʔil-buyūt/
'the houses'
Adult Form. /kubār/ ~ /kæbīra/
'big (pl.)' 'big (f.sing.)'

This familiar adjective (elicited before in Item 1) was repeated with an inanimate noun, and the cue was the uninflected masculine form. The plural of the inanimate noun was used to elicit the modifying adjective, which could be either the plural or the feminine singular form, in free variation.

A few children (Children 3, 6, 7, 17, and 24) left the adjective uninflected, which was incorrect. Seven children used the feminine form and 14 used the plural; if the plural was used, it was inflected with the correct irregular pattern.

7. Cue Sentence. /ʔil-bēḍa læzīza/
'The egg (is) delicious (f.sing.).'
Cue Word. /ʔil-bēḍ/
'the eggs (collective pl.)'
Adult Form. /læzīz/
'delicious (m.sing.)'

This adjective was familiar and was elicited modifying a collectively pluralized noun. The cue form was the feminine adjective modifying a feminine noun, and the collective plural must be modified by the uninflected masculine singular adjective.

Only Children 3, 9, 29 and 31 used the correct masculine singular form /læzīz/ after the collective plural (and probably the two youngest children were partially imitating the model rather than using the correct form intentionally). Children 6, 12, 17, 18 and 21 used the feminine adjective, possibly treating the noun like an inanimate noun with a counted plural.

Most children treated the noun like other plurals and used the plural adjective. In fact, some repeated the sentence using /dōl/ 'these' as the head word before the plural adjective. Of those who used a plural form, most knew the irregular plural /luzǣz/. Child 8 regularized it with the suffix /-īn/, saying /læzizīn/. Children 15 and 23 patterned the plural on the other common irregular pattern /lúzaza/, and Child 14 invented two irregular plural forms, /luzūza/ and /luzīza/.

8. Cue Sentence. /ʔil-bit kamīna/
'The girl (is) (nonsense adjective, f.sing.).'
Cue Words. (a) /ʔil-wād/ 'the boy' (b) /humma/ 'they'
Adult Form. (a) /kamīn/ (b) /______/

This item was a nonsense adjective, of the same singular pattern as many adjectives elicited in the test. The cue adjective was inflected for feminine, and it was elicited in the masculine and plural forms. There is no 'correct' form for plural, although the plurals for real adjectives of this pattern would suggest the forms /kumān/, /kumǣn/, /kúmana/ as the most likely.

All children used the uninflected masculine singular form correctly.

For the plural, most chose one of the irregular patterns, /kumān/, /kumǣn/, or /kúmana/. Children 6, 8, 12, 14, 17 and 18 did not inflect the adjective for plural; Children 3 and 7 used the regular /-īn/ suffix, saying /kaminīn/, and Child 19 used the /-āt/ noun plural suffix, saying /kaminǣt/, which is not used for pluralizing adjectives in adult language.

9. Cue Sentence. /ʔir-rājul mændūb/
'The man (is) delegated (m.sing.).'
Cue Words. (a) /ʔis-sitt/ 'the woman' (b) /humma/ 'they'
Adult Forms. (a) /mændūba/ 'delegated (f.sing.)' (b) mændubīn/ 'delegated (pl.)'

This adjective is a real word in the language, but since it is not in the children's vocabulary, it was used as a nonsense noun here. It is the passive participle form, and has a regular plural with the suffix /-īn/.

It was expected that this item would be inflected with the regular forms. All children inflected it correctly for feminine.

Children 11, 18, 20 and 30 used the uninflected form for plural. All other children used the regular plural suffix /-īn/ except Child 15, who used an irregular pattern /mænadīb/ (like the word /mæjnūn/ 'crazy', which has the plural /mæjanīn/).

6.3.3. *Child Rules and Stages for Adjective Inflection and Agreement*

The stages and characteristics of development for adjective inflection and agreement will be discussed, based mainly on data from the adjective test. Relevant data from spontaneous conversation and the elicitation test for noun plurals will also be considered.

6.3.3.1. *Adjective Inflections for Gender and Number*

6.3.3.1.1. *The Inflection for Gender*

1. Quantitative Results of the Test: quantitative results of items in the adjective test in which the feminine inflection was elicited were definitive. In fully 100% of the responses for all items, the adjective was inflected correctly for feminine with the suffix /-a/ added to the masculine stem form.
2. Development of the Use of the Inflection for Gender: since no children inflected the adjectives for feminine incorrectly in the adjective test, no stages can be postulated for the acquisition of the feminine inflection. Apparently the inflection is acquired very early and since it is simple and always regular, errors are not made.

In the noun plural test, the feminine inflection for adjectives of color was used and repeated accurately in phrases, but was not elicited directly from the masculine form for these adjectives (it has a different vowel pattern; not the suffix /-a/). In many cases, children demonstrated their awareness of the relationship between the masculine and feminine forms of color adjectives by substituting the masculine for the feminine form. For example, in Item 16 of the noun plural test, several pluralized /kūra ḥamra/ 'a red (f.sing.) ball' as /kuwar ʔaḥmar/ 'red (m.sing.) balls' (although this is incorrect agreement here). When the adjective was inflected for feminine, it was correct.

6.3.3.1.2. *The Inflections for Plural*

1. Quantitative Results of the Test: quantitative results of items in the adjective test in which the plural inflections were elicited are presented in Table 19. Where both a correct and an incorrect response were given for an item, the correct response is counted.

The number of correct plurals for adjectives varied with the item. The number of responses was a high of about 90% for the adjective /kwayyis/ 'good', which has a regular plural, and a low of 50% for the adjective /fagīr/ 'poor', which has an uncommon irregular plural. For the adjective /fagīr/, a large number of irregular 'invented' plurals were also given. The other two

Table 19

Number of children using types of adjective plural inflections

Adjective[a]	Total Responses (31 children)	Correct	Incorrect (-īn)	Incorrect Irregular Pattern	Incorrect Feminine Form	Not Pluralized	
/kæbīr(kubār)/ (dual; plural)	22–23	20–17	0–4	1–0	0–1	1–1	
/fagīr/ (fúgara)	25	12	4	8	1	0	
/kwayyis/ (kwayyisīn)	26	24	–	1	1	0	
/ṭawīl/ (ṭuwāl)	27	20	1	1	3	2	
		/-ān/ /-ǣn/	/CúCaCa/	/-īn/	Other Irregular Pattern	Feminine Form	Not Pluralized
/*kamīn/	25	13	3	2	1	0	6
/*mændūb/	25	–	–	20	1	0	4

[a] Nonsense adjectives are marked with (*).

real adjectives have the same singular and plural vowel patterns. For the first, /kæbīr/ 'big', 90% of the responses were the correct plural with a dualized noun, and 75% with a plural noun. For /ṭawīl/ 'tall', 75% of the responses were with the correct plural form.

The two nonsense adjectives were of very different singular patterns and consequently elicited different types of plurals. For /kamīn/, about 65% of the plurals were the 'intuitive' irregular patterns usually given this type of adjective, and 25% of the responses were with the uninflected adjective (as compared to almost no responses with the uninflected form for the real adjectives). For /mændūb/, the passive participle, the regular suffix /-īn/ was used in 80% of the responses; the other responses were mostly with the uninflected form.

2. Development of the Use of the Inflections for Plural: the development of plural inflections for adjectives appears to follow the same stages of development found for the acquisition of noun plurals.

The younger children sometimes used the uninflected adjective for plural. Examples of responses from the adjective test are:

	Cue	Child's Response	Gloss for Cue	Gloss for Response
Child 3	/ʔil-wadēn/	/ʔitnēn kæbīr/	'the two boys'	'two big (m.sing.)'
Child 6	/ʔil-wilǣd/	/kæbīr/	'the children'	'big (m.sing.)'
Child 8	/ʔil-mudarrisīn/	/ṭawīl/	'the teachers'	'tall (m.sing.)'
Child 3, 7, 17, 24	/ʔil-buyūt/	/kæbīr/	'the houses'	'big (m.sing.)'
Child 6, 8, 12, 14, 17, 18	/humma/	/kamīn/	'they'	'/kamīn/ (m.sing.)'
Child 11, 18, 20	/humma/	/mændūb/	'they'	'/mændūb/ (m.sing.)'

This can be called Stage I, and the rule for pluralization of adjectives at this stage may be written:

Stage I:

T Opt Pl:

$$N_{sing} + Adj_{sing} \Rightarrow N_{pl} + Adj_{sing}$$

The frequency of use of this pattern was correlated with the children's age (although not strongly), and more so with the familiarity of the item. Only younger children used the uninflected adjective for plural with familiar words, and even this was not common. With the nonsense word /kamīn/, which would seem intuitively to have some irregular pattern as plural, six children of various ages left the adjective uninflected in the plural. The nonsense word /mændūb/ was left uninflected by fewer children, probably because it was 'easier' to pluralize with the regular suffix. The other item for which the uninflected adjective was used for plural was the noun /buyūt/ 'houses', which is an inanimate noun, and this may have led to a confusion as to which adjective form to use with it.

When the children used plural inflections for adjectives, there was a clear tendency for younger ones to regularize all plurals with the regular suffix /-īn/. This may be considered Stage II in the acquisition of the plural inflection. Some children overgeneralized the plural for almost every adjective in the test. Examples of responses with overgeneralized plurals are:

	Cue	Child's Response	Gloss for Cue	Gloss for Response
Child 3, 5, 7, 13	/ʔil-wilǣd/	/kæbirīn/	'the children'	'big'
Child 3, 5, 7, 9	/humma/	/fagirīn/	'they'	'poor'
Child 3	/ʔil-mudarrisīn/	/ṭawilīn/	'the teachers'	'tall'
Child 8	/ʔil-bēḍ/	/læzizīn/	'the eggs'	'delicious'
Child 3, 7	/humma/	/kaminīn/	'they'	'/kamīn/'

Although the /-āt/ suffix was used for regularization of noun plurals (and never the masculine plural /-īn/), the children apparently had learned that adjectives are not pluralized with /-āt/. Only two examples were found where children pluralized the adjective with this suffix. In the noun plural test, Item 9, Child 9 produced /ṣuɣayyarāt/ as the plural for the adjective /ṣuɣayyar/ 'small'. In the adjective test, Item 8, Child 19 pluralized the nonsense adjective as /kaminǣt/.

The rule for pluralization in Stage II may be written:

Stage II:

T Opt Pl:

$$N_{sing} + Adj_{sing} \Rightarrow N_{pl} + Adj_{pl_{1,2}}$$
$$Adj_{pl_1} \rightarrow Adj\ s + /\text{-īn}/$$
$$Adj_{pl_2} \rightarrow non\text{-}/\text{-īn}/ \text{ plural patterns.}$$

Other types of plurals are grouped as one plural form, as opposed to the /-īn/ suffix plural, because they are not used for regularization.

As with the noun plurals, the various stages postulated for adjective pluralization overlap. Children of all ages used both 'rules', and individual children varied in the type of plural used according to item. Younger children did tend more often to make errors in using both types of pluralization rules; most were made by children ages 3–5 (Children 3 to 9). Unlike the use of the uninflected adjective for plural, which was common for all ages, the only older child who overregularized the adjective with the suffix /-īn/ was Child 13, age 6.

Stage III would be the acquisition of the irregular plural patterns for adjectives. Apparently this is acquired much earlier than plural patterns for nouns, probably because there is a stronger, more predictable pattern relation between singular and plural adjectives of various types.

High percentages of children did not err in producing the irregular plurals of familiar adjectives. There was little 'inventing' of irregular adjective plurals; for unfamiliar adjectives or in incorrect responses, the patterns chosen were still very common irregular patterns (this was also the case with the adjective /laṭīf/ 'nice', used in Item 19 in the noun plural test, in which the two incorrect forms were /ḷúṭafa/ and /luṭf/).

It may be noted that there is a striking difference in the number of correct responses for adjective plurals as compared to noun plurals.

The regular plural for adjectives of color was elicited in some items in the noun plural test. Almost all children used the correct plural form /CuCC/ with plural nouns. A few errors were the attempts of Children 3 and 5 to dualize an adjective with a dualized noun in Item 5, resulting in the form /ṣafritēn/ 'yellow'. In this same item, Children 14 and 24 used /ṣafr/ as the plural pattern, which does not exist in adult language. In Item 8 all correctly pluralized the adjective /sumr/ 'dark'. In Item 9, the adjective /kæbīr/ was pluralized correctly; the adjective /ṣuɣayyar/ was pluralized by Child 9 with the suffix /-āt/. In Item 16, the correct plural, /ḥumr/ 'red', was correctly given by all children.

Inflections of active participles were not elicited in the adjective test. In imitations and spontaneous conversation, however, inflected forms of the active participles were common. Children repeated the participles correctly and inflected them correctly for gender and plural in conversation.

6.3.3.2. *Agreement of Adjectives and Nouns*

6.3.3.2.1. *Agreement for Gender*

1. Quantitative Results of the Test: quantitative results of the adjective test showing gender agreement between nouns (and nominals) and adjectives are presented in Table 20.

These results show nearly 100% agreement in the gender of nouns and the adjectives modifying them for the responses of all children. There are only three responses out of the total 205 which are incorrect.

In the noun plural test, adjectives of color which modified nouns were more often not in agreement. The errors for gender were:

Item 5	Child 18	/warda ʔaṣfar/	'yellow (m.sing.)	flower (f.sing.)'
Item 9	Child 13	/ḥidāšar ʕayil sumr/	'eleven dark (pl.)	children (sing.)'
	Child 19, 27, 31	/ḥidāšar walad sumr/	'eleven dark (pl.)	boys (sing.)'
Item 18	Child 14	/kūra ʔaḥmar/	'red (m.sing.)	ball (f.sing.)'
	Child 19, 25	/kūra ḥumr/	'red (pl.)	ball (f.sing.)'

Table 20

Number of children using correct nominal-adjective Agreement, gender

Gender of Nominal	Total Responses (31 children)	Masculine Adjective	Feminine Adjective	Plural Adjective
(Masculine)				
(ʔæna/ (m.) (mabsūṭ)	14	13	0	1
(ʔaḥmad/ (kwayyis)	27	27	0	0
/wād/(kamīn)	25	25	0	0
(Feminine)				
/bit/ (kæbīra)	28	1	27	0
/ʔæna/ (f.) (mabsūṭa)	9	0	9	0
/ʔinti/ (mabsūṭa)	25	0	25	0
/sitt/ (fagīra)	25	0	25	0
/ʔil-mudarrisa/ (ṭawīla)	27	0	27	0
/sitt/ (mændūba)	25	1	24	0

In data from conversation, a few examples of non-agreement for gender were also found:

Child 4	/lōnu wiḥša/	'It's color (m.sing.) (is) ugly (f.sing.).'
Child 7	/da warda w da ʔit-tænya/	'That (m.sing.) (is) a flower (f.sing.) and that (m.sing.) (is) the other (f.sing.).'

There were many examples of correct agreement. Present participles were used correctly; for example, Children 1 and 2 used /ʕayza/ 'I want' (lit., 'wanting') inflected for feminine when referring to themselves. Child 4 used the form /gaʕda/ 'sitting', inflected for feminine to refer to her mother. Some other examples are:

Child 4	/warda ḥilwa/	'a pretty (f.sing.) flower (f.sing.)'
	/lōnu ʔaḥmar/	'It's color (m.sing.) (is) red (m.sing.).'

Child 7	/ʔæna ʕayza ʕarabiya/	'I want (f.sing.) a car.'
	/da ʕāwiz yāxud di/	'That one (m.sing.) wants (m.sing.) to take this.'
	/šayfa/	'See (f.sing.)?' (to a girl)

2. Development of Agreement for Gender: in these data, the children observed had already acquired the gender inflections and mastered the basic concept of adjective agreement. It appears that this is learned early, since Child 1 was already using the pattern productively. Few errors were observed either in the adjective and noun plural tests or in conversation. The children used adjectives inflected for feminine even with nouns which were unmarked for gender, such as /sitt/ 'lady' and /bit/ 'girl'. (Further investigation is needed to determine the extent of use of feminine adjectives with unmarked feminine nouns which are inanimate.)

In the few errors of agreement made, usually the masculine, uninflected adjective was used for a feminine noun (two examples occur in the adjective test), although one example of the use of a feminine adjective with a masculine noun is Child 4's utterance /lōnu wiḥša/ 'It's color (m.sing.) (is) ugly (f.sing.)'.

There were not a sufficient number of errors observed to characterize their patterns of development.

There was no parallel to Slobin's observation that Russian-speaking children tend to learn the grammatical gender of nouns late, at first generalizing with one inflectional ending.[48] This is probably because the marking for gender in Arabic is not as complex as in some inflected languages, and there is a stronger semantic correlation.

6.3.3.2.2. *Agreement for Number*

1. Quantitative Results of the Test: the quantitative results of the adjective test showing number agreement between nominals and adjectives are presented in Table 21.

The first five nouns should be followed by an adjective inflected for plural, and few children erred in this agreement. The adjective /ṭawīl/ 'tall' was most often left uninflected or used in the feminine, although it is as familiar as the adjective /kæbīr/ 'big' and has the same irregular pattern.

The next item with the inanimate noun /buyūt/ 'houses' may take either a feminine singular or a plural adjective. Over half of the children responded with the plural adjective, twice as many as used the feminine singular alternative. 20% of the responses were with the uninflected adjective.

[48] Slobin, 1966a, 142.

The noun /bēḍ/ 'eggs', a collective plural, should have been followed by the uninflected masculine adjective. The children showed a strong tendency to treat this noun like other pluralized nouns. Only five, or about 20%, of the responses were correct, and these were usually made by older children. About 50% of the responses were with the plural adjective, and 25% with the feminine adjective, indicating that the correct modification of collectively pluralized nouns is learned late.

Table 21

Number of children using correct nominal-adjective Agreement, number

Plural Nominals[a]	Total Responses (31 children)	Masculine Singular (Uninflected)	Feminine Singular	Plural
/ʔil-wadēn/ (kubār)	22	1	0	21
/ʔil-wilǣd/ (kubār)	23	1	1	21
/humma/ (fúgara)	25	0	1	24
/ʔaḥmad w ʔuxtū/ (kwayyisīn)	26	0	1	25
/ʔil-mudarrisīn/ (ṭuwāl)	27	2	3	22
/ʔil-buyūt/ (kæbīra) (kubār)	26	5	7	14
/ʔil-bēd/ (læzīz)	24	5	6	13
/*humma/ (kumān) (kúmana)	25	6	0	19
/*humma/ (mændubīn)	25	4	0	21

[a] Nonsense adjectives are marked with (*).

The two nonsense adjectives were usually inflected for plural, although they showed a higher percentage of responses with the uninflected form than that found for the first five real adjectives (about 20% as compared to about 5%).

In the noun plural test, similar results were found. There were more examples of not using a plural adjective (usually the uninflected masculine form was used instead), and some examples of incorrectly modifying a collectively pluralized noun with a plural adjective. Examples of incorrect modification are:

Item 9	Child 14	/ṣubyān ʔasmar/	'dark (m.sing.) boys'
	Child 15	/wilǣd ʔaṣmar/	'dark (m.sing.) boys'
Item 10	Child 8, 9, 11, 14, 18, 20, 21, 23	/rijjǣla laṭīf/	'nice (m.sing.) men'
Item 11	Child 21, 23	/sajar kubār/	'big (pl.) trees (coll. pl.)'
	Child 10	/kulluhum kæbīra/	'All of them (are) big (f.sing.)'
Item 15	Child 14, 24	/ward ṣafr/	'yellow (pl.) flowers (coll.pl.)'
Item 18	Child 9, 14, 18	/kuwar ʔaḥmar/	'red (m.sing.) balls'

For the inanimate noun /kuwar/ 'balls', the adjective may be feminine singular or plural, and as in the adjective test, more than half of the responses were with the plural adjective.

In imitations and conversation, the agreement was almost always correct. Some nominal-adjective constructions modified correctly for number were:

Child 2	/bit kæbīra/	'a big girl'
	/guṭṭa ṣafra/	'a yellow cat'
Child 4	/ʕayǣl ṣuɣayyarīn/	'small children'
Child 5	/ʕayzīn nīji fiṣ-ṣubḥ/	'(We) want to come in the morning.' (present participle)

The only error observed was:

Child 4	/humma kæbīr/	'They (are) big (m.sing.).'

2. Development of Agreement for Number: it is clear that the tendency to use the uninflected masculine adjective with plural nouns corresponds with the age of the children, because it is used more often by younger ones (see Stage I of adjective plural inflection). Results of the adjective test show that it also corresponds with familiarity of the adjective and with uncertainty as to how to modify a particular noun, such as an inanimate noun. The adjective /kwayyis/ 'good', which has the regular plural /-īn/, was never left uninflected for plural, while the irregular adjective /laṭīf/ 'nice' (in the noun plural test) was often uninflected with both dual and plural nouns.

Based on this evidence, it is possible to speculate that children may begin by using uninflected adjectives at first, especially with unfamiliar nouns, but they probably acquire the concept of inflecting adjectives for plural as early as they acquire the noun pluralization concept. They may even use the plural adjectives with more consistency thereafter, since the pluralization is simpler. Correct agreement between the nominal and adjective is probably acquired as early as the acquisition of the inflections themselves.

6.4. SUMMARY

The results of this study show some general characteristics in the children's acquisition of morphology:

1. In the speech of the youngest children, early morphology was characterized by the use of uninflected or 'unmarked' words.
2. Some types of inflections were acquired and mastered before others.
3. The first to be acquired were the regular, most commonly recurring inflections. The regular inflections were productive patterns, and were overgeneralized and used with words which required irregular inflections.

4. The regular inflections for adjectives and their use in agreement with modified words was mastered by about age 3; irregular inflections were learned by age 5.
5. Regular inflections for noun plurals and the use of the plural noun with some numerals were acquired by about age 3; the dual inflection and most irregular noun plurals were acquired by about age 5 or 6. Errors were still made for some noun plural inflections by the oldest children studied, who were ages 13–15.
6. Nonsense words were left uninflected more often than real words, and the use of regular inflections was usually preferred for nonsense words.
7. There was no significant difference in the performance of boys and girls. There were, however, individual differences in the level of mastery of inflections.

7

CONCLUSION

7.1. REVIEW OF FINDINGS IN THIS STUDY

The data obtained in this study revealed many facts about the manner in which children acquire Egyptian Arabic as a native language. Data will be reviewed regarding the phonological, syntactic, and morphological levels of language structure, with considerations for semantic development as well.

The order of acquisition of various structures was approximately as expected, and was similar in most respects to the acquisition of language structures observed in other languages.

The babbling stage began at about six months, which is the same age as that observed in other linguistic communities. In early imitation, children simplified the phonology of model words, but retained stressed syllables. The sounds produced were mainly front consonants and a variety of vowels.

Phonology was acquired in stages, and the increase in phonemes was more sudden than that observed for some middle-class children learning other languages. Stage I of phonemic development began at about age 1–1½, with the acquisition of bilabial and laryngeal stops and nasal consonants, and the three primary vowels. There was no voiced-voiceless opposition. Stage II, at about age 2½, included other stops, fricatives, and sounds with different points of articulation; not yet acquired were pharyngeal and alveo-palatal consonants, some consonant clusters, and diphthongs. There was no contrast for emphasis or doubling of vowels and consonants. Stage III, adult mastery, was achieved at about age 5. This may be compared to a similar order of acquisition of phonemes in other languages; however, these children acquired them at later ages than children in other studies.

In imitations, model words were reduced to the children's phonological level, and often final consonants were omitted. Stressed words and reference words were imitated, with function words and some inflections omitted. Inversion and substitution were also observed. These characteristics are similar to those observed in children's imitation in other studies. There was hypercorrection of some difficult sounds. Imitation tended to improve with age.

The comprehension test showed that most grammatical contrasts and contrasts with obvious semantic reference such as opposite adjectives or persons are learned early, by age 3. Colors and numbers are learned as late as age 6, which is later than that found for children in other studies.

Vocabulary development is about the same as in other languges; children began acquiring words at about age 1–1½, most of which were nouns, referring to people, foods, and objects in their environment. Much early vocabulary included 'baby talk' words, which generally had a simplified phonology and were uninflected.

On the grammatical level, most aspects of syntax were mastered before morphology, which is similar to observations in other languages.

Children were found to begin syntactic development by advancing from single-word utterances to utterances composed of two and three words, at about age 2½–3. The words could be distinguished as having Pivot or Open functions. These early sentences were reductions of adult sentences, in which function words, articles, and inflections were usually omitted. Word order was more flexible than that observed for children learning other languages. The semantic content of the sentences was similar to that in other languages. Children in this stage of development were about a year older than children observed in a similar stage learning English.

Three stages of development were found in the acquisition of the optional negative and interrogative transformations. For the negative, a negative word was used before a negative affix was acquired. For the interrogative, intonation was acquired first, then question words and their use with prepositions. The negative transformation was acquired by about age 3½, and the interrogative by age 5 or before. For both transformations, fewer complexities exist in the adult language and fewer syntactic errors were observed as compared with a language like English.

Inflections on the morphological level were the last to be mastered, and the order of acquisition was determined by their regularity and essentiality for conveyence of meaning. Rather than being suddenly acquired as 'rules', the use of inflections increased in frequency and accuracy with age, which was more like habit formation than rule learning.

Early morphology was characterized by the tendency to use uninflected words; in later development, there was a correlation between the frequency of use of uninflected words and age. Overregularized use of some inflections was common for nouns and adjectives. Unmarked strings were not found, as they have been in some other languages; by the time syntactic combinations were beginning, most inflections were also being used, at age 2½ or 3.

The first use of inflections began by age 2½, about the same age as found in studies in other languages. The age of mastery of inflections varied.

Some regular noun and adjective plural inflections and the adjective gender inflection were mastered by age 3. Adjective agreement and the use of plural nouns with numerals was learned by about age 3½. The dual inflection for nouns was mastered at age 5 or 6; irregular plural inflections for nouns and adjectives were not mastered, however, until age 6 and later, some as late as adolescence. For both noun and adjective inflections, stages of development were found.

For all parts of speech, there was a greater tendency not to inflect unfamiliar words, with a preference for using the unmarked form; this was demonstrated in the data as corresponding with age. It was also seen in the comparative amount of non-inflection for nonsense items.

Over-all mastery of the language system is not achieved until age 6 or 7; errors are still made in noun pluralization as late as age 14 and 15. This may be compared to estimates of age 4–5 for mastery of English, and 7–8 for Russian. Besides complexity of the native language, other factors which may account for this later development may be environmental.

Table 22 summarizes the approximate ages (within the nearest half-year) and relative order in which children acquire the various aspects of Arabic language structure.

7.2. IMPLICATIONS FOR THEORIES REGARDING LANGUAGE AND PRIMARY LANGUAGE ACQUISITION

Characteristics of children's acquisition of language may provide insights into both the nature of language structure and the nature of human learning. The way in which language is acquired is fairly uniform for all children in all linguistic communities, despite their lack of direct instruction and their finite and arbitrary linguistic experience. Some hypotheses about universal characteristics of language acquisition have been discussed in preceding chapters.

It may be assumed that universals of language learning reflect more general universals of the structure of the object learned, language. Some observers believe that there must be an innate linguistic structure which is the basis for every language; only such a universal nature of language would permit first-language learning to take place.[1]

Greenberg has investigated in some detail possible characteristics shared by all human languages, and arrived at some probable universals of structure on all linguistic levels.[2] He postulates that for all aspects of language, if more than one unit can function as a member of a category, one will be "unmarked" and

[1] Paul M. Postal, "Epilogue", *English Transformational Grammar*, eds., Roderick A. Jacobs and Peter S. Rosenbaum (Waltham, Mass., Blaisdell Publishing Co., 1968) p. 283.

[2] Joseph H. Greenberg, "Language Universals", *Current Trends in Linguistics*, Vol. 3, *Theoretical Foundations*, ed., T. A. Sebeok (The Hague, Mouton, 1966) pp. 61–112.

Table 22

Age and order of acquisition of Arabic language structure

Age	Aspect of Language Acquired
.6	Babbling stage.
1.0–1.6	Stage I of phonemic development: acquisition of bilabial stop and nasal, laryngeal consonants, semivowels, primary vowels.
1.6	Acquisition of first (uninflected) words; one-word sentences.
2.0	Intermediate stage of phonemic development: acquisition of dental stops, sibilants, velar consonants. Stage I in development of interrogation: beginning of use of interrogative intonation.
2.6	Stage II of phonemic development: acquisition of fricative consonants, lateral, all vowels. Earliest stage of syntactic development: two- and three-word sentences. Stage I in development of negation: beginning of use of negative words. Stage II in development of interrogation: beginning of use of question words. Beginning of use of morphological inflections. Stage I in development of noun pluralization: use of singular uninflected nouns for plural and with numerals.
3.0	Stage II in development of negation: use of negative words. Mastery of some regular noun and adjective inflections, and adjective gender inflection. Comprehension of basic grammatical and semantic contrasts.
3.6	Intermediate stage of phonemic development: acquisition of contrasts of vowel length and consonant gemination, emphasis, and diphthongs. Later stage of syntactic development: further development of the noun phrase. Stage III in development of negation: use of all types of negative. Stage II in development of noun pluralization: use of overregularized noun plural inflection. Stage II in development of adjective pluralization: use of overregularized adjective plural inflection. Mastery of adjective agreement. Use of plural nouns with numerals.
4.0	Stage I in development of dual inflection: use of numeral 2 with singular noun.
4.0–5.0	Stage III in development of interrogation: mastery of question words and their use with prepositions.
5.0	Complete mastery of phonological system.
5.0–5.6	Beginning of mastery of some irregular noun plural inflections. Stage II in development of dual inflection: use of numeral 2 with plural noun. Stage III in development of dual inflection: beginning of mastery of dual inflection.
6.0	Learning of colors and numbers.
6.0–7.0	General over-all mastery of language system.
7.0+	Further acquisition of some irregular noun plural inflections.

the others "marked". The unmarked item will be the most "basic" to the language, the most independent (less often neutralized or assimilated), and the most frequent. (Thus, it would presumably be the first to be recognized and acquired by the child.)

Some of Greenberg's findings regarding the marking of items in all languages are listed below.

1. Oral phonemes are unmarked; nasalized phonemes are marked.
2. The singular number is unmarked for nouns, adjectives, pronouns and verbs. It occurs the most frequently, with plural number next, and if dual number occurs, it is the least frequent.
3. If the language has only two genders, usually the masculine gender is unmarked.
4. The positive adjective is unmarked; comparative and superlative adjectives are marked. Often the superlative is formed with an additional affix.
5. For persons, the third person is the "least marked", the first person intermediate, an the second person is the "most marked".
6. The active voice is unmarked; the passive is marked.
7. The present tense is usually unmarked; the past tense is marked, and the future is always marked with an auxiliary or an affix.
8. The indicative mood is unmarked; other moods such as subjunctive are marked. However, the imperative mood is commonly a zero expression.
9. Lower numerals are unmarked, as compared to higher numerals. Inflectional distinctions may be neutralized above a certain number.
10. Positive sentences usually have zero expression; negation always has overt expression.
11. Declarative sentences are unmarked; the interrogative is marked, even if only by special intonation.

Greenberg states that "when, in a particular environment, no contrast occurs within a set of phonemes or lexemes which differ from each other only in a single feature, it is the unmarked feature which appears in this environment".[3] There is also greater allophonic or allomorphic variability of the unmarked member. The number of marked units in a language is never greater than the number of unmarked ones.

In Arabic, some of these generalizations can be applied to the language structure, and this may give an insight into why certain features are acquired before others.

For example, emphatic and fricative consonants could be considered marked. They are less frequent and were acquired later than non-emphatic and non-fricative consonants. Similarly, doubled vowels and consonants may be regarded as the marked members of pairs, which were acquired later than their

[3] Greenberg, 1966, 92.

single counterparts. The singular, unmarked form of nouns and adjectives was the first acquired and used by children. The unmarked masculine gender for adjectives and imperative verbs was preferred. The neutralized number agreement between nouns and higher numerals was at first applied with all numerals. Children tended to keep negative and interrogative elements outside the structure of unmarked positive and declarative sentences in early stages.

Many similar observations could be made for the acquisition of English, Russian, Spanish, and other languages. The same types of unmarked forms and structures are preferred in early language acquisition, which is possibly related to their greater frequency of occurrence, and to their greater simplicity for expressing meaning and fulfilling the function of communication.

Besides language universals helping account for language acquisition, characteristics of language acquisition may in turn have implications about other theoretical universals of language. One would look at the early 'reduced' utterances of children to find the most basic and primitive structure of a language. It can be seen that these child utterances are approximately the same for all languages thus far observed, regardless of some major differences in adult language structure.

Children tend to choose between alternatives on the basis of simplicity and essentiality. Recurring preferences for certain types of phonemes (stops, nasal consonants, the primary vowels), lexemes (uninflected nouns, active verbs), and structures *(P–O* and *O–O* types) suggest that these might be considered as universal components of all languages at the deep structure level. It may be concluded that stops, nouns, verbs and the subject-predicate relations are more innate to language than, for example, affricates, adverbs, or syntactic concord relations. The existence of 'semantic primitives' is also attested by children's early use of words with wide referential meaning referring to immediate objects, needs, and situations. Surface structure interpretations of the deep structure are unique to each language and their later acquisition implies their lesser importance in the role of communication.

This would further imply that the 'base' subcomponent of the syntax of a language, which generates deep structures (as input for the semantic component) would be more essential and innate to language structure than the transformational subcomponent, which generates the surface structure (as input for the phonological component).

In discussing language universals and some universals of language acquisition, we are discussing the competence of language speakers, as partially seen through their performance. The fundamental distinction between the two is important. The children must acquire competence in the language (the ability to generate infinite structures and sentences) in spite of the finiteness of input data and constraints on performance such as memory limitations. How to arrive at an evaluation and description of the children's competence at various stages of development is problematical; the observer must try to determine the child's whole language from a corpus of utterances.

Even more of a problem is how to account for language acquisition–how to explain it, on the basis of the children's performance. Several theories have been proposed which may help explain how and why children learn language with such rapidity and uniformity.

McNeill, Chomsky, Fodor, Katz and others account for this ability in a nativistic theory in which they postulate the existence of an internal "Language Acquisition Device" in the child, which consists of linguistic universals, both substantive and formal.[4] The "Language Acquisition Device" receives input linguistic data and scans it for distinctions drawn from a universal hierarchy of categories.[5] Distinctions are found and incorporated into the child's grammar. The final result or output of the "Language Acquisition Device" is grammatical competence. Jacobs and Rosenbaum suggest that the child "... comes into the world knowing, quite unconsciously, what to look for in a language ... He uses his innate knowledge to construct the particular transformations of his language, to piece together in a remarkably short time the grammar of the language to which he is exposed. This explains in part how a human child can learn any native language at all."[6]

Slobin suggests that it may be more accurate to characterize the "Language Acquisition Device" as containing potentialities to develop language, rather than positing "innate knowledge" in this component.[7]

Fodor states that the child has a body of "intrinsic" learning principles by which it can organize observations of linguistic information, converting language data into syntactic information about the underlying structures of strings.[8] The child chooses the correct base structures for types of sentences by an inductive process of selecting among several available hypotheses and arrives at tentative rules. The child can recognize abstract relations–presumably it must know the *N* class before developing *NP*'s.

McNeill has theorized that the recognition and use of certain "basic grammatical relations" such as subject, predicate, object, modifier-noun, noun-verb,

[4] McNeill, 1966a, 49; Noam Chomsky, *Aspects of the Theory of Syntax* (Cambridge, MIT Press, 1965) pp. 27–30; Jerry A. Fodor, "How to Learn to Talk: Some Simple Ways", *The Genesis of Language*, eds., Frank Smith and George A. Miller (Cambridge, MIT Press, 1966) pp. 105–122.

[5] McNeill, 1966a, 49.

[6] Jacobs and Rosenbaum, 1968, 28.

[7] Dan I. Slobin, "Comments on 'Developmental Psycholinguistics'", *The Genesis of Language*, eds., Frank Smith and George A. Miller (Cambridge, MIT Press, 1966) pp. 87–89.

[8] Fodor, 1966, 106, 115.

and verb-object are part of the child's "innate capacity" to perceive similarities and organize them.[9] These form classes are not equivalent to adult ones.

Presumably the child has acquired certain grammatical or functional relationships in terms of universal categories and a deep structure configuration. The child must somehow distinguish between the base structures and transformed sentences, because definitions of functional relations will apply only to the former. This would be the case if the child's comptence in earliest stages is "pre-transformational"; as McNeill states, ". . . it is not too unreasonable to think of children 'talking' base structures directly"[10] in most cases, rather than the surface structure of sentences.

The essential properties of sentences which are necessary to convey meaning (the deep structure) are retained in children's speech, while the form of the sentence (the surface structure) may be reduced or changed. The deep structure (meaning) is an abstract object, and is related to the surface structure through transformations in each language. These universal deep structures are what children first acquire in their early attempts to manipulate language.

In terms of a transformational model of language structure, it could be said that children master the obigatory phrase structure rules or underlying structure first, then optional transformations, and finally refinements on the morphological level, such as inflections. Menyuk found that almost all "base structures" used by adults are used by English-speaking children at age 2.10–3.0.[11] Optional transformations and morphological inflections are acquired later, and are used more accurately with age.[12]

Braine has proposed the controversial theory that "contextual generalization" can be applied to first language learning to account in part for the child's learning of grammatical structure.[13] This is more within the framework of the traditional psychological explanation of the child learning directly from the language data to which it is exposed. Braine suggests that the child experiences sentences in which a segment (morpheme, word, or phrase) occurs in a certain position in a context, and it then tends to place the segment in the same position in other contexts. Thus, the context is generalized and the child has shown "contextual generalization". This is a process of "stimulus generalization", whereby a word learned in one context could generalize to another context even though no associations were previously formed between the word and the new context. This process would especially help to explain aspects related to learning restrictions on word order.

[9] McNeill, 1966a, 46.
[10] McNeill, 1966a, 51.
[11] Menyuk, 1963a, 419.
[12] Menyuk, 1963a, 429.
[13] Martin D. S. Braine, "On Learning the Grammatical Order of Words", *Readings in the Psychology of Language*, eds., Leon A. Jakobovits and Murray S. Miron (Englewood Cliffs, N. J., Prentice-Hall, Inc., 1967) pp. 232–256. Braine, 1963.

Braine further postulates that as well as learning the locations of units, children also form "paired associations", or associative links between morphemes of the "closed-class" type (articles, prepositions, inflections, etc.) and links (although less strong) between "open-class" morphemes such as articles and nouns, or verb inflections and stems. He feels that the learning of positional regularities and forming of paired associations between morphemes can help in deducing the conditions for phenomena in child language such as the "overgeneralization" of irregular inflections. The learning of positions of words can help explain how children learn the position of pivot words and later form classes. For example, in Weir's data, the following paradigms with words in a recurring position and context were "practiced" by her child:[14]

sit down
sit down on the blanket
block
yellow block
look at all the yellow block
what color blanket
what color mop
what color glass

This theory has been questioned by Bever *et al.*, among others.[15] They point out that different types of expressions may have the same ordinal position, while expressions with the same ordinal relation among the segments may be different syntactic types, so a stimulus-response relation cannot be inferred. The child learns the underlying structures and produces ordered sequences of classes for which the verbal environment provides no explicit models. In this case, the child would be imposing internal ordering of linguistic data which is unordered. There need not be a direct relationship between the grammar acquired and the data on which it is based.

Braine's theory is probably less useful in explaining the acquisition of syntax in languages where syntactic relations are signalled by inflection more than by word order, such as Russian.[16] In Arabic, word order can signal grammatical

[14] Weir, 1962, 82, 109. Slobin reports the same kind of 'practicing' observed for a Russian child in his article, "Psycholinguistic Similarities", Slobin, 1965a, 5.

[15] T. G. Bever, J. A. Fodor, and W. Weksel, "On the Acquisition of Syntax: A Critique of 'Contextual Generalization'", *Readings in the Psychology of Language*, eds., Leon Jakobvits and Murray S. Miron (Englewood Cliffs, N. J., Prentice-Hall, 1967) pp. 257–273. T. G. Bever, J. A. Fodor, and W. Weksel, "Is Linguistics Empirical?", *Readings in the Psychology of Language*, pp. 285–293. The first article is rebutted by Braine in the article, "On the Basis of Phrase Structure: A Reply to Bever, Fodor, and Weksel", Braine, 1967.

[16] Slobin, 1965a, 6. He feels that Russian data cast serious doubt on Braine's theory.

meaning, but there is also much more inflection and a more flexible word order than in English, which is the language to which Braine mainly confined his applications.

Others have suggested similar processes of learning linguistic structure, such as Jenkins and Palermo, who also discuss mediation, stimulus and response equivalence, and "paired association" learning with respect to learning linguistic sequences and classes.[17] McNeill suggests that words are classified into *P* and *O* types in terms of which symbol *(NP*, *VP*, etc.) forms the context of the word sorted.[18] Thus, a word fulfilling the definition of MODIFIER in English would be tagged *(-N)*, and a word fulfilling the definition of PREDICATE *(NP-)*.

It would seem that in Arabic, the level of morphology rather than syntax is more appropriate for applying some theories of primary language acquisition.

Theories that children may begin speaking in 'base structures' or at the deep structure level of language are better illustrated at this level. The simplest unmarked word forms are used first. Using the transformational model of language structure, it could be said that the children studied mastered the inflections of the morphological level (M-Rules) last. The tendency to reduce unfamiliar words to their unmarked, stem form is seen in the children's preference for uninflected nonsense forms and in the utterances of children under age 2, where the children obviously distinguish morpheme boundaries.

Braine's theory of contextual generalization may also be applied here to help account for the children's early recognition and correct use of inflections for different parts of speech. Apparently the children learn to differentiate particular inflections by their regular recurrence in certain contexts and in certain positions with words. Children may make some type of 'paired associations' between words of certain parts of speech and inflections required for them. This could be demonstrated by the regular use of the /-āt/ suffix for pluralizing nouns, whereas the /-īn/ suffix was used for pluralizing adjectives.

More detailed information about how this and other languages are acquired should contribute further to expansions and revisions of theories about language universals and universal characteristics of language acquisition. Clearly, only a beginning has been made into an investigation of this important area.

7.3. SUGGESTIONS FOR FURTHER RESEARCH

A few suggestions may be made as to further research needed in the area of language acquisition and specifically, the acquisition of Arabic.

[17] James J. Jenkins and David S. Palermo, "Mediation Processes and the Acquisition of Linguistic Structure", *The Acquisition of Language*, eds., Ursula Bellugi and Roger Brown (Lafayette, Ind., Child Development Publication of the Society for Research in Child Development, 1964) pp. 141–169.

[18] McNeill, 1966, 112–13.

One of the limitations of this study was the lack of time in which to observe the children studied, which precluded making longitudinal case studies and comparisons of individual development. A longer stay in the village, or at least recurrent sampling of language data from some of the children, would give valuable supplementary information into the nature of language development.

More linguistic data are needed especially from the younger children, from the babbling stage to about age 3. Youngest children did not produce many utterances, and those who are in the early stages of phonological, syntactical, and morphological development are precisely the ones whose development should be followed the most closely and intensively.

Case studies would yield more information regarding the interrelationships of developments for various aspects of language structure, and the stages of their acquisition. Information regarding certain aspects of development was not obtained in this study, such as the use of verbs and auxiliary words, the acquisition of embedding transformations in sentences, the acquisition and use of clauses and the conditional, the relation of children's word order to that in adult language, and the development of comprehension. Another area of language development not investigated was that of paralinguistic communication-the use of gestures, voice quality, and situations in association with language.

To obtain a broader perspective in which to evaluate the data obtained, comparative studies should be made in other dialects of Arabic, and with children of other socio-economic classes. Especially useful would be investigation of language acquisition among children in Cairo or another large city. It would also be helpful to administer some of the elicitation tests to adults in the speech community, for comparative purposes.

It is assumed that children at all stages of grammatical development can understand more complex grammatical constructions than they can produce.[19] Most studies, including this one, have concentrated on investigation of children's performance through discovering their generative and grammatical systems. Chomsky and others have called for additional research relating to the important aspect of competence in early syntactic acquisition.[20]

If possible, the relation between the grammar produced and children's grammatical competence should be determined. One way of testing competence would be to obtain children's reactions to, and judgments of, examples of grammatical and ungrammatical utterances, if this is practicable at young ages.

Environmental and ethnolinguistic factors should be considered when observ-

[19] Fraser, Bellugi and Brown found that three-year-old American children could imitate and comprehend more complex grammatical contrasts than they could produce. C. R. Fraser, U. Bellugi, and R. Brown, "Control of Grammar in Imitation, Comprehension and Production", *Journal of Verbal Learning and Verbal Behavior* 2 (1963), 121–135.

[20] Chomsky, 1964, 35–39. McNeill, 1966a, 76–82.

ing linguistic development. Lévi–Strauss has pointed out that language is a result of culture, a part of culture, and a condition of culture.[21]

The relations between the children's environment and lifespace and their conceptual and linguistic development need to be more fully studied and compared to the development of children in other environments. Varying cultural attitudes regarding the value and functions of language, or its varieties and styles, may have an effect on the nature and rate of language acquisition. Hymes has discussed the importance of determining not only how children learn what to say, but also how they learn what not to say, and when and where.[22] He feels that environment is an extremely important factor in language acquisition, and has stated, "Language development in children can be expected to vary with any social, cultural or ecological conditions affecting the makeup of the household".[23]

It must be more clear to what extent linguistic development reflects cognitive development, and factors affecting cognitive development should be determined. Other features of development and behavior such as perception of reality, physical characteristics, and general intelligence, should also be correlated with linguistic development.

[21] Claude Lévi-Strauss, *Anthropologie structurale* (Paris, Librairie Plon, 1958) p. 78.

[22] Dell H. Hymes, "Introduction: Toward Ethnographies of Communication", *The Ethnography of Communication*, eds., John Gumperz and Dell Hymes (=Special publication of *American Anthropologist*, Part 2, 66.6) (Menasha, Wisc., American Anthropological Assn., 1964) p. 27.

[23] Dell H. Hymes, "Linguistic Aspects of Cross-Cultural Personality Study", *Studying Personality Cross-Culturally*, ed., Bert Kaplan (Elmsford, N. Y., Row, Peterson and Co., 1961) p. 342.

BIBLIOGRAPHY

PRIMARY LANGUAGE ACQUISITION

Albright, Robert W., and Joy B. Albright

1958 "The Application of Descriptive Linguistics to Child Language", *Journal of Speech and Hearing Research* 1.3: 257–261.

Bellugi, Ursula

1965 "The Development of Interrogative Structures in Children's Speech", *The Development of Language Functions,* ed., K. F. Riegel, (=Center for Human Growth and Development Report No. 8) (Ann Arbor, Univ. of Michigan) pp. 103–137.

1967 "The Acquisition of Negation", Unpublished Ph. D. dissertation (Harvard University).

Berko, Jean

1961 "The Child's Learning of English Morphology", *Psycholinguistics, A Book of Readings,* ed., Sol Saporta (New York, Holt, Rinehart, and Winston) pp. 359–375.

Bever, T. G., J. A. Fodor, and W. Weksel

1967 "Is Linguistics Empirical?", *Readings in the Psychology of Language,* eds., Leon A. Jakobovits and Murray S. Miron (Englewood Cliffs, N. J., Prentice-Hall) pp. 285–293.

1967 "On the Acquisition of Syntax: A Critique of 'Contextual Generalization'", *Readings in the Psychology of Language,* eds., Leon A. Jakobovits and Murray S. Miron (Englewood Cliffs, N. J., Prentice-Hall) pp. 257–273.

Braine, Martin D. S.

1963 "The Ontogeny of English Phrase Structure: The First Phase", *Language* 39: 1–13.

1967 "On the Basis of Phrase Structure: A Reply to Bever, Fodor, and Weksel", *Readings in the Psychology of Language,* eds., Leon A. Jakobovits and Murray S. Miron (Englewood Cliffs, N. J., Prentice-Hall) pp. 274–284.

1967 "On Learning the Grammatical Order of Words", *Readings in the Psychology of Language,* eds., Leon A. Jakobovits and Murray S. Miron (Englewood Cliffs, N. J., Prentice-Hall) pp. 232–256.

Brown, Roger, and Ursula Bellugi

1964 "Three Processes in the Child's Acquisition of Syntax", *New Directions in the Study of Language,* ed., Eric Lenneberg (Cambridge, MIT Press) pp. 131–161.

Brown, Roger, and Colin Fraser

1964 "The Acquisition of Syntax", *The Acquisition of Language,* eds., Ursula Bellugi and Roger Brown (Lafayette, Ind., Child Development Publication of the Society for Research in Child Development) pp. 43–79.

Carmichael, Leonard

1964 "The Early Growth of Language Capacity in the Individual", *New Directions in the Study of Language*, ed., Eric Lenneberg (Cambridge, MIT Press) pp. 1–22.

Carroll, John B.

1961 "Language Development in Children", *Psycholinguistics, A Book of Readings*, ed., Sol Saporta, (New York, Holt, Rinehart and Winston, Inc.) pp. 331–345.

Chao, Yuen Ren

1951 "The Cantian Idiolect. An Analysis of the Chinese Spoken by a Twenty-Eight-Months Old Child", *Semitic and Oriental Studies: A Volume Presented to William Popper*, ed., Walter J. Fischel (Berkeley, Univ. of California Press) pp. 27–44.

Chomsky, Noam

1964 "Formal Discussion", *The Acquisition of Language*, eds., Ursula Bellugi and Roger Brown (Lafayette, Ind., Child Development Publication of the Society for Research in Child Development) pp. 35–39.

Chukovsky, Kornei

1963 *From Two to Five*, trans., ed., Miriam Morton (Berkeley, Univ. of California Press).

Dato, Daniel P.

1969 *The Child's Acquisition of Spanish Syntax in the Foreign Environment* (Washington, D. C., U.S. Office of Education).

1970 "Development of Spanish Interrogatives in Children's Second Language Learning", Memorial Volume to Ruth Weir, ed., M. J. Hardman-de-Bautista and V. Honsa, forthcoming.

Ervin, Susan M.

1964 "Imitation and Structural Change in Children's Language", *New Directions in the Study of Language*, ed., Eric Lenneberg, (Cambridge, MIT, Press) pp. 163–189.

Ervin, Susan M., and Wick Miller

1963 *Language Development*, Offprint of Chapter III of the 62nd Yearbook, Part I, of the National Society for the Study of Education (Chicago, Univ. of Chicago Press).

Ferguson, Charles A.

1956 "Arabic Baby Talk", *For Roman Jakobson*, ed., Morris Halle (The Hague, Mouton) pp. 121–128.

1964 "Baby Talk in Six Languages", *The Ethnography of Communication*, ed., John J. Gumperz and Dell Hymes (→Special publication of *American Anthropologist*, Part 2, 66.6) (Menasha, Wisc., American Anthropological Assn.) pp. 103–114.

1968 "Contrastive Analysis and Language Development", *Georgetown University Monograph Series on Languages and Linguistics* 21, ed., James E. Alatis (Washington, D. C., Georgetown Univ. Press), 101–112.

Fodor, Jerry A.

1966 "How to Learn to Talk: Some Simple Ways", *The Genesis of Language*, eds., Frank Smith and George A. Miller (Cambridge, MIT Press) pp. 105–122.

Fraser, Colin

1966 "Discussion", *Psycholinguistic Papers*, ed., J. Lyons and R. J. Wales (Edinburgh, Edinburgh Univ. Press) pp. 115–120.

Fraser, Colin, Ursula Bellugi, and Roger Brown

1963 "Control of Grammar in Imitation, Comprehension and Production", *Journal of Verbal Learning and Verbal Behavior* 2: 121–135.

Fry, D. B.

1966 "The Development of the Phonological System in the Normal and the Deaf

Child", *The Genesis of Language*, eds., Frank Smith and George A. Miller (Cambridge, MIT Press) pp. 187–206.

Gili y Gaya, Samuel

1960 *Funciones Gramaticales en el Habla Enfantil* (=*Publicaciones Pedagogicas*, Serie II, No. XXIV) (Rio Piedras, Univ. de Puerto Rico).

Gregoire, Antoine

1937, 1947 *L'Apprentissage du language*, 2 vols. (Paris, Droz).

Irwin, Orvis C., and H. P. Chen

1947 "Development of Speech in Infancy: Curve of Phonemic Frequencies", *Journal of Experimental Psychology* 37.2, 187–193.

Jakobson, R., and M. Halle

1961 "Phonemic Patterning", *Psycholinguistics, A Book of Readings*, ed., Sol Saporta (New York, Holt, Rinehart, and Winston, Inc.) pp. 346–350.

Jenkins, James J., and David S. Palermo

1964 "Mediation Processes and the Acquisition of Linguistic Structure", *The Acquisition of Language*, eds., Ursula Bellugi and Roger Brown (Lafayette, Ind., Child Development Publication of the Society for Research in Child Development) pp. 141–169.

Kahane, Henry, Renee Kahane, and Sol Saporta

1958 "The Development of the Verbal Categories in Child Language", *IJAL* 24.4, Part II: 1–65.

Kernan, Keith T., and B. G. Blount

1966 "The Acquisition of Spanish Grammar by Mexican Children", *Anthropological Linguistics* 8.9, 1–14.

Klima, E. S., and Ursula Bellugi

1966 "Syntactic Regularities in the Speech of Children", *Psycholinguistic Papers*, eds., J. Lyons and R. J. Wales (Edinburgh, Edinburgh Univ. Press) pp. 183–219.

Kroeber, A. L.

1916 "The Speech of a Zuñi Child", *American Anthropologist* 18.4, 529–534.

Lenneberg, Eric H.

1964 "A Biological Perspective of Language", *New Directions in the Study of Language*, ed., Eric Lenneberg (Cambridge, MIT Press) pp. 65–88.

1964a "The Capacity for Language Acquisition", *The Structure of Language: Readings in the Philosophy of Language*, ed., J. A. Fodor and J. J. Katz (Englewood Cliffs, N. J., Prentice-Hall) pp. 579–603.

1966 "The Natural History of Language", *The Genesis of Language*, eds., Frank Smith and George A. Miller (Cambridge, MIT Press) pp. 219–252.

1967 *Biological Foundations of Language* (New York, John Wiley and Sons).

Leopold, Werner F.

1948 "Study of Child Language and Infant Bilingualism", *Word* 4, 1–17.

1961 "Patterning in Children's Language Learning", *Psycholinguistics, A Book of Readings*, ed., Sol Saporta (New York, Holt, Rinehart and Winston, Inc.) pp. 350–358.

Lewis, Morris M.

1951 *Infant Speech: A Study of the Beginnings of Language* (New York, Humanities Press).

1959 *How Children Learn to Speak* (New York, Basic Books).

1964 *Language, Thought and Personality in Infancy and Childhood* (New York, Basic Books).

Luria, Aleksandr R.

1959 "The Directive Function of Speech in Development and Dissolution. Part I:

Development of tne Directive Function of Speech in Early Childhood", *Word* 15, 341–352.

Luria, Aleksandr R., and F. I. Yudovich
1959 *Speech and the Development of Mental Processes in the Child,* trans., O. Kovasc and J. Simon (London, Staples Press).

McCarthy, Dorothea A.
1954 "Language Development in Children", *Manual of Child Psychology,* ed., L. Carmichael, 2d ed. (New York, John Wiley and Sons) pp. 492–630.

McNeill, David
1966 "The Creation of Language by Children", *Psycholinguistic Papers,* eds., J. Lyons and R. J. Wales (Edinburgh, Edinburgh Univ. Press) pp. 99–132.
1966a "Developmental Psycholinguistics", *The Genesis of Language,* eds., Frank Smith George A. Miller (Cambridge, MIT Press) pp. 15–84.

Menyuk, Paula
1963 "A Preliminary Evaluation of Grammatical Capacity in Children", *Journal of Verbal Learning and Verbal Behavior* 2, 429–439.
1963a "Syntactic Structures in the Language of Children", *Child Development* 34, 407–422.
1968 "The Role of Distinctive Features in Children's Acquisition of Phonology", *Journal of Speech and Hearing Research* 11.1, 138–146.

Miller, Wick, and Susan Ervin
1964 "The Development of Grammar in Child Language", *The Acquisition of Language,* eds., Ursula Bellugi and Roger Brown (Lafayette, Ind., Child Development Publication of the Society for Research in Child Development) pp. 9–34.

Olmsted, D. L.
1966 "A Theory of the Child's Learning of Phonology", *Language* 42.2, 531–535.

Osgood, Charles E., and James J. Jenkins
1965 "Diachronic Psycholinguistics – First Language Learning", *Psycholinguistics: A Survey of Theory and Research Problems,* ed., Charles E. Osgood and Thomas A. Sebeok (Bloomington, Indiana Univ. Press) pp. 126–135.

Piaget, J., and K. Paul
1955 *The Language and Thought of the Child,* trans., Marjorie Gabain (New York, Meridian Books).

Slobin, Dan I.
1965 *Grammatical Development in Russian-Speaking Children* (=Center for Human Growth and Development Report No. 8) (Ann. Arbor, Univ. of Michigan).
1965a *Psycholinguistic Similarities in the Acquisition of English and Russian as Native Languages* (Washington, D. C., U.S. Office of Education).
1966 "Abstracts of Soviet Studies of Child Language", *The Genesis of Language,* eds., Frank Smith and George A. Miller (Cambridge, MIT Press) pp. 363–386.
1966a "The Acquisition of Russian as a Native Language", *The Genesis of Language,* eds., Frank Smith and George A. Miller (Cambridge, MIT Press) pp. 129–148.
1966b "Comments on 'Developmental Psycholinguistics'", *The Genesis of Language,* eds., Frank Smith and George A. Miller (Cambridge, MIT Press) pp. 87–89.
1967 (ed.) *A Field Manual for the Cross-Cultural Study of the Acquisition of Communicative Competence,* 2d draft (Berkeley, Univ. of California Press).
1969 *Universals of Grammatical Development in Children* (=Working Paper No. 22, Language-Behavior Research Laboratory) (Berkeley, Univ. of California).

Slobin, Dan I., and Charles A. Welsh
1968 *Elicited Imitation as a Research Tool in Developmental Psycholinguistics* (=Work-

ing Paper No. 10, Language-Behavior Research Laboratory) (Berkeley, Univ. of California).

Smith, Frank, and George A. Miller, eds., (no author)

1966 "General Discussion, McNeill and Slobin Presentations", in *The Genesis of Language* (Cambridge, MIT Press) pp. 93–103.

Stross, Brian

1969 *Language Acquisition by Tenejapa Tzeltal Children* (=Working Paper No. 20, Language-Behavior Research Laboratory) (Berkeley: Univ. of California).

Templin, Mildred C.

1947 "Spontaneous versus Imitated Verbalization in Testing Articulation in Preschool Children", *Journal of Speech and Hearing Disorders* 12, 293–300.

Velten, H. V.

1943 "The Growth of Phonemic and Lexical Patterns in Infant Language", *Language* 19, 281–292.

Weir, Ruth H.

1962 *Language in the Crib* (→*Janua Linguarum*, series major 14) (The Hague, Mouton).

1966 "Some Questions on the Child's Learning of Phonology", *The Genesis of Language*, eds., Frank Smith and George A. Miller (Cambridge, MIT Press) pp. 153–168.

GENERAL LINGUISTICS

Chomsky, Noam

1965 *Aspects of the Theory of Syntax* (Cambridge, MIT Press).

Firth, J. R.

1966 "Sounds and Prosodies", *Readings in Linguistics II*, ed., Eric P. Hamp, Fred W. Householder, and Robert Austerlitz (Chicago, Univ. of Chicago Press) pp. 175–191.

Greenberg, Joseph H.

1966 "Language Universals", *Current Trends in Linguistics*, Vol. 3 (=*Theoretical Foundations)* ed. by T. A. Sebeok (The Hague, Mouton) pp. 61–112.

Jakobson, Roman, C. Fant, and Morris Halle

1963 *Preliminaries to Speech Analysis* (Cambridge, MIT Press).

Lieberman, Philip

1967 *Intonation, Perception and Language* (Cambridge, MIT Press).

Malmberg, Bertil

1963 *Phonetics* (New York, Dover).

Piaget, Jean

1950 *The Psychology of Intelligence* (London, Routledge and Kegan Paul, Ltd.).

Postal, Paul M.

1968 "Epilogue", *English Transformational Grammar*, eds., Roderick A. Jacobs and Peter S. Rosenbaum (Waltham, Mass., Blaisdell Publishing Co.).

1964 *The Principles of the International Phonetic Association* (London, International Phonetic Association).

Vygotsky, Lev S.

1965 *Thought and Language*, ed., trans., Eugenia Hanfmann and Gertrude Vakar (Cambridge, MIT Press).

ARABIC LANGUAGE

Abdel-Malek, Zaki N.
1965 "Numerals in Colloquial Egyptian Arabic", Unpublished Master's thesis (Georgetown Univ.).

Cantineau, Jean
1960 "Esquisse d'une phonologie de l'arabe classique", *Etudes de linguistique arabe* (Paris, Librairie Klincksieck).

Erwin, Wallace M.
1963 *A Short Reference Grammar of Iraqi Arabic* (Washington, D. C., Georgetown Univ. Press).

Ferguson, Charles A.
1956 "The Emphatic L in Arabic", *Language* 32, 446–452.

Gamal-Eldin, Saad M.
1967 *A Syntactic Study of Egyptian Colloquial Arabic* (The Hague, Mouton).

Hanna, Hanna M.
1962 "The Phrase Structure of Egyptian Colloquial Arabic", Unpublished Ph.D. dissertation (Cornell University).

Harrell, Richard S.
1957 *The Phonology of Colloquial Egyptian Arabic* (New York, American Council of Learned Societies).
1960 "A Linguistic Analysis of Egyptian Radio Arabic", *Contributions to Arabic Linguistics*, ed., Charles A. Ferguson (Cambridge, Harvard Univ. Press) pp. 1–77.

Harrell, Richard S., Laila Tewfik, and George D. Selim
1963 *Lessons in Colloquial Egyptian Arabic* (Washington, D. C., Georgetown Univ. Press).

Khalafallah, Abdelghany A.
1961 "A Descriptive Grammar of Saʕiidi Colloquial Egyptian Arabic" Unpublished Ph. D. dissertation (Univ. of Texas).

Lehn, Walter
1963 "Emphasis in Cairo Arabic", *Language* 39, 29–39.

Lehn, Walter, and Peter Abboud
1965 *Beginning Cairo Arabic* (Austin, Univ. of Texas Press).

Selim, George D.
1967 "Some Contrasts between Classical Arabic and Egyptian Arabic", *Linguistic Studies in Memory of Richard Slade Harrell*, ed., D. G. Stuart (Washington, D. C., Georgetown Univ. Press) pp. 133–152.

Tomiche, Nada
1964 *Le Parler Arabe du Caire* (The Hague, and Paris, Mouton).

Wolfe, Ronald G.
1965 *An Introduction to the Arabic Language for Americans* (Washington, D.C., American Friends of the Middle East, Inc.).

OTHER SUBJECTS

Ammar, Hamed
1954 *Growing Up in an Egyptian Village: Silwa, Province of Aswan* (London, Routledge and Paul).

Hymes, Dell H.
1961 "Linguistic Aspects of Cross-Cultural Personality Study", *Studying Personality Cross-Culturally*, ed., Bert Kaplan (Elmsford, N. Y., Row, Peterson) pp. 313–359.

1964 "Introduction: Toward Ethnographies of Communication", *The Ethnography of Communication*, ed., John J. Gumperz and Dell Hymes (=Special publication of American Anthropologist, Part 2, 66.6), (Menasha, Wisc., American Anthropological Assn.) pp. 1–34.

Labov, William

1966 "Hypercorrection by the Lower Middle Class as a Factor in Linguistic Evolution", *Sociolinguistics*, ed., William Bright (→*Janua Linguarum*, series major 20) (The Hague, Mouton).

Lévi-Strauss, Claude

1958 *Anthropologie Structurale* (Paris, Librairie Plon).

Scrimshaw, Nevin S.

1969 "Infant Malnutrition and Adult Learning", *The Development Digest* VII. 1, 20–24.